FUNDAMENTALS OF MANAGEMENT PROCESS AND ORGANIZATIONAL BEHAVIOUR

Fundamentals of
Management Process and Organizational Behaviour

Y. VENKATA RAO
H. RAMANAND SINGH

AKANSHA PUBLISHING HOUSE
NEW DELHI • GUWAHATI • VISAKHAPATNAM

AKANSHA PUBLISHING HOUSE
4649-B/21, Ansari Road
Daryaganj, New Delhi-110002
Phones: 23268193, 09435116718
Email: ektabooks@yahoo.com
visit us: www.akanshapublishinghouse.com

Fundamentals of Management Process and Organizational Behaviour

First Published 2010

ISBN 978-81-8370-228-7

PRINTED IN INDIA

Published by Akansha Publishing House, New Delhi-110002 and printed at S.N. Offset Press, Delhi.

Dedicated
to
Our Beloved Parents

Foreword

The book consists of two parts. Part I is on Management Process with seven chapters and Part II is on Organizational Behaviour with 15 chapters. The book gives the complete coverage of the topics on the subject presented in a very logical and sequential order. Besides all the important topics normally covered in an MPOB book. The authors have thoughtfully included and elaborated the new emerging topics in the subject like transactional analysis, *yoga* and stress, organizational creativity and innovation. The well-knitted structure and depth and detailed feel with fact presentation reflects the authors' clarity of understanding in the subject. I have been the student and teacher of organizational behaviour for over three decades, but I find the present book unique to other books in the subject on various aspects such as its easy language to understand. Self-learning style, jargon-free presentation, concepts and principles duly exemplified with the help of caselets and anecdotes, and case studies from the Indian context to explain the issues relating to people behaviour at work. In nutshell, the book is rich with concepts, experiences, case studies, and research findings. The book joins the list of books that have made a lasting impression on me.

In writing the 'Foreword' of this book, I find myself fortunate and delighted on two counts. *First* that the authors have been my erstwhile colleagues in Assam University, Silchar, Assam and *second* that the authors have done a wonderful job of putting together a rich and contemporary text for the benefits of the readers of the subject. I extend my heartiest congratulations to both the authors for making such an academic contribution to the subject. Being elder to them, my usual saying goes: *"Well done. Keep it up"*. I have gone through the book with great academic interest and delight. The discernible readers like students teachers and management professionals, I am sure, will feel likewise.

Prof. S.S. KHANKA
National Institute of Financial Management,
Ministry of Finance
Government of India
Faridabad

Preface

In the present era, understanding human element in the organized system is felt more than ever before. The dizzying rate of change with the uncertainty and continuous impact of technology are influencing dynamics between human activities and organizational structure. In the given context, management as well as engineering graduates is needed to equip with the knowledge of management process and behavioural implications in organizations. In the light of these, the present book is a modest attempt to bring out the fundamental issues of management and organizational behaviour in an illustrative way to reach the targeted readers. We hope that this piece of work would be helpful not only to the students and teachers of management but also for management professionals for their personal introspection and self-development. Especially topic such as perception, attitude, personality, stress management and so on would be relevant in exploring one's own self too.

First of all, we are immensely thankful to Prof. J.A.K. Tareen, Vice-Chancellor, Pondicherry University and Prof. A. Balasubramanian, Director, Directorate of Culture and Cultural Relations, Pondicherry University for their encouragement and advice to think out of the box. Their ideas and beliefs over academia supported us to come up with this piece of academic work. We also owe our gratitude to Prof. Topodhir Bhattacharjee, Vice-Chancellor, Assam University for his moral support and inspiring words that have enabled us to complete this book.

We could not have imagined the final shape of this work without the direction and guidance given by Prof. S.S Khanka, National Institute of Financial Management,

Ministry of Finance, Fridabad. We are also thankful to him for his support and encouragement in our academic work by writing Foreword of this book. We are also privileged to record our profound gratitude to our teachers Prof. G. Anjaneya Swamy, Dr. M. Srimannarayana, G. Machala and Dr. G. Singiaih, who have been our spirit and strength in finalizing this work. We are highly thankful to our counselors Prof. N.S.R.K. Murty, Andhra University, and Prof. N. Sudhakara Rao, University of Hyderabad.

Thanks are also due to our well-wishers Prof. P. Satyanarayanchari (Rtd. Principal), Shri. M. Jayprakash Chowdury (Manager) of C.R. Reddy College, Shri Steven-Doraswamy, Mrs. Garapati. Kamala Kumari, Dr. G.B.V.L. Narsimha Rao, Dr. Nirmala Devi, Dr. B.V.V. Balakrishana, Dr. K. Siva Rama Krishan, Shri LCh. Srimanth, Dr. K. Krishnaiah Chowdury and Shri. A. Kishore Babu, who in some way or the other have contributed in the development and production of this piece of work. We are also thankful to our colleagues Dr. Sampad Kumar Swain, Dr. Jitendra Mohan Mishra, Mr. Anu Chandran, Sibi George of the Department of Tourism Studies, Pondicherry University, for their valuable helps and suggestions in the finalization of this book. We also wish to express our sincere thanks to Prof. A. Mazumdar, Prof. R.K Raul, Dr. A.L. Ghosh, Dr. Arup Barrrian, Mr. Debomalya Ghosh, Dr. Anurag Singh and Mr. N. Biswas of Department of Business Administration, Assam University, for their continued moral support and encouragement right from the beginning.

We are also indebted to Mr. M.P. Misra of Akansha Publishing House, New Delhi without his support and encouragement, this piece of work might not have shaped into a fine piece of book.

Finally, we are earnestly thankful to mother Smt. Venkamma, Mrs. Padmini, Nikhita, Akhil Venkat Ram and Aditya Singh Haomom for bearing all inconveniences during the period of preparing this work.

Y. VENKATA RAO
H. RAMANANDA SINGH

Contents

PART I
MANAGEMENT PROCESS

1 Introduction to Management

If you command wisely, you'll be obeyed cheerfully.
– *Thomas Fuller*

Human and Management

Managing activity is the most important for human beings. Since human beings began to live together, in an organized form for achieving certain common tasks, management existed in their activities for coordination of individuals. Thus, organizations come into existence for the people and inherently management needed to avoid complexity and to bring clarity in their activities. As a result, management exists in organizations among identified human activities. In due course of time, management has become as an essential for integration of individual work. As team work is highly needed for organizations in the globalizing society, role of proper management has been increasing.

More broadly, management is the process of designing and maintaining an environment in which individuals, working together in groups, efficiently accomplish selected aims. In its expanded form, this basic definition means several things. First, as managers, people carry out the managerial functions of planning, organizing, staffing, leading, and controlling. Second, management applies to any kind of organization. Third, management applies to managers at all organizational levels. Fourth, the aim of all managers is the same – to create surplus. Finally, managing is concerned with productivity – this implies effectiveness and efficiency.

Organization and Management

Organizations are two or more people working together in a structured, formal environment to achieve common goals. Managers provide guidance, implementation, and coordination so those organizational goals can be reached. The modern manager coaches employees of the organization to develop teamwork, which effectively fulfils their needs and achieves organizational objectives. The traditional autocratic organization with its hierarchical system of management and an overbearing "boss" that forces performance out of people is no longer needed. The modern manager provides an atmosphere of empowerment by letting workers make decisions and inspiring people to boost productivity. The practices of management functions are needed for all types of organizations (Fig. 1.1).

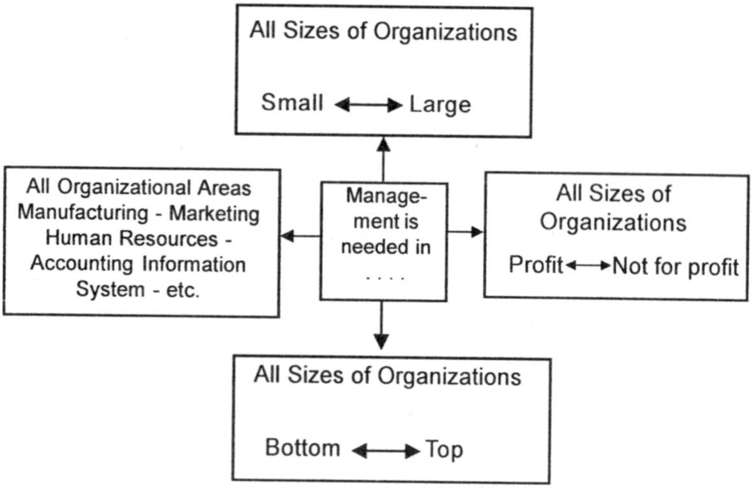

Fig. 1.1: Organization and Management

First and foremost, management is about solving problems that keep emerging all the time in the course of an organization struggling to achieve its goals and objectives. Problem-solving should be accompanied by problem identification, analysis and the implementation of remedies to managerial problems. Second, administration involves following laid down procedures (although procedures or rules should not be seen as ends in themselves) for the execution, control, communication, delegation and crisis management. Third, human resource management should be based on strategic integration of human resource, assessment of workers, and exchange of ideas between shareholders and workers. Finally, organizational leadership should be developed along lines of interpersonal relationship, teamwork, self-motivation to perform, emotional strength and maturity to handle situations, personal integrity, and general management skills.

What is Management?

A human organization is not a natural system in the sense that its functioning is not directed by any invisible force. It is an artificial creation and innovation of human ingenuity and therefore has to be directed by a specific organ, which may be referred to as *Management.* Since an organization is *a* man-made entity of co-operative group effort, someone has to take charge and coordinate its activities in a meaningful manner. An individual or a sub-group, which takes charge of the organization and directs its activities, is its *Management.* Hence, the management is existing very much in an *organization* where planned coordination of activities of two or more people on a common goals in a hierarchy of authority and responsibility.

The term *Management* is popularly viewed as a synonym to administration, leadership, and even supervision. However, the following concepts describe some of the facets of management. Management is perceived by many people in different ways. This concept is sometimes called the *universality of management* in which managers perform the same functions regardless of their place in the organizational structure or the type of enterprise in which they are managing. *Management* can be defined as all the activities and tasks undertaken by one or more persons for the purpose of planning and controlling the activities of others. In order to achieve an objective or complete an activity that could not be achieved by the others acting independently. Although there are good numbers of definitions, Mary Parker Follett, a notable management scholar, defined the management in very simple as "*the art of getting things done through people.*" It is interesting to observe the changes of the concept in the words of the General Motors

Chairman as "the *art of getting things done along with others*". Management as defined by well-known authors in the field of management contains the following components:

Peter F. Drucker	Management is a function, a discipline, a task to be done, and mangers practice this discipline, carry out the functions and discharge these tasks.
Joseph Massie	Management is the process by which a cooperative group directs actions towards common goals.
Henry Sisk	Management is the coordination of all resources through the process of planning, organization, directing and controlling in order to attain stated goals.
Dalton McFarland	Management is the process by which manager's crate, direct, maintain and operate purposive organizations through system - attic, coordinated a cooperative human effort.

Nature and Purpose of Management

Management is the process of designing and maintaining an environment in which individuals, working together in groups, accomplish efficiently selected aims. As managers, people carry out the managerial functions of planning, organizing, staffing, leading, and controlling. Management practices can be applied to any kind of organization. The aim of all managers is to create a surplus and highly concerned productivity that implies effectiveness and efficiency. In fact, effective and efficient management is in the hands of right human beings, who decide the future of today's organizations. To ensure the efficiency and effectiveness in human activities, understanding human beings and adopting appropriate management practices is the need of hour. *Efficiency* is getting the most output from the least input, whereas *Effectiveness* is completing activities so that the organization's goals are attained (See Fig 1.2).

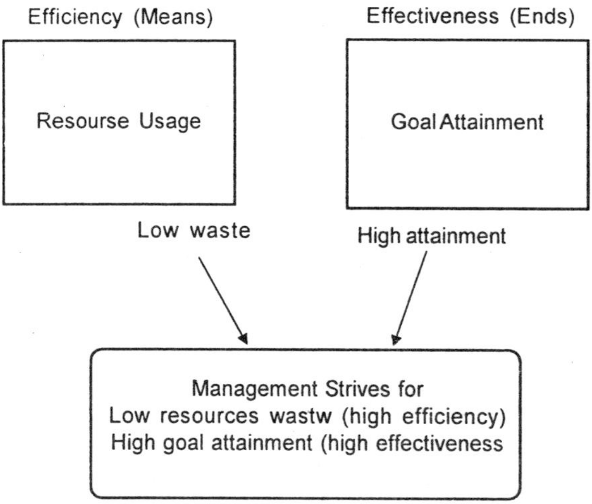

Fig. 1.2: Nature and Purpose of Management

Five Dimensions of Management

Five-dimensional management (5DM), based on the principle that everyone is a manager and focusing on managing people the way they need to be managed, is an innovative technique in management training which is set to challenge conventional thinking. The character types are then dealt with through five dimensions of management responsibility, where all managers have to perform in five separate areas:

- *Self* - everyone must understand and know themselves before they can begin to manage others;
- *Boss* - individuals should consciously manage their superiors;
- *Internal* - colleagues and peers over whom they have no authority, but with whom they communicate and therefore "manage";
- *External* - including customers and external human resources;
- *Subordinates* - to traditional managers, man-management is exclusively about managing subordinates and telling

them what to do. It is within the five management skills of communication, planning, selling, motivating and measuring that a 5DM manager can apply his or her ability to interact with, or effectively manage, others.

Management Objectives, Functions, Goals, and Essentiality

Management Objectives

There are basically three management objectives.

- Ensuring organizational goals and targets are met – with least cost and minimum waste.
- Looking after health and welfare, and safety of staff.
- Protecting the machinery and resources of the organization, including the human resources.

Management Functions

To understand management, it is imperative that we break it down into four managerial functions, namely; planning, organizing, leading, and controlling.

- Planning involves selecting missions and developing future course of action.
- Organizing involves establishing an intentional structure of roles for people to fill in an organization.
- Leading is the influencing of people so that they will contribute to organization and group goals. It has to do predominantly with the interpersonal aspect of managing.
- Controlling involves measuring and correcting of activities of subordinates to ensure that events conform to plans. It measures performance against goals and plans, shows where negative deviations exist, and, by putting in motion actions to correct deviations, helps ensure accomplishment of plans.

Goals of All Managers

First and foremost, the logical and publicly desirable aim of all managers in all kinds of organizations, whether business or non-business, should be a surplus. Thus, managers must establish an environment in which people can accomplish group goals with the least amount of time, money, materials, and personal dissatisfaction or in which they can achieve as much as possible of a desired goal with available resources.

The Essentiality of Management in Any Organization: Managers are charged with the responsibility of taking actions that will make it possible for individuals to make their best contributions to group objectives. Thus, management applies to small and large organizations, to profit and not for-profit enterprises, to manufacturing as well as service industries. However, a given situation may differ considerably among various levels in an organization or various types of enterprises. The scope of authority held may vary and the types of problems dealt with may be considerably different.

Management Process

Managers create and maintain an internal environment, commonly called the organization, so that others can work efficiently in it. A manager's job consists of planning, organizing, directing, and controlling the resources of the organization. These resources include people, jobs or positions, technology, facilities and equipment, materials and supplies, information, and money. Managers work in a dynamic environment and must anticipate and adapt to challenges.

The job of every manager involves what is known as the functions of management: planning, organizing, directing, and controlling. These functions are goal-directed, interrelated and interdependent. Planning involves devising a systematic process for attaining the goals of the organization. It prepares the organization for the future. Organizing involves arranging the necessary resources to carry out the plan. It is the process of creating structure, establishing relationships, and allocating resources to accomplish the goals of the organization. Directing

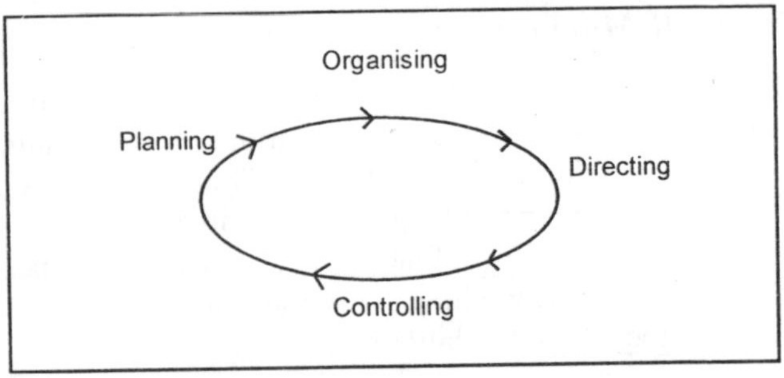

Fig. 1.3: Management Functions and Process

involves the guiding, leading, and overseeing of employees to achieve organizational goals. Controlling involves verifying that actual performance matches the plan. If performance results do not match the plan, corrective action is taken (See the Figure).

Management Levels

The extent to which managers perform the functions of management - planning, organizing, directing, and controlling- varies by level in the management hierarchy. The term manager could be applied at all management levels of the organization to those who direct the work of others. In common usage, however, the title tends to be used only in the first level of the management hierarchy. If an organization were divided into top, middle, and lower managerial levels, the term generally applies to the lower level (See Fig. 1.4).

Managers are managers whose major functions emphasize directing and controlling the work of employees in order to achieve the team goals. They are the only level of management managing non-managers. Thus, most of the manager's time is allocated to the functions of directing and controlling. In contrast, top managers spend most of their time on the functions of planning and organizing. The top manager determines the mission and sets the goals for the organization. His or her primary function is long-range planning. Top management is accountable for the overall management of the organization. Middle management implements top management goals. Managers direct the actual work of the organization at the operating level.

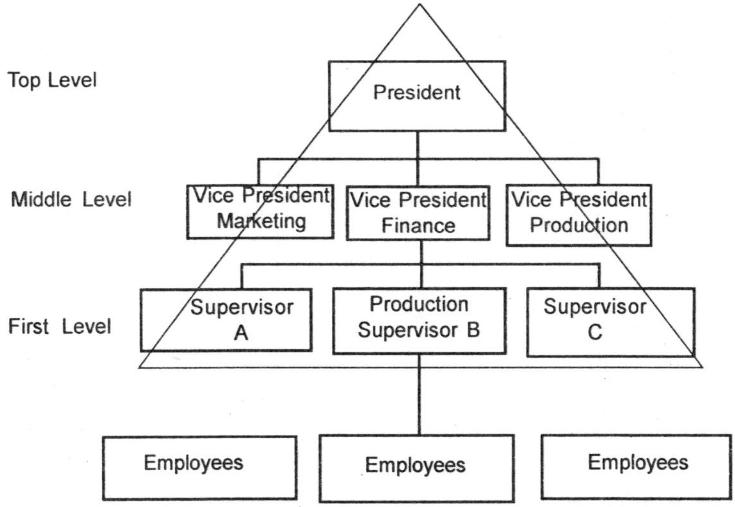

Fig. 1.4: Levels of Management

Management Roles

To meet the many demands of performing their functions, managers assume multiple roles. A role is an organized set of behaviors. Henry Mintzberg has identified ten roles common to the work of all managers. The ten roles are divided into three groups: interpersonal, informational, and decisional. The *informational roles* link all managerial work together. The *interpersonal roles* ensure that information is provided. The *decisional roles* make significant use of the information. The performance of managerial roles and the requirements of these roles can be played at different times by the same manager and to different degrees depending on the level and function of management. The ten roles are described individually, but they form an integrated whole (See Fig. 1.5).

The three interpersonal roles are primarily concerned with interpersonal relationships. In the figurehead role, the manager represents the organization in all matters of formality. The top level manager represents the company legally and socially to those outside of the organization. The manager represents the work group to higher management and higher management to

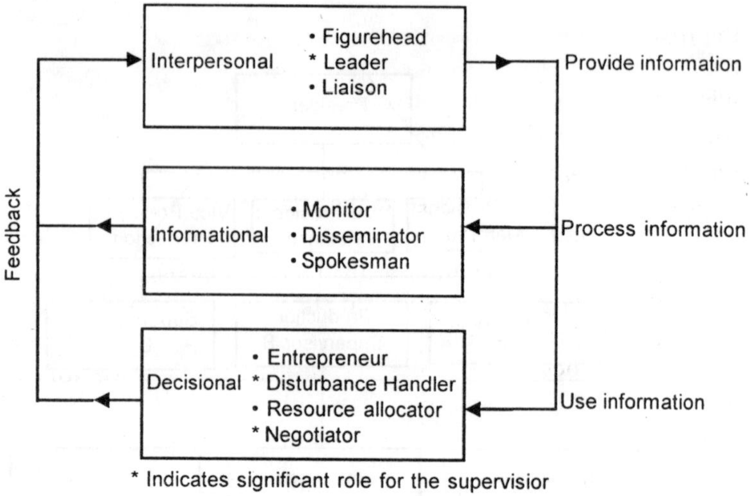

Fig. 1.5: FeedbackThe Managerial Roles

the work group. In the liaison role, the manger interacts with peers and people outside the organization. The top level manager uses the liaison role to gain favors and information, while the manager uses it to maintain the routine flow of work. The leader role defines the relationships between the manger and employees.

The direct relationships with people in the interpersonal roles place the manager in a unique position to get information. Thus, the three informational roles are primarily concerned with the information aspects of managerial work. In the monitor role, the manager receives and collects information. In the role of disseminator, the manager transmits special information into the organization. The top level manager receives and transmits more information from people outside the organization than the manager. In the role of spokesperson, the manager disseminates the organization's information into its environment. Thus, the top level manager is seen as an industry expert, while the manager is seen as a unit or departmental expert.

The unique access to information places the manager at the center of organizational decision-making. There are four decisional roles. In the entrepreneur role, the manager initiates change. In the disturbance handler role, the manger deals with threats to the organization. In the resource allocator role, the manager chooses where the organization will expend its efforts. In the negotiator role, the manager negotiates on behalf of the organization. The top level manager makes the decisions about the organization as a whole, while the manager makes decisions about his or her particular work unit. The manager performs these managerial roles but with different emphasis than higher managers. Managery management is more focused and short-term in outlook. Thus, the figurehead role becomes less significant and the disturbance handler and negotiator roles increase in importance for the manager. Since leadership permeates all activities, the leader role is among the most important of all roles at all levels of management.

Managers play multiple roles especially at higher levels in the organization. Besides discharging specific responsibilities allocated to them such as those related to functions like marketing, production, finance or personnel management, managers play strategic, leadership, operating, and other roles. A role is "... a set of expected behaviour patterns attributed to someone occupying a given position in a social unit". The performance of the manager depends considerably on how well his/her multiple roles are played. In turn, how well these roles are played by the managers of an organization influences the performance of the organization. The question, therefore, is: What are the competencies required to play various managerial roles effectively especially at senior levels in the organization? In response to this question, we present data on a large number of managerial roles and associated managerial competencies from a study of 73 senior level Indian corporate managers.

Management Skills

In order to perform the functions of management and to assume multiple roles, managers must be skilled. Robert Katz identified three managerial skills that are essential to successful management: technical, human, and conceptual. *Technical skill* involves process or technique knowledge and proficiency. Managers use the processes, techniques and tools of a specific area. *Human skill* involves the ability to interact effectively with people. Managers interact and cooperate with employees. *Conceptual skill* involves the formulation of ideas. Managers understand abstract relationships, develop ideas, and solve problems creatively. Thus, technical skill deals with things, human skill concerns people, and conceptual skill has to do with ideas.

A manager's level in the organization determines the relative importance of possessing technical, human, and conceptual skills. Top level managers need conceptual skills in order to view the organization as a whole. Conceptual skills are used in planning and dealing with ideas and abstractions. Managers need technical skills to manage their area of specialty. All levels of management need human skills in order to interact and communicate with other people successfully. As the pace of change accelerates and diverse technologies converge, new global industries are being created (for example, telecommunications). Technological change alters the fundamental structure of firms and calls for new organizational approaches and management skills (See Fig. 1.6).

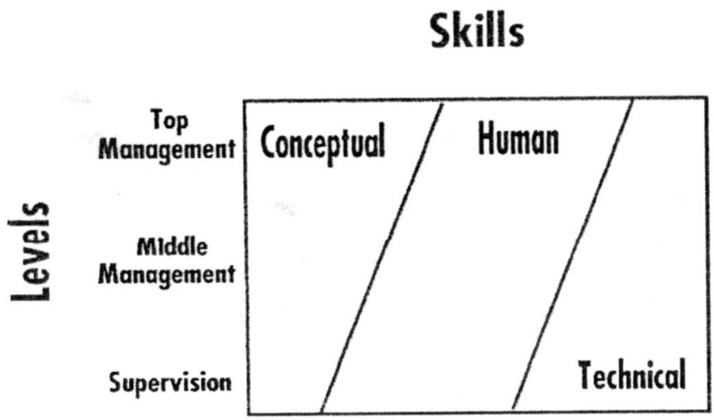

Fig. 1.6: Skill Distribution at Various Management Levels

Nature of Indian Management

The present Indian management system is a product of a mixture of social, economic, religious and political factors, which have now prevailed in India for a long time. Indians are socialized in an environment that values strong family ties and extended family relationships; thus they are more likely to develop stronger affiliate tendencies or greater dependence on others. So, in the work context, interpersonal relations are more relevant to them and, as a result, their job-related decisions might be influenced more by interpersonal considerations than by task demands. Moreover, Indian organizations in both the past and the present have made attempts to emulate Western or Eastern patterns of management. This is because Indian managers are often trained in the West and most of the Indian management institutes have adopted the Western education system.

Presently, Indian managers are equipping themselves with new management techniques and the various aspects of the management function which are helpful in maintaining good relations suggests serious consideration is being given to the development of human resources in Indian organizations. Such relation is based on the understanding that without the development of human resources, Indian organizations will not be able to adopt successfully the new technology, improve the quality of their products, reduce costs of production, capacity utilization of resources and rationalize the workforce and hence compete with overseas competitors.

Management in Information Age

Management is transformed by the communication and information technology in modern organizations. In order to keep pace with the increased speed and complexity of business, new means of calculating, sorting and processing information were invented. An interesting description of the modern era is the Information Age that describes the general use of technology to transmit information. Managers realized that they could profit from immediate knowledge of relevant information. The telegraph was the first instrument to transform information into electrical form over long distances.

Communication and processing technologies are an essential tool in almost every field of business. The Internet, with its interconnection of millions of computers, has evolved to potentially become one of the greatest resources available to businesses today. The World Wide Web (www) offers access to vast information resources and an immense number of sites on the Internet. Managers can access, store and move digital information (voice, sound, text and numbers). Private corporate intranets provide a universal interface for sharing company-wide information and work group level information. Employees can access information, collaborate, and distribute results anywhere, anytime (Fig. 1.7).

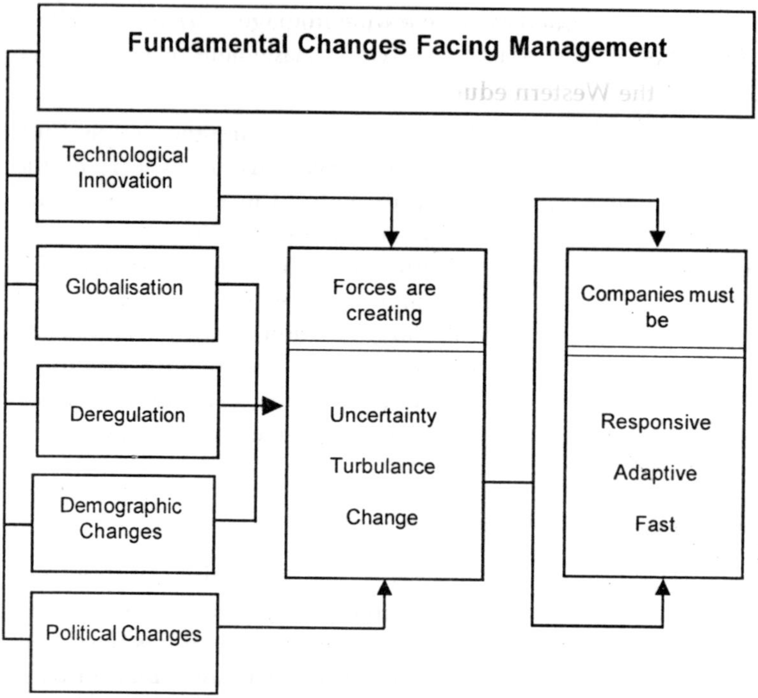

Fig. 1.7: Management in Information Age

The computer and telecommunications industries continue to converge and have resulted in advances in two-way pagers, digital cellular service, desktop video-conferencing, portable satellite phones, mini-dishes and high-speed Internet access. Business documents include graphics and text on computers around the world, sound, video and simultaneous voice communications. Thus, the Information Age implies a time for a revolution in the information environment for business and management. The changes that are taking place may be more significant to management than the Industrial Revolution.

Changing Profile of Executive

Nature of the Work: All organizations have specific goals and objectives that they strive to meet. Top executives devise strategies and formulate policies to ensure that these objectives are met. Although they have a wide range of titles—such as chief executive officer, board chair, president, vice president, school superintendent, county administrator, and tax commissioner—all formulate policies and direct the operations of businesses and corporations, nonprofit institutions, governments, and other organizations.

The chief executive officer in collaboration establishes a corporation's goals and policies with other top executives, who are overseen by a board of directors. In a large corporation, the chief executive officer meets frequently with subordinate executives to ensure that operations are implemented in accordance with these policies. The chief executive officer of a corporation retains overall accountability; however, a chief operating officer may be delegated several responsibilities, including the authority to oversee executives who direct the activities of various departments and implement the organization's policies on a day-to-day basis. In publicly held and nonprofit corporations, the board of directors is ultimately accountable for the success or failure of the enterprise, and the chief executive officer reports to the board.

The nature of other high-level executives' responsibilities depends upon the size of the organization. In large organizations, their duties are highly specialized. Managers of cost and profit centers, for instance, are responsible for the overall performance of one aspect of the organization, such as manufacturing, marketing, sales, purchasing, finance, personnel, training, administrative services, electronic data processing, property management, transportation, or the legal services department. In smaller organizations, such as independent retail stores or small manufacturers, a partner, owner, or general manager often is responsible for purchasing, hiring, training, quality control, and day-to-day manager's duties.

Chief financial officers direct the organization's financial goals, objectives, and budgets. They oversee the investment of funds and manage associated risks, supervise cash management activities, execute capital-raising strategies to support a firm's expansion, and deal with mergers and acquisitions.

Chief information officers are responsible for the overall technological direction of their organizations. They are increasingly involved in the strategic business plan of a firm as part of the executive team. To perform effectively, they also need knowledge of administrative procedures, such as budgeting, hiring, and supervision. These managers propose budgets for projects and programs, and make decisions on staff training and equipment purchases. They hire and assign computer specialists, information technology workers, and support personnel to carry out specific parts of the projects. They supervise the work of these employees, review their output, and establish administrative procedures and policies. Chief information officers also provide organizations with the vision to master information technology as a competitive tool.

Chief executive officers carry out a number of other important functions, such as meeting with legislators and constituents to determine the level of support for proposed programs. In addition, they often nominate citizens to boards and commissions, encourage business investment, and promote economic development in their communities. To do all of these varied tasks effectively, chief executives of large governments rely on a staff of highly skilled aides and assistants to research issues that concern the public. Executives that control small governmental bodies, however, often do this work by themselves.

General and operations managers plan, direct, or coordinate the operations of companies or public and private sector organizations. The duties include formulating policies, managing daily operations, and planning the use of materials and human resources, but are too diverse and general in nature to be classified in any one area of management or administration, such as personnel, purchasing, or administrative services. In some organizations, the duties of general and operations managers may overlap the duties of chief executive officers.

Conclusion

In conclusion, it has to be restated that management is the process of designing and maintaining an environment for the purpose of efficiently accomplishing selected aims. Managers carry out the functions of planning, organizing, staffing, leading, and controlling. Managing is an essential activity at all organizational levels.

However, the managerial skills required vary with organizational levels. Although women have made progress in obtaining responsible positions, they still have a long way to go. The goal of all managers is to create a surplus and to be productive by achieving a favorable output-input ratio within a specific time period with due consideration for quality. Productivity implies effectiveness (achieving of objectives) and efficiency (using the least amount of resources).

REFERENCES

Akhouri, N. (2002). "Aligning HRM Strategies with Competitiveness," in Singh, S. (ed.), *High Performance Organizations*, New Delhi: New Age, 333-343.

Budhwar, P. (2001). "Doing Business in India", *Thunderbird International Businesss Review*, Vol. 43, No.4. pp. 549-68

Davis, Keith (1957). *Human Relations at Work: The Dynamics of Organizational Behavior*, New York: McGraw-Hill, 1957 is now in its 10th edition.

Harold, Koontz and Weihrich Heinz (1990) *Essentials of Management*, Fifth Edition, New York: McGraw-Hill.

Herbert, Samir, Chatterjee and Mark (2006), *Management in India: Trends and Transition*, Response Books, New Delhi

Holt, David H. (1993). *Management – Principles and Practices*, Prentice-Hall, Englewood Cliffs, New Jersey, 1993.

Kanungo, R.N. and Mendonca, M. (1994), 'Culture and Performance Improvement,' *Productivity*, Vol. 35, No. 3, pp. 447-53

Katz, Robert (1974). "Skills of an effective administrator", *Harvard Business Review*, September-October 1974, pp. 90-101.

Luthans, Fred (1988). "Successful Vs. Effective Real Mangers", *The Academy of Management Executive*, Vol. II, No. 2, 1988.

Mintzberg, Henry (1973). *The Nature of Managerial Work*, New York: Harper & Row, 1973.

Newstrom, John W. and Keith Davis, (1996). *Organizational Behavior: Human Behavior at Work* 10th Edition, New York: McGraw-Hill.

Olum, Yasin (2004), *Modern Management Theories and Practices*, a paper presented at the 15th East African Central Banking Course, held on 12th July 2004, at Kenya School of Monetary Studies.

Rangnekar, S. (2006). "The Temple Ethos in Indian Management," *Science Tech Entreprenurship*, January 2006. pp. 4-7, 31 Neelamber, 37-G, Deshmukh Marg, Mumbai - 400026.

Robbins, S. (1998). *Organizational Behaviour*, 8th edition, New Delhi: Prentice-Hall of India, 16th Indian reprint.

Sahay, S. and Walsham, G. (1997), Social structure and managerial agency in India, *Organization Studies*, Vol. 18, pp. 415-44.

Stuart, Naomi (2008). *5DM*, Salisbury House, 15-17 The Broadway, Old Hatfield, Herts AL9 5HZ.

2 Evolution of Management

Leaders grow; they are not made.

– Peter F. Drucker

While appreciating the past success of 'management' we would also recognize that today's accelerating pace of change is putting pressure on our organizations to be at the forefront of management thinking. If we want to maintain our standard of living our rate of change has to be comparative to the rest of the world. But our present day management thinking has evolved from a whole range of influences over an extraordinary long period of time. In his comprehensive book '*The Evolution of Management Thought*' Daniel A Wren writes:

> "Within the practices of the past there are lessons of history for tomorrow in a continuous stream. We occupy but one point in this stream. The purpose.. is to present...the past as a prologue to the future."

So with the aim of accelerating the development of our management practice for the future let us examine that stream of evolving management thought of the past. Modern managers use many of the practices, principles, and techniques developed from earlier concepts and experiences. The Industrial Revolution brought about the emergence of large-scale business and its need for professional managers. Early military and church organizations provided the leadership models.

Classical School of Management

The Classical school of thought began around 1900 and continued into the 1920s. Traditional or *classical management* focuses

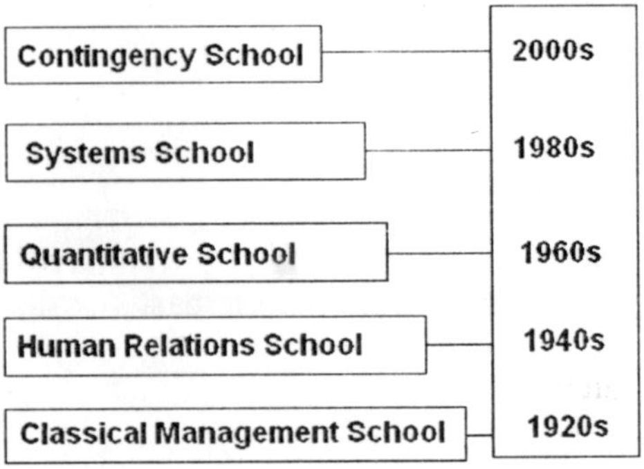

Fig. 2.1: Management Thoughts

on efficiency and includes bureaucratic, scientific and administrative management. Bureaucratic management relies on a rational set of structuring guidelines, such as rules and procedures, hierarchy, and a clear division of labor. Scientific management focuses on the "one best way" to do a job. Administrative management emphasizes the flow of information in the operation of the organization.

Bureaucracy

Max Weber (1864-1920), known as the Father of Modern Sociology, analyzed *bureaucracy* as the most logical and rational structure for large organz-iations. Bureaucracies are founded on legal or *rational authority* which is based on law, procedures, rules, and so on. *Positional authority* of a superior over a subordinate stems from legal authority. *Charismatic authority* stems from the personal qualities of an individual. Efficiency in bureaucracies comes from:

(1) clearly defined and specialized functions;

(2) use of legal authority;

(3) hierarchical form;

(4) written rules and procedures;

(5) technically trained bureaucrats;

(6) appointment to positions based on technical expertise;

(7) promotions based on competence;

(8) clearly defined career paths.

Scientific Management

It focuses on worker and machine relationships. Organizational productivity can be increased by increasing the efficiency of production processes. The efficiency perspective is concerned with creating jobs that economize on time, human energy, and other productive resources. Jobs are designed so that each worker has a specified, well controlled task that can be performed as instructed. Specific procedures and methods for each job must be followed with no exceptions.

Frederick Taylor (1856-1915)

Many of Frederick Taylor's definitive studies were performed at Bethlehem Steel Company in Pittsburgh. To improve productivity, Taylor examined the time and motion details of a job, developed a better method for performing that job, and trained the worker. Furthermore, Taylor offered a piece rate that increased as workers produced more.

In 1911, Frederick Taylor, known as the Father of Scientific Management, published *Principles of Scientific Management* in which he proposed work methods designed to increase worker productivity. One of his famous experiments had to do with increasing the output of a worker loading pig iron to a rail car. Taylor broke the job down into its smallest constituent movements, timing each one with a stopwatch. The job was redesigned with a reduced number of motions as well as effort and the risk of error. Rest periods of specific interval and duration and a differential pay scale were used to improve the output. With scientific management, Taylor increased the worker's output from 12 to 47 tons per day! The Taylor model gave rise to dramatic productivity increases.

Frank Gilbreth (1868-1924) and Lillian Gilbreth (1878-1972)

Frank and Lillian Gilbreth emphasized method by focusing on identifying the elemental motions in work, the way these motions were combined to form methods of operation, and the basic time each motion took. They believed it was possible to design work methods whose times could be estimated in advance, rather than relying upon observation-based time studies. Frank Gilbreth, known as the Father of Time and Motion Studies, filmed individual physical labor movements. This enabled the manager to break down a job into its component parts and streamline the process. His wife, Lillian Gilbreth, was a psychologist and author of *The Psychology of Work.* In 1911 Frank Gilbreth wrote *Motion Study* and in 1919 the couple wrote *Applied Motion Study.* Frank and Lillian had 12 children. Two of their children, Frank B. Gilbreth, Jr. and Ernestine Gilbreth Careyone, wrote their story, *Cheaper by the Dozen.*

One of Frank Gilbreth's first studies concerned bricklaying. (He had worked as an apprentice bricklayer.) He designed and patented special scaffolding to reduce the bending and reaching which increased output over 100 per cent. However, unions resisted his improvements, and most workers persisted in using the old, fatiguing methods.

Henry Gantt (1861-1919)

Henry Gantt developed the Gantt chart, which is used for scheduling multiple overlapping tasks over a time period. He focused on motivational schemes, emphasizing the greater effectiveness of rewards for good work (rather than penalties for poor work). He developed a pay incentive system with a guaranteed minimum wage and bonus systems for people on fixed wages. Also, Gantt focused on the importance of the qualities of leadership and management skills in building effective industrial organizations.

Administrative management emphasizes the manager and the functions of management. Henri Fayol (1841-1925), known as the Father of Modern Management, was a French industrialist who developed a framework for studying management. He wrote *General and Industrial Management.* His five functions of managers were plan, organize, command, coordinate, and control. His fourteen principles of management included division of work, authority and responsibility, discipline, unity of command, unity of direction, subordination of individual interests to general interests, renumeration of personnel, centralization, scalar chain, order, equity, stability of tenure of personnel, initiative, and esprit de corps (union is strength).

Mary Parker Follett's concepts included the universal goal, the universal principle, and the Law of the Situation. The **universal goal** of organizations is an integration of individual effort into a synergistic whole. The **universal principle** is a circular or reciprocal response emphasizing feedback to the sender (the concept of two-way communications). **Law of the Situation** emphasizes that there is no one best way to do anything, but that it all depends on the situation.

Human Relations School of Management

Behavioural or *human relations* management emerged in the 1920s and dealt with the human aspects of organizations. It has been referred to as the neoclassical school because it was initially a reaction to the shortcomings of the classical approaches to management. The human relations movement began with the Hawthorne Studies which were conducted from 1924 to 1933 at the Hawthorne Plant of the Western Electric Company in Cicero, Illinois.

The Hawthorne Studies

Harvard Business School researchers, T.N. Whitehead, Elton Mayo, and George Homans, were led by Fritz Roethlisberger. Elton Mayo, known as the Father of the Hawthorne Studies, identified the *Hawthorne Effect* or the bias that occurs when people know that they are being studied. The Hawthorne Studies are significant because they demonstrated the important influence of human factors on worker productivity. There were four major phases to the Hawthorne Studies: the illumination experiments, the relay assembly group experiments, the interviewing program, and the bank wiring group studies. The intent of these studies was to determine the effect of working conditions on productivity.

The illumination experiments tried to determine whether better lighting would lead to increased productivity. Both the control group and the experimental group of female employees produced more whether the lights were turned up or down. It was discovered that this increased productivity was a result of the attention received by the group. In the relay assembly group experiments, six female employees worked in a special, separate area; were given breaks and had the freedom to talk; and were continuously observed by a researcher who served as the manager. The manager consulted the employees prior to any change. The bank wiring group studies were analyzed thoroughly by Homans and were included in his now classic book, *The Human Group*. The bank wiring groups involved fourteen male employees and were similar to the relay assembly group experiments, except that there was no change of supervision. Again, in the relay and bank wiring phases, productivity increased and was attributed to group dynamics. The conclusion was that there was no cause-and-effect relationship between working conditions and productivity. Worker attitude was found to be important. An extensive employee interviewing program of 21,000 interviews was conducted to determine employee attitudes toward the company and their jobs. As a major outcome of these interviews, managers learned that an employee's complaint frequently is a symptom of some underlying problem on the job, at home, or in the person's past.

Chester Barnard (1886-1961)

When Chester Barnard retired as the CEO of New Jersey Bell Telephone, he recorded his insights about management in his book, *Functions of the Executive*. It outlined the legitimacy of the manager's directives and the extent of the subordinates' acceptance. He developed the concepts of strategic planning and the acceptance theory of authority. Strategic planning is the formulation of major plans or strategies, which guide the organization in pursuit of major objectives. Barnard taught that the three top functions of the executive were to

(1) establish and maintain an effective communication system,

(2) hire and retain effective personnel, and

(3) motivate those personnel.

His *Acceptance Theory of Authority* states that managers only have as much authority as employees allow them to have. The acceptance theory of authority suggests that authority flows downward but depends on acceptance by the subordinate. The acceptance of authority depends on four conditions:

(1) Employees must understand what the manager wants them to do.

(2) Employees must be able to comply with the directive.

(3) Employees must think that the directive is in keeping with organizational objectives.

(4) Employees must think that the directive is not contrary to their personal goals.

Barnard believed that each person has a *zone of indifference* or a range within each individual in which he or she would willingly accept orders without consciously questioning authority. It was up to the organization to provide sufficient inducements to broaden each employee's zone of indifference so that the manager's orders would be obeyed.

Integrating the Management Theories

Systems theory and a contingency view can help integrate the theories of management. Appropriate managerial techniques can be applied as required by environmental conditions. A broad perspective is valuable to managers when overseeing one unit or the total integration of all subunits.

Quantitative School Management

During the 1940s and World War II, quantitative perspective in management emerged. The historic origins of this school are found in World War II, when the Allies developed hunt-and-kill tactics for enemy submarines. Using statistical models, military experts were able to locate German submarines with some degree of probability. This approach is also called management science. It uses mathematical models for quantified decision-making. Its methods involve rather sophisticated techniques, extensive use of statistics, and complex decisions-making models. This viewpoint uses quantitative approaches from mathematics, statistics, engineering, and other related fields to solve problems.

It is a contemporary approach to management that focuses on the use of rigorous quantitative techniques to help managers make maximum use of organizational resources to produce goods and services. In essence, management science theory is a contemporary extension of scientific management, which, as developed by Taylor, also took a quantitative approach to measuring the worker–task mix in order to raise efficiency. There are many branches of management science; each of them deals with a specific set of concerns:

- *Quantitative management* utilizes mathematical techniques—such as linear and nonlinear programming, modelling, simulation, queuing theory, and chaos theory—to help managers decide, for example, how much inventory to hold at different times of the year, where to locate a new factory, and how best to invest an organization's financial capital.
- *Operations management (or operations research)* provides managers with a set of techniques that they can use to analyze any aspect of an organization's production system to increase efficiency.
- *Total quality management (TQM)* focuses on analyzing an organization's input, *Management information systems (MIS)* help managers design information systems that provide information about events occurring inside the organization as well as in its external environment—information that is vital for effective decision-making. All these subfields—

of management science provide tools and techniques that managers can use to help improve the quality of their decision-making and increase efficiency and effectiveness, conversion, and output activities to increase product quality.

Systems Theory

During the 1940s and World War II, systems analysis emerged. A system is an interrelated and interdependent set of elements functioning as a whole. It is an open system that interacts with its environment. It is composed of inputs from the environment (material or human resources), transformation processes of inputs to finished goods (technological and managerial processes), outputs of those finished goods into the environment (products or services), and feedback (reactions from the environment).

Subsystems are systems within a broader system. Interdependent subsystems (such as production, finance, and human resources) work toward synergy in an attempt to accomplish an organizational goal that could not otherwise be accomplished by a single subsystem. Systems develop synergy (See Fig. 2.3). This is a condition in which the combined and coordinated actions of the parts of a system achieve more than all the parts could have achieved acting independently. Entropy is the process that leads to decline.

Contingency Theory

Another milestone in management theory was the development of *contingency theory* in the 1960s by Tom Burns and G.M. Stalker in the United Kingdom and Paul Lawrence and Jay Lorsch in the United States. In the mid-1960s, the contingency view of management or situational approach emerged. The crucial message of contingency theory is that *there is no one best way to organize*: The organizational structures and the control systems that managers choose depend on—are contingent on—characteristics of the external environment in which the organization operates. According to contingency theory, the characteristics of the environment affect an organization's ability to obtain resources. To maximize the likelihood of gaining access

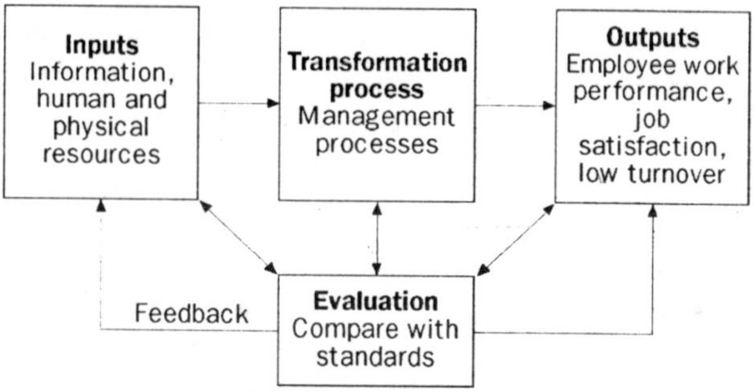

Fig. 2.2: A System appraoch to expatriate management

to resources, managers must allow an organization's departments to organize and control their activities in ways most likely to allow them to obtain resources, given the constraints of the particular environment they face. In other words, how managers design the organizational hierarchy, choose a control system, and lead and motivate their employees is contingent on the characteristics of the organizational environment (see Fig 2.4).

An important characteristic of the external environment that affects an organization's ability to obtain resources is the degree to which the environment is changing. Changes in the organizational environment include: changes in technology, which can lead to the creation of new products (such as compact discs) and result in the obsolescence of existing products (eight-track tapes); the entry of new competitors (such as foreign organizations that compete for available resources); and unstable economic conditions. In general, the more quickly the organizational environment is changing, the greater are the problems associated with gaining access to resources and the greater is the manager's need to find ways to coordinate the activities of people in different departments in order to respond to the environment quickly and effectively. The basic idea behind contingency theory – that there is no one best way to design or lead an organization – has been incorporated into other areas of management theory, including leadership theories. This view emphasizes the fit between organization processes and the characteristics of the situation. It calls for fitting the structure of the organization to various

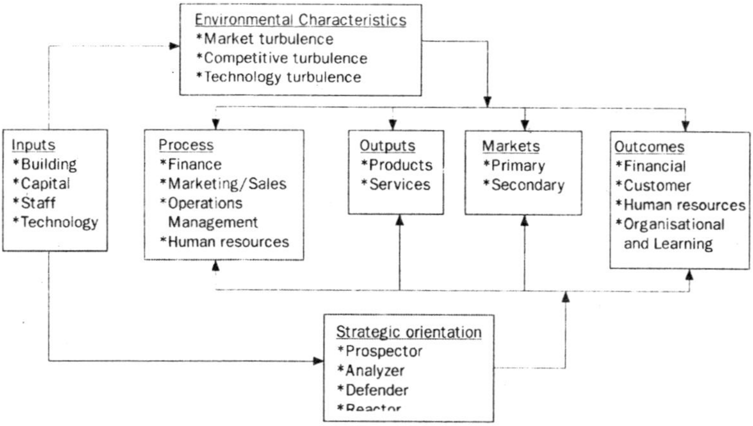

Fig. 2.4: The Characteristics of the Organizational Environment

possible or chance events. It questions the use of universal management practices and advocates using traditional, behavioural, and systems viewpoints independently or in combination to deal with various circumstances. The contingency approach assumes that managerial behaviour is dependent on a wide variety of elements. Thus, it provides a framework for integrating the knowledge of management thought.

Emerging Management Thoughts

New management viewpoints are emerging. Quality management emphasizes achieving customer satisfaction by providing high quality goods and services. Reengineering the organization redesigns the processes that are crucial to customer satisfaction. Chaos models the corporation as a complex adaptive system that interacts and evolves with its surroundings. Many seemingly random movements in nature exhibit structured patterns. Living systems operate at their most robust and efficient level in the narrow space between stability and disorder – poised at "the edge of chaos." It is here that the agents within a system conduct the fullest range of productive interactions and exchange the greatest amount of useful information.

REFERENCES

Bennis, W. (1989) *On Becoming a Leader*, Reading, MA: Addison-Wesley Publishers.

Drucker, P. (1992) "Innovation and Entrepreneurial Practices and Principles", *Hardvard Business Rewiew*: 19.

Friesen and J.A. Johnson, M. (1995): *The Success Paradigm*, Westport, CT: Quorum Books.

Harold, Koontz (1961). "The Management Theory Jungle", *Journal of the Academy of Management*, December.

Harold, Koontz (1962). "Making Sense of Management Theory", *Harvard Business Review*, July-August.

Harold, Koontz (1980). "The Management Theory Revisited", *Academy of Management Review*, April.

Harold, Koontz and Weihrich Heinz (1990). *Essentials of Management*, Fifth Edition, McGraw-Hill.

Hetterick, Jr., R. (1994), "Technological Change and Higher Education Policy," *AGB Priorities 1* (Spring).

Homans, G. C. (1958) *The Human Group*, New York: Harcour, Brace and World.

Johnson, J. A. (1998). "Interview with Warren Bennis," *Journal of Healthcare Management* (July/August): 293.

Miller, L. (1989). *Barbarians to Bureaucrats: Corporate Lifestyle Strategies*, New York: Fawcett.

Mintzberg, H. (1996). "The Manager's Job: Folklore and Fact," in *Management 96/97*, 4th ed., ed. F.H. Maidment, Sluice Dock, Guilford, CT: Brown & Benchmark Publishers.

Stoner, James A.F., Freeman R. Edward, and Gilbert, Jr. Daniel R. (2003). *Management*, New Delhi: Prentice-Hall of India, Sixth Edition.

Van, Fleet David D. and Peterson Tim O. (1994) *Contemporary Management*, Houghton Mifflin Company, Third Edition.

3 Planning

A vision without a plan is just a dream. A plan without a vision is just drudgery. But a vision with a plan can change the world.

Planning

Planning is a complex process that can take many forms. There are different kinds of planning and different ways of planning. *Planning* refers to the process of deciding what to do and how to do it. Planning is the process of defining an organizational objectives and then articulating strategies, tactics, and operations necessary to achieve those objectives. George Steiner describes the planning function as one in which mangers must decide "what is to be done, when it is to be done, how it is to be done, and who is to do it." A plan, therefore, is a navigational tool that maps out a destination and chats a course to get there. Planning occurs at many levels, from day-to-day decisions made by individuals and families, to complex decisions made by businesses and governments. This paper focuses on community land use and transport planning, but most principles described apply to any planning activity. *Planners* are professionals who facilitate decision-making. Planners do not make decisions themselves; rather, they support decision-makers (managers, public officials, citizens) by coordinating information and activities. Their role is to create a logical, systematic decision-making process that results in the best actions.

Planning Principles

Good planning requires a methodical process that clearly defines the steps that lead to optimal solutions. This process should reflect the following principles:

- *Comprehensive* - all significant options and impacts are considered.
- *Efficient* - the process should not waste time or money.
- *Inclusive* - people affected by the plan have opportunities to be involved.
- *Informative* - results are understood by stakeholders (people affected by a decision).
- *Integrated* - individual, short-term decisions should support strategic, long-term goals.
- *Logical* - each step leads to the next.
- *Transparent* - everybody involved understands how the process operates.

The Planning Hierarchy and Categories

Planning responsibilities are different for mangers at each organizational level. Planning requires clear and effective method of communication. The purpose of plan is effective and efficient use of resources. Efficiency is doing things right. An efficient manger achieves results that match up to the inputs. Effectiveness is doing the right things. It is the ability to choose appropriate course of actions. The hierarchy and categories of plans are as follows:

Levels	*Plans*	*Time Span*	*Category*
Corporate	Purpose and Mission Board and CEO Long-term strategic vision	No time horizon	Strategic Plan • Corporate level strategy • Business unit strategy • Functional strategy
Top	Strategic Plans Executing Management Facilitating goals/Targets	Five Years	
Middle	Tactical Plans Middle Management and Functional Staff Supporting operational objectives	Annual	Operations Plan (a) Single use Plan Budget Programmes Projects
Lower	Operational Plans First line Management Department Heads Managers First line Implementation, Individual Objectives	Short-term	(b) Standing Plans Policies Rules Standard Procedure Regulations

Strategic Planning

Strategic planning produces fundamental decisions and actions that shape and guide what an organization is, what it does, and why it does it. It requires broad-scale information gathering, an exploration of alternatives, and an emphasis on the future implications of present decisions. Top level managers engage chiefly in strategic planning or long range planning. They answer such questions as "What is the purpose of this organization?" "What does this organization have to do in the future to remain competitive?" Top level managers clarify the mission of the organization and set its goals. The output needed by top management for long range planning is summary reports about finances, operations, and the external environment.

Strategic planning is the process of developing and analyzing the organization's mission, overall goals, general strategies, and allocating resources. A strategy is a course of action created to achieve a long-term goal. The time length for strategies is arbitrary, but is probably two, three, or perhaps as many as five years. It is generally determined by how far in the future the organization is committing its resources. Goals focus on desired changes. They are the ends that the organization strives to attain. Traditionally strategic planning has been done annually. However, many companies are doing away with annual business plans altogether and moving to a system of continuous planning, to permit quicker response to changing conditions. Thus, the strategic plan involves adapting the organization to take advantage of opportunities in its constantly changing environment.

Tactical Plans

Top level managers set very general, long-term goals that require more than one year to achieve. Examples of long-term goals include long-term growth, improved customer service, and increased profitability. Middle managers interpret these goals and develop tactical plans for their departments that can be accomplished within one year or less. In order to develop tactical plans, middle management needs detail reports (financial, operational, market, external environment). Tactical plans have shorter time frames and narrower scopes than strategic plans. Tactical planning provides the specific ideas for implementing the strategic plan. It is the process of making detailed decisions about what to do, who will do it, and how to do it.

Operational Plans

Managers implement operational plans that are short-term and deal with the day-to-day work of their team. Short-term goals are aligned with the long-term goals and can be achieved within one year. Managers set standards, form schedules, secure resources, and report progress. They need very detailed reports about operations, personnel, materials, and equipment. The manager interprets higher management plans as they apply to his or her unit. Thus, operational plans support tactical plans. They are the manager's tools for executing daily, weekly, and monthly activities. An example is a budget, which is a plan that shows how money will be spent over a certain period of time. Other examples of planning by managers include scheduling the work of employees and identifying needs for staff and resources to meet future changes. Resources include employees, information, capital, facilities, machinery, equipment, supplies, and finances.

Operational plans include policies, procedures, methods, and rules. The terms themselves imply different degrees of scope.

- *Policy* is a general statement designed to guide employees' actions in recurring situations. It establishes broad limits, provides direction, but permits some initiative and discretion on the part of the manager. Thus, policies are guidelines.
- *Procedure* is a sequence of steps or operations describing how to carry out an activity and usually involves a group. It is more specific than a policy and establishes a customary way of handling a recurring activity. Thus, less discretion on the part of the manager is permissible in its application. An example of a procedure is the sequence of steps in routing of parts.
- *Method* sets up the manner and sequence of accomplishing a recurring, individual task. Almost no

discretion is allowed. An example of a method is the steps in cashing a check.

- *Rule* is an established guide for conduct. Rules include definite things to do and not to do. There are no exceptions to the rules. An example of a rule is "No Smoking".

Monitor the plan

A systematic method of monitoring the environment must be adopted to continuously improve the strategic planning process. To develop an environmental monitoring procedure, short-term standards for key variables that will tend to validate the long-range estimates must be established. Although favorable long-range values have been estimated, short-term guidelines are needed to indicate if the plan is unfolding as hoped. Next, criteria must be set up to decide when the strategy must be changed. Feedback is encouraged and incorporated to determine if goals and objectives are feasible. This review is used for the next planning cycle and review.

Planning Process

Leaders are proactive. They make change happen instead of reacting to change. The future requires corporate leadership with the skills to integrate many unexpected and seemingly diverse events into its planning. Every organization must plan for change in order to reach its ultimate goal. Effective planning helps an organization adapt to change by identifying opportunities and avoiding problems. It sets the direction for the other functions of management and for teamwork. Planning improves decision-making. All levels of management engage in planning.

Strategic goals and objectives are developed to bridge the gap between current capability and the mission. They are aligned with the mission and form the basis for the action plans. Objectives are sometimes referred to as performance goals. Generally, organizations have long-term objectives for such factors as return on investment, earnings per share, or size. Furthermore, they set minimum acceptable standards or common-sense minimums. In addition, certain limitations, either explicit or implicit, such as "must provide jobs for existing employees" may exist. Objectives elaborate on the mission statement and constitute a specific set of policy, programmatic, or management objectives for the programmes and operations covered in the strategic plan. They are expressed in a manner that allows a future assessment of whether an objective has been achieved.

Tactical plans are based on the organization's strategic plan. In turn, operational plans are based on the organization's tactical plans. These are specific plans that are needed for each task or supportive activity comprising the whole. Strategic, tactical, and operational planning must be accompanied by controls. Monitoring progress or providing for follow-up is intended to assure that plans are carried out properly and on time. Adjustments may need to be made to accommodate changes in the external and/or internal environment of the organization. A competitive advantage can be gained by adapting to the challenges.

Operating Guidelines

Successful organizations continually innovate and change based upon customer needs and feedback. Values, mission, and vision form the foundation for the execution of the functions of management. They are an organization's guidelines that affect how it will operate. They work only if visible and used in everyday activities and decisions. An organization's values are its beliefs or those qualities that have intrinsic worth and will not be compromised. Its mission is its purpose for existing. The vision is the image of itself in the future.

Values

Each manager's approach to management will reflect his or her values, as well as those of the organization. Building trust starts with creating culture based on shared values. Values are traits or qualities having intrinsic worth, such as courage, respect, responsibility, caring, truthfulness, self-discipline, and fairness. Values serve as a baseline for actions and decision-making and guide employees in the organization's intentions and interests. The values driving behavior define the

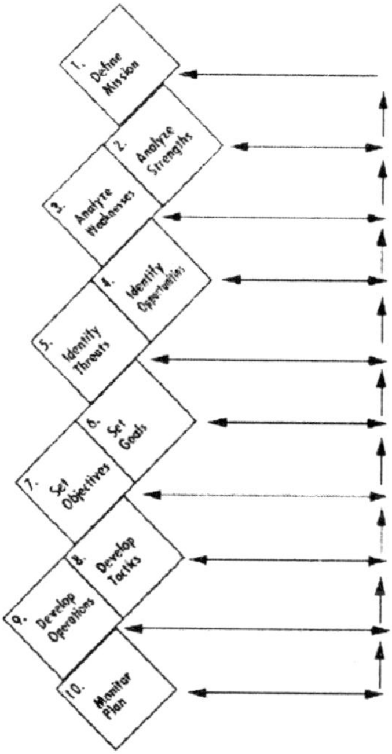

Fig. 3.1: Steps in Planning

organizational culture. A strong value system or clearly defined culture turns beliefs into standards such as best quality, best performance, most reliable, most durable, safest, fastest, best value for the money, least expensive, most prestigious, best designed or styled, easiest to use. If asked, "What do we believe in?" or "List our organization's values" all employees in the organization should write down the same values. For example, McDonald's values were captured in its motto of "Q.S.C. & V." which stands for quality, service, cleanliness, and value.

Planning Framework

A *planning framework* defines the basic planning process structure. This typically includes the following components.

- *Principles* - A basic rule or concept used for decision-making.
- *Vision* - A general description of the desired result of the planning process.

- *Problem* – An undesirable condition to be *mitigated* (solved, reduced or compensated).
- *Goals* – A general desirable condition to be achieved.
- *Objectives* – Specific ways to achieve goals.
- *Scope* – The range (area, people, time, activities, etc.) to be included in a process.
- *Options* – Possible solutions to a problem or ways to achieve an objective.
- *Evaluation methodology* – The process of valuing and comparing options, such as cost
- Effectiveness, benefit/cost, or lifecycle cost analysis.
- *Evaluation criteria* – The impacts (costs and benefits) considered in an analysis.
- *Policies* – A general course of action.
- *Plans* – A scheme or set of actions. This may be a *strategic* (general and broad) or an
- *Action* (specific and narrow) plan.
- *Programmes* – A specific set of objectives, responsibilities and tasks within an organization.
- *Tasks* or *Actions* – A specific thing to be accomplished.
- *Targets* – Something specific to be achieved.
- *Performance indicators* – Practical ways to measure progress toward objectives.

Sustainability Planning

Sustainability emphasizes the integrated nature of human activities and therefore the need to balance economic, social and environmental objectives. Interest in sustainability can be considered a reaction to overly specialized decision-making focused on easily measured goals and impacts, while ignoring those that are indirect or more difficult to measure. Sustainability planning requires comprehensive analysis that accounts for all significant impacts, including those distant in space and time. It strives for *development* (increased quality) rather than *growth* (increased quantity), and recognizes resource constraints and ecological risks such as fossil fuel depletion, habitat loss and climate change. Conventional planning asks, "Does it work?" Sustainability planning tends to ask "Does it fit?" That is, whether individual decisions fit into overall long-term goals.

Steps to Effective Planning

- Planning should be integrated, so individual, short-term decisions are consistent with broader, strategic goals.
- Analysis should be comprehensive, reflecting all significant perspectives, impacts and objectives. A broad range of options and impacts should be considered.
- Planners should be objective, fair and respectful.
- Insure adequate public involvement. Stakeholders should be kept informed and have opportunities for involvement.
- Clearly define the goals (what you ultimately want), and regularly revisit the question, "what exactly are we trying to accomplish?"
- The planning process should be understood by all stakeholders, with clearly defined vision or problem statement, goals, objectives, evaluation criteria and performance indicators.
- Consider a wide range of possible solutions including some that may initially seem unrealistic but could be appropriate as part of an integrated programme. Support innovation: recognizing that some new strategies fail, but even unsuccessful experiments provide useful information.
- Identify resources, constraints, and conflicts. Draw attention to potential problems.
- Make sure results are comprehendible to the intended audience, using suitable language and visual information (graphs, maps, images, etc.). Highlight differences between options.
- Identify and avoid token solutions which fail to really address a problem. Modest actions may be appropriate if it is the beginning but not the end of more substantial solutions.
- Be prepared for setbacks. A planning process sometimes initially fails, but succeed if repeated due to changing

circumstances, more stakeholder understanding and commitment.

- Changes should be implemented as predictably and gradually as possible.
- When appropriate use contingency-based planning, which identifies a wide range of potential solutions and implements the most cost-effective strategies justified at each point in time, with additional strategies available for quick deployment if needed in the future.

REFERENCES

Allen, LA. (2002). *Management and Organization*, McGraw-Hill Publishing Co., Ltd.

Black, Stewart and Lyman W. Porter (2000). *Management – Meeting New Challenges*, Prentice-Hall.

Blanchard, B.S. and W.J. Fabrycky, (1990). *System Engineering and Analysis*, 2nd ed., Prentice-Hall, Englewood Cliffs, N.J.

Certo (2002), *Modern Management*, 9th Edition, Prentice-Hall of India, New Delhi.

Fayol, H. (1949), *General and Industrial Administration*, Sir Isaac Pitman & Sons, London, UK.

Hellriegel, Jackson and Slocum (2002). *Management: A Competency-based Approach*, South Western, 9th edition.

Kerzner, H. (1989). *Project Management: A Systems Approach to Planning, Scheduling, and Controlling*, 3rd ed., Van Nostrand Reinhold, New York, N.Y.

Koontz, H. and C. O'Donnell, (1972). *Principles of Management: An Analysis of Managerial Functions*, 5th ed., McGraw-Hill, New York, N.Y.

MacKenzie, R.A. (1969). "The Management Process in 3-D," *Harvard Business Review*, Nov.-Dec. pp. 80-87.

Sathyaraju (2002), *Management : Text & Cases*, Prentice-Hall of India.

Snell, Bateman (2002). *Management: Competing in the New Era*, McGraw-Hill, Irwin, 2002.

Thayer, R.H. and A.B. Pyster (1984). "Guest Editorial: Software Engineering Project Management," *IEEE Transactions on Software Engineering*, Vol. SE-10, No. 1, Jan.

Weihrich, H. and H. Koontz (1993). *Management: A Global Perspective*, 10th ed., McGraw-Hill, New York, NY.

4 Organizing

"Processes are assembled from flows, directed at flows, and summarize flows."

– *Karl Weick*

Organizing, like planning, must be a carefully worked out and applied process. This process involves determining what work is needed to accomplish the goal, assigning those tasks to individuals, and arranging those individuals in a decision-making framework i.e. organizational structure. Organizing is that part of the manager's task which involves coordinating and directing the company's resources in such a way that the company can carry out its objectives. Managers can control very substantial resources in terms of people, money, time, materials, equipment, etc., although it is the organization of the first of these, i.e. people, which takes up most of a manager's time and attention. Organizing is the process of identifying activities and making structure of the organization fit with its planned objectives. Organizing as a function gathering resources, allocating resources, and structuring tasks to fulfill organizational plans. Organizational structure is the arrangement and interrelationship of the different departments and positions.

Purpose of Organizing

Urwick defined the purpose of organizing, from the view of an administrator: Much of the task of organizing involves establishing a framework or structure of roles for people in the organization to fill. This means that all the tasks which have to be done to allow the company to accomplish its objectives are assigned to people who are able to carry them out competently.

Organizing, therefore, involves identifying the activities which need to be done to achieve these objectives; grouping these activities together into departments; assigning such groups of activities to managers; delegating to the managers the authority to carry the tasks out; and setting up a structure for coordinating all these activities, both horizontally and vertically within the organization.

Elements of Organizing

There are various elements (or principles) of organizational structure which tend to be common to most businesses. One set of these principles was published by Urwick in the 1940s (which he subsequently revised in the early 1950s). They provide a useful starting point for bdiscussion, and so are listed here:

- *The principle of the objective.* Every part of the organization must be an expression of the purpose of the undertaking concerned, or else it is meaningless and, therefore, redundant.
- *The principle of specialization.* The activities of every member of any organized group should be confined, as far as possible, to the performance of a single function.
- *The principle of coordination.* The purpose of organizing, as distinguished from the purpose of the undertaking, is to facilitate co-ordination and unity of effort.
- *The principle of authority.* In every organized group supreme authority must rest somewhere. There should be a clear line of authority from the holder of supreme authority down to every individual in the group.
- *The principle of responsibility.* Managers have absolute responsibility for the acts of their subordinates.
- *The principle of definition.* The content of each position (the duties involved, the authority and responsibility it contains, and the relationships with other positions) should be clearly defined in writing and given to all concerned.

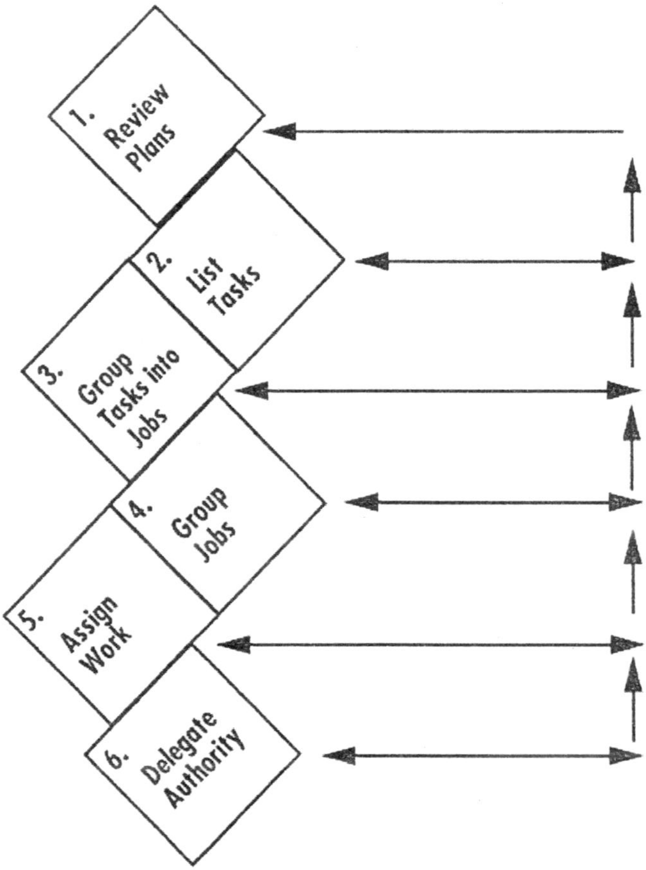

Fig. 4.1: Steps in Organizing Process

- *The principle of correspondence.* In every position the degree of responsibility it carries and the authority it confers should correspond. The principle of the span of control. No person should supervise more than five, or at the most six, direct subordinates whose work interlocks.
- *The principle of balance.* It is essential that the various elements of the organization should be kept in balance.
- *The principle of continuity.* Organizing is a continuous process, and in every undertaking specific provision should be made for it.

Organizing Process

A key issue in accomplishing the goals identified in the planning process is structuring the work of the organization. Organizations are groups of people, with ideas and resources, working toward common goals. The purpose of the organizing function is to make the best use of the organization's resources to achieve organizational goals. Organizational structure is the formal decision-making framework by which job tasks are divided, grouped, and coordinated. Formalization is an important aspect of structure. It is the extent to which the units of the organization are explicitly defined and its policies, procedures, and goals are clearly stated. It is the official organizational structure conceived and built by top management. The formal organization can be seen and represented in chart form. An organization chart displays the organizational structure and shows job titles, lines of authority, and relationships between departments (See Fig. 4.2).

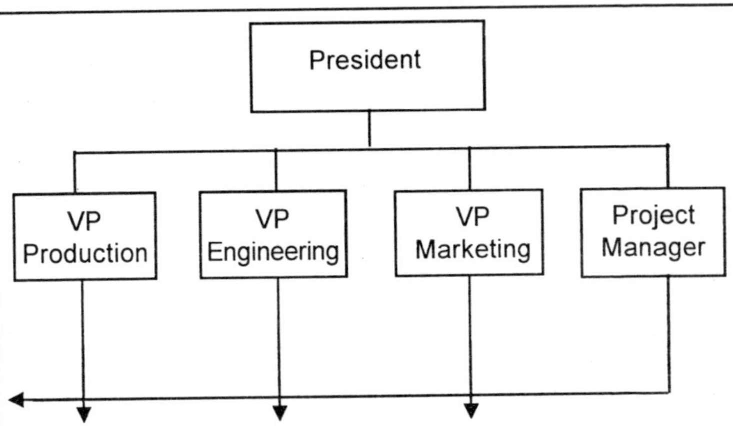

Fig. 4.2: Organisational Structure

The informal organization is the network, unrelated to the firm's formal authority structure, of social interactions among its employees. The manager must realize that the informal organization affects the formal organization. The informal organization can pressure group members to conform to the expectations of the informal group that conflict with those of the formal organization. This can result in the generation of false information or rumors and resistance to change desired by management. The manager should recognize the existence of information groups, identify the roles member play within these groups, and use knowledge of the groups to work effectively with them. The informal organization can make the formal organization more effective by providing support to management, stability to the environment, and useful communication channels.

Organizational Structure

Even though the differences among organizations are enormous, there are many similarities that enable them to be classified. One widely used classification is the twofold system (mechanistic versus organic forms of organizational structure) developed by Tom Burns and G. M. Stalker in their study of electronics firms in the United Kingdom. The mechanistic structure is the traditional or classical design, common in many medium- and large-size organizations. Mechanistic organizations are somewhat rigid in that they consist of very clearly delineated jobs, have a well-defined hierarchical structure, and rely heavily on the formal chain of command for control. Bureaucratic organizations, with their emphasis on formalization, are the primary form of mechanistic structures.

According to Max Weber, bureaucracy is a form of organization characterized by a rational, goal-directed hierarchy, impersonal decision-making, formal controls, and subdivision into managerial positions and specialization of labor. Bureaucratic organizations are tall consisting of hierarchies with many levels of management. In a tall structure, people become relatively confined to their own area of specialization. Bureaucracies are driven by a top-down or command and control approach in which managers provide considerable direction and have considerable control over others. Other features of the bureaucratic organization include functional division of labor and work specialization. On the other hand, the organic structure is more flexible, more adaptable to a participative form of management, and less concerned with a clearly defined structure. The organic organization is open to the environment in order to capitalize upon new opportunities.

Organization Design

Designing an organization involves choosing an organizational structure that will enable the company to most effectively achieve its goals. Organization design is the creation of an organization's structure, traditionally functional, divisional, and/or matrix. Functions or divisions arrange traditional organizations. In a functional organization, authority is determined by the relationships between group functions and activities. Functional structures group similar or related occupational specialties or processes together under the familiar headings of finance, manufacturing, marketing, accounts receivable, research, surgery, and photo finishing. Economy is achieved through specialization. However, the organization risks losing sight of its overall interests as different departments pursue their own goals.

In a divisional organization, corporate divisions operate as relatively autonomous businesses under the larger corporate umbrella. In a conglomerate organization, divisions may be unrelated. Divisional structures are made up of self-contained strategic business units that each produces a single product. For example, General Motors' divisions. A central headquarters, focusing or results, coordinates and controls the activities, and provides support services between divisions. Functional departments accomplish division goals. A weakness however, is the tendency to duplicate activities among divisions.

In a matrix organization, teams are formed and team members report to two or more managers. Matrix structures utilize functional and divisional chains of command simultaneously in the same part of the organization, commonly for one-of-a-kind projects. It is used to develop a new product, to ensure the continuing success of a product to which several departments directly contribute, and to solve a difficult problem. By superimposing a project structure upon the functional structure, a matrix organization is formed that allows the organization to take advantage of new opportunities. This structure assigns specialists from different functional departments to work on one or more projects being led by project managers. The matrix concept facilitates working on concurrent projects by creating a dual chain of command, the project (programme, systems, or product) manager and the functional manager. Project managers have authority over activities geared toward achieving organizational goals while functional managers have authority over promotion decisions and performance reviews. An example is an aerospace firm with a contract.

Matrix organizations are particularly appealing to firms that want to speed up the decision-making process. However, the matrix organization may not allow long-term working relationships to develop. Furthermore, using multiple managers for one employee may result in confusion as to manager evaluation and accountability. Thus, the matrix system may elevate the conflict between product and functional interests.

Boundaryless organizations are not defined or limited by horizontal, vertical, or external boundaries imposed by a predetermined structure. They share many of the characteristics of flat organizations, with a strong emphasis on teams. Cross-functional teams dissolve horizontal barriers and enable the organization to respond quickly to environmental changes and to spearhead innovation. Boundaryless organizations can form relationships (joint ventures, intellectual property, distribution channels, or financial resources) with customers, suppliers, and/or competitors. Telecommuting, strategic alliances and customer-organization linkages break down external barriers, streamlining work activities. Jack Welch, former CEO of General Electric, to facilitate interactions with customers and suppliers, first used this unstructure.

A boundaryless environment is required by learning organizations to facilitate team collaboration and the sharing of information. When an organization develops the continuous capacity to adapt and survive in an increasingly competitive environment because all members take an active role in identifying and resolving work-related issues, it has developed a learning culture. A learning organization is one that is able to adapt and respond to change. This design empowers employees because they acquire and share knowledge and apply this learning to decision-making. They are pooling collective intelligence and stimulating creative thought to improve performance. Managers facilitate learning by sharing and aligning the organization's vision for the future and sustaining a sense of community and strong culture.

Organizing Function

The organizing function deals with all those activities that result in the formal assignment of tasks and authority and a coordination of effort. The manager staffs the work unit, trains employees, secures resources, and empowers the work group into a productive team. The steps in the organizing process include:

- View plans
- List all tasks to be accomplished
- Divide tasks into groups one person can accomplish - a job
- Group related jobs together in a logical and efficient manner
- Assign work to individuals
- Delegate authority to establish relationships between jobs and groups of jobs.

The nature and scope of the work needed to accomplish the organization's objectives is needed to determine work classification and work unit design. Division of labor, or work specialization, is the degree to which tasks in an organization are divided into separate jobs. Work process requirements and employee skill level determine the degree of specialization. Placing capable people in each job ties directly with productivity improvement. In order to maximize productivity, managers match employee skill level with task requirements.

Managers should perform workflow analysis to examine

how work creates or adds value to the ongoing processes in an organization. Workflow analysis looks at how work moves from the customer or the demand source through the organization to the point at which the work leaves the organization as a product or service to meet customer demand. Thus, workflow analysis can be used to tighten the connection between employees' work and customers' needs. Also, it can help to make major performance breakthroughs throughout business process reengineering (BPR), a fundamental rethinking and radical redesign of business processes to achieve dramatic improvements in costs, quality, service, and speed. BPR uses workflow analysis to identify jobs that can be eliminated or recombined to improve company performance.

Departmentalization

After reviewing the plans, usually the first step in the organizing process is departmentalization. Once jobs have been classified through work specialization, they are grouped so those common tasks can be coordinated. Departmentalization is the basis on which work or individuals are grouped into manageable units. There are five traditional methods for grouping work activities (Fig. 4.2).

Departmentalization by function organizes by the functions to be performed. The functions reflect the nature of the business. The advantage of this type of grouping is obtaining efficiencies from consolidating similar specialties and people with common skills, knowledge and orientations together in common units.

Departmentalization by product assembles all functions needed to make and market a particular product are placed under one executive. For instance, major department stores are structured around product groups such as home accessories, appliances, women's clothing, men's clothing, and children's clothing.

Departmentalization by geographical regions groups jobs on the basis of territory or geography. For example, Merck, a major pharmaceutical company, has its domestic sales departmentalized by regions such as Northeast, Southeast, Midwest, Southwest, and Northwest.

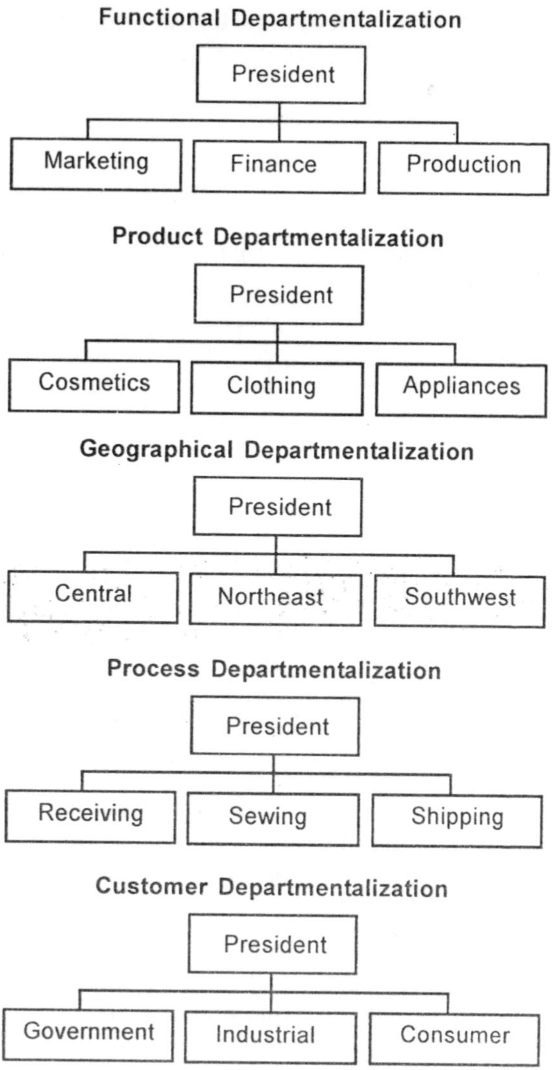

Fig. 4.3: Departmentalization: Five Traditional Methods for Grouping Work Activities

Departmentalization by process groups jobs on the basis of product or customer flow. Each process requires particular skills and offers a basis for homogeneous categorizing of work activities. A patient preparing for an operation would first engage in preliminary diagnostic tests, then go through the admitting process, undergo a procedure in surgery, receive post operative care, be discharged and perhaps receive out-patient attention. These services are each administered by different departments.

Departmentalization by customer groups jobs on the basis of a common set of needs or problems of specific customers. For instance, a plumbing firm may group its work according to whether it is serving private sector, public sector, government, or not-for-profit organizations. A current departmentalization trend is to structure work according to customer, using cross-functional teams. This group is chosen from different functions to work together across various departments to interdependently create new products or services. For example, a cross-functional team consisting of managers from accounting, finance, and marketing is created to prepare a technology plan.

Power and Authority

Organizational structure is a means of facilitating the achievement of organizational objectives. Such structures are not static, but dynamic. They reorganize in response to changing conditions that occur in the environment, new technology, or organizational growth. Organization structures are dependent upon the employees whose activities they guide. Managers rely upon power and authority to ensure that employees get things done.

Authority

The organizational structure provides the framework for the formal distribution of authority. Formalization is the degree to which tasks are standardized and rules and regulations govern employee behavior. It influences the amount of discretion an employee has over his or her job. In an organization with high degrees of formalization, job descriptions and policies provide clear direction. Where formalization is low, employees have a great deal of freedom in deciding how they conduct their work. Within the same organization, different departments may have different degrees of formalization. For example, in a hospital, doctors have freedom in selecting treatments, drugs, and methods for treating patients. However, the hospital physical plant staff has a strict schedule for cleaning buildings, mowing lawns, and maintaining the facilities. Authority is the legitimate power of a manager to direct subordinates to take action within the scope of the manager's position. Formal authority in the organization can be traced all the way back to the U.S. constitutional right to own property. The owner of the organization has the authority to make decisions. For example, entrepreneurial firms have an informal arrangement of employees and centralization of decision-making authority, the owner.

Power

In addition to authority, managers have more personal sources of power to draw upon for getting things done. Everyone has power in one form or another and it is by exercising this power that organizations get things accomplished. Managers who are capable of achieving their objectives independently of others are said to possess strength. When these "strong" managers involve and incorporate others into their plans and activities they are making use of power, and in fact increasing the total amount of power available to incorporate into a particular situation or problem. Involving employees in setting objectives and making decisions as it relates to their jobs empowers everyone, and results in greater job satisfaction and commitment, as well as increased productivity. Empowering employees provides them with greater autonomy.

Power is the ability to exert influence in the organization beyond authority, which is derived from position. The manager's personal power could include job knowledge, personal influence, interpersonal skills, and ability to get results, empathetic ability, persuasive ability, and physical strength.

Sources of Power

there are six sources of power - legitimate, coercive, reward, expert, referent, and information. Legitimate power is a result of the position a person holds in the organization hierarchy. This position power is broader than the ability to reward and punish, as members need to accept the authority of the position.

Coercive power is the threat of sanctions. It is dependent on fear and includes, but is not limited to the ability to dismiss, assign undesirable work, or restriction of movement. Reward power results in people doing what is asked because they desire positive benefits or rewards. Rewards can be anything a person values (praise, raises, and promotions). Expert power comes from expertise, skill, or knowledge. Referent power refers to a person who has desirable resources or personal traits. It results in admiration and the desire to emulate. Information power is based upon the persuasiveness or content of a communication and is independent of the influencing individual.

Centralization versus Decentralization

Centralization is the degree to which decision-making is concentrated in top management's hands. Decentralization is the extent to which decision-making authority is pushed down the organization structure and shared with many lower-level employees. Centralized organizations have more levels of management with narrow spans of control. Employees are not free to make decisions. Decentralized organizations have fewer levels of management with wide spans of control giving employees more freedom of action. All other things being equal, a wide span of control is more efficient because it requires fewer managers. However, it is important to recognize that, at some point, effectiveness will decline.

The current trend is toward broadening decentralization. As competition intensifies, the need for organizations to be responsive increases. This has made employees, usually those at the lower levels, who are closest to customers extremely important. They are an excellent source of knowledge and implement changes that directly impact performance. Giving this group more input into certain decision-making activities can result in increased firm performance.

Delegating

It is impractical for the manager to handle all of the work of the department directly. In order to meet the organization's goals, focus on objectives, and ensure that all work is accomplished, managers must delegate authority. Authority is the legitimate power of a manager to direct subordinates to take action within the scope of the manager's position. By extension, this power, or a part thereof, is delegated and used in the name of a manager. Delegation is the downward transfer of formal authority from superior to subordinate. The employee is empowered to act for the manager, while the manager remains accountable for the outcome. Delegation of authority is a person-to-person relationship requiring trust, commitment, and contracting between the manager and the employee.

The manager assists in developing employees in order to strengthen the organization. He or she gives up the authority to make decisions that are best made by subordinates. This means that the manager allows subordinates the freedom to make mistakes and learn from them. He or she does not supervise subordinates' decision-making, but allows them the opportunity to develop their own skills. The manager lets subordinates know that he or she is willing to help, but not willing to do their jobs for them. The manager is not convinced that the best way for employees to learn is by telling them how to solve a problem. This results in those subordinates becoming dependent on the manager. The manager allows employees the opportunity to achieve and be credited.

An organization's most valuable resource is its people. By empowering employees who perform delegated jobs with the authority to manage those jobs, managers free themselves to manage more effectively. Successfully training future managers means delegating authority. This gives employees the concrete skills, experience, and the resulting confidence to develop themselves for higher positions. Delegation provides better managers and a higher degree of efficiency. Thus, collective effort, resulting in the organization's growth, is dependent on delegation of authority.

Responsibility and Accountability

Equally important to authority is the idea that when an employee is given responsibility for a job, he or she must also be given the degree of authority necessary to carry it out. Thus, for effective delegation, the authority granted to an employee must equal the assigned responsibility. Upon accepting the delegated task, the employee has incurred an obligation to perform the assigned work and to properly utilize the granted authority. Responsibility is the obligation to do assigned tasks. The individual employee is responsible for being proficient at his or her job. The manager is responsible for what employees do or fail to do, as well as for the resources under their control. Thus, responsibility is an integral part of a manager's authority.

Responsibilities fall into two categories: individual and organizational. Employees have individual responsibilities to be proficient in their job. They are responsible for their actions. Nobody gives or delegates individual responsibilities. Employees assume them when they accept a position in the organization. Organizational responsibilities refer to collective organizational accountability and include how well departments perform their work. For example, the manager is responsible for all the tasks assigned to his or her department, as directed by the manager.

When someone is responsible for something, he or she is liable, or accountable to a superior, for the outcome. Thus, accountability flows upward in the organization. All are held accountable for their personal, individual conduct. Accountability is answering for the result of one's actions or omissions. It is the reckoning, wherein one answers for his or her actions and accepts the consequences, good or bad. Accountability establishes reasons, motives and importance for actions in the eyes of managers and employees alike. Accountability is the final act in the establishment of one's credibility. It is important to remember that accountability results in rewards for good performance, as well as discipline for poor performance.

The Delegation Process

The delegation process has five phases (See Figure):

- Preparing;
- Planning;
- Discussing;

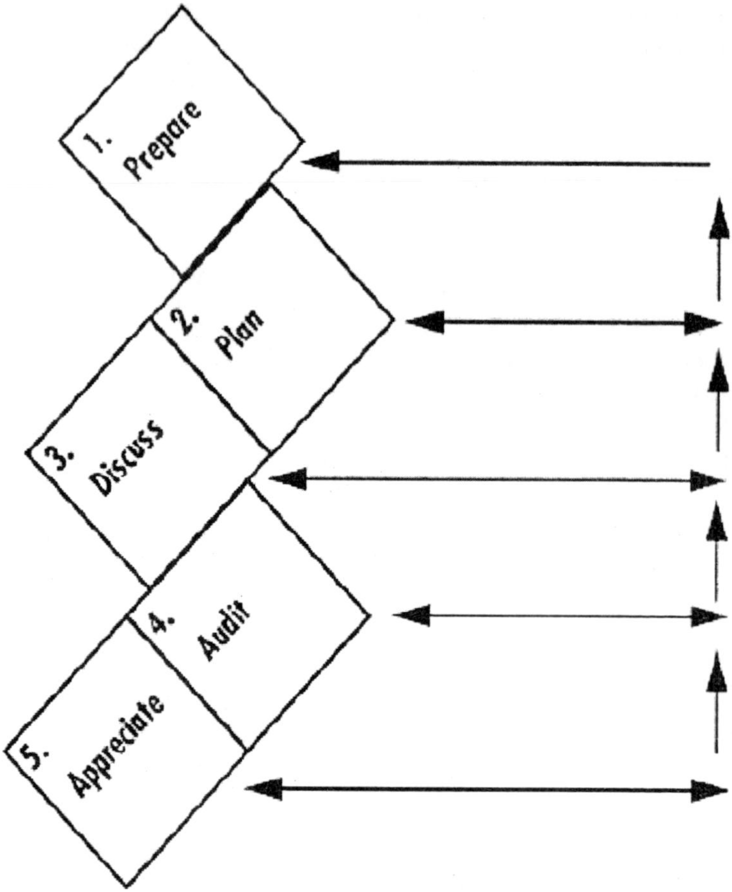

Fig. 4.4: Steps in Delegating

- auditing and
- appreciating.

The first step in delegating is to identify what should and should not be delegated. The manager should delegate any task that a subordinate performs better. Tasks least critical to the performance of the manager's job can be delegated. Any task that provides valuable experience for subordinates should be delegated. Also, the manager can delegate the tasks that he or she dislikes the most. But, the manager should not delegate any task that would violate a confidence.

Preparing includes establishing the objectives of the delegation, specifying the task that needs to be accomplished, and deciding who should accomplish it. Planning is meeting with the chosen subordinate to describe the task and to ask the subordinate to devise a plan of action. As Andrew Carnegie once said, "The secret of success is not in doing your own work but in recognizing the right man to do it." Trust between the manager and employee that both will fulfil the commitment - is most important. Discussing includes reviewing the objectives of the task as well as the subordinate's plan of action, any potential obstacles, and ways to avoid or deal with these obstacles. The manager should clarify and solicit feedback as to the employee's understanding. Clarifications needed for delegation include the desired results (what not how), guidelines, resources available, and consequences (good and bad). Delegation is similar to contracting between the manager and employee regarding how and when the work will be completed. The standards and time frames are discussed and agreed upon. The employee should know exactly what is expected and how the task will be evaluated. Auditing is monitoring the progress of the delegation and making adjustments in response to unforeseen problems. Appreciating is accepting the completed task and acknowledging the subordinate's efforts.

REFERENCES

Aldag, Raymond J. and Timothy M. Stearns (1987). *Management*, Cincinnati: Southwestern.

Barton, Cunningham J. and Ted Eberle (1990) "A Guide to Job Enrichment and Redesign," *Personnel* (February): 56–61.

Borsenik, Frank D. and Alan T. Stutts (1997) *The Management of Maintenance and Engineering Systems in the Hospitality Industry*, 4th ed. (New York: John Wiley & Sons, Inc.

Dann and Timothy Hornsey, D. (1986) "Towards a Theory of Interdepartmental Conflict in Hotels," *International Journal of Hospitality Management*, 23.

Dumaine, Brian (1993) "A Checklist of Qualities That Make a Good Boss," *Nation's Business* (November).

Dumaine, Brian (1993) "The New Non-Managers," *Fortune*, February 22, pp. 80–84.

Galbraith, Jay (2002). *Designing Organizations*, San Francisco, Jossey-Bass.

Hammer, Michael, "Process Management and the Future of Six Sigma", *MIT Sloan Management Review*, 42: 2, Winter.

Ivancevich, John M., Peter Lorenzi, and Steven J. Skinner, with Philip B. Crosby, *Management: Quality and Competitiveness*, Boston: Richard D. Irwin, 254.

Majchrzak, Ann and Qianwei Wang (1996). "Breaking the Functional Mindset in Process Organizations", *Harvard Business Review*, Sept-Oct.

Ostroff, Frank (1999). *The Horizontal Organization*, New York, Oxford University Press.

Peters, Tom, *Thriving on Chaos*, New York: Knopf.

Robert, D. Dewar and Donald P. Simet (1981). "A Level-Specific Prediction of Spans of Control Examining the Effects of Size, Technology, and Specialization," *Academy of Management Journal* (March): 5.

Shippes, Frank and Charles C. Manz (1988) "Employee Self-Management Without Formally Designated Teams: An Alternative Road to Empowerment," *Organizational Dynamics* (Winter 1992): 48–61.

Weick, K. E. (2001). *Making Sense of the Organization*, Blackwell Publishing.

5 Leading

> If your actions inspire others to dream more, learn more, do more and become more, you are a leader.
>
> *– John Quincy Adams*

Once the plans have been made, the structure of the organization has been determined; it is the function of the manager to lead employees. The leading/directing involves influence, communication, and motivation of others to strive towards performance that achieves organizational objectives. This function aims at getting the members of the organization to perform in a way that will of all the members lead the organization to its goals. Hence this section of the discussion includes detailed description of leadership, communication and motivation.

Leadership

An organization has the greatest chance of being successful when all of the employees work toward achieving its goals. Since leadership involves the exercise of influence by one person over others, the quality of leadership is a critical determinant of success.

Definition of Leadership

A traditional definition of leadership is an interpersonal influence directed toward the achievement of a goal or goals. Three important parts of this definition are the terms interpersonal, influence, and goal. *Interpersonal* means relations between persons. Thus, a leader has more than one person (group) to lead. *Influence* is the power to affect others. *Goal* is the end one strives to attain. Basically, this traditional definition of leadership says that a leader influences more than one person toward a goal.

Leadership is a dynamic relationship based on mutual influence and common purpose between leaders and collaborators in which both are moved to higher levels of motivation and moral development as they affect real, intended change. Three important parts of this definition are the terms—relationship, mutual, and collaborators. *Relationship* is the connection between people. *Mutual* means shared in common. *Collaborators* cooperate or work together. This definition of leadership says that the collaborators influence the leader while they work together to achieve an important goal.

Leadership Vs Management

A leader can be a manager, but a manager is not necessarily a leader. The leader of the work group may emerge informally as the choice of the group. If a manager is able to influence people to achieve the goals of the organization, without using his or her formal authority to do so, then the manager is demonstrating leadership.

According to John P. Kotter, managers must know how to lead as well as manage. Without leading as well as managing, today's organizations face the threat of extinction. *Management* is the process of setting and achieving the goals of the organization through the functions of management: planning, organizing, directing (or leading), and controlling. A manager is hired by the organization and is given formal authority to direct the activity of others in fulfilling organization goals. Thus, leading is a major part of a manager's job. Yet a manager must also plan, organize, and control. Generally speaking, leadership deals with the interpersonal aspects of a manager's job, whereas planning, organizing, and controlling deal with the administrative aspects. Leadership deals with change, inspiration, motivation, and influence. Management deals more with carrying out the organization's goals and maintaining equilibrium.

The key point in differentiating between leadership and management is the idea that employees willingly follow leaders because they want to, not because they have to. Leaders may not possess the formal power to reward or sanction performance. However, employees give the leader power by complying with what he or she requests. On the other hand, managers may have to rely on formal authority to get employees to accomplish goals.

Leadership and Management

These two are inter-linked. The ideal top leader is one who combines leadership with the skills and knowledge, which a general manager requires. Not all managers are leaders. The key tasks in management may revolve around planning, organising and directing with the achievement of acceptable compromise. For leaders the key tasks are defining purpose, creating shared vision and values and alignment with the organisation's purpose. Leadership resides in trust based on perceived competence and integrity and often involves intangibles such as emotional intelligence, intuition and motivation. There is often an intense, emotional attachment on the part of staff towards effective leaders beyond managerial successes. When the attitude and/or behaviours of staff are influenced significantly and as a consequence they achieve goals that otherwise would not have been attainable, then leadership is effective. The Leadership Framework seeks to identify those characteristics that can influence this process.

The Two Most Important Keys to Effective Leadership

A Hay's study examined over 75 key components of employee satisfaction. They found that:

1. Trust and confidence in top leadership was the single most reliable predictor of employee satisfaction in an organization.
2. Effective communication by leadership in three critical areas was the key to winning organizational trust and confidence:
   a) Helping employees understand the company's overall business strategy.
   b) Helping employees understand how they contribute to achieving key business objectives.
   c) Sharing information with employees on both how the company is doing and how an employee's own division is doing - relative to strategic business objectives.

So in a nutshell – you must be trustworthy and you have to be able to communicate a vision of where the organization needs to go. The next section, "Principles of Leadership," ties in closely with this key concept.

Principles of Leadership

To help you be, know, and do; (U.S. Army, 1973) follow these eleven principles of leadership (later chapters in this guide expand on these and provide tools for implementing them):

1. *Know yourself and seek self-improvement* - In order to know yourself, you have to understand your be, know, and do, attributes. Seeking self-improvement means continually strengthening your attributes. This can be accomplished through self-study, formal classes, reflection, and interacting with others.

2. *Be technically proficient* - As a leader, you must know your job and have a solid familiarity with your employees' tasks.

3. *Seek responsibility and take responsibility for your actions* – Search for ways to guide your organization to new heights. And when things go wrong, they always do sooner or later - do not blame others. Analyze the situation, take corrective action, and move on to the next challenge.

4. *Make sound and timely decisions* - Use good problem solving, decision making, and planning tools.

5. *Set the example* - Be a good role model for your employees. They must not only hear what they are expected to do, but also see. We must become the change we want to see - Mahatma Gandhi

6. *Know your people and look out for their well-being* - Know human nature and the importance of sincerely caring for your workers.

7. *Keep your workers informed* - Know how to communicate with not only them, but also seniors and other key people.

8. *Develop a sense of responsibility in your workers* - Help to develop good character traits that will help them carry out their professional responsibilities.

9. *Ensure that tasks are understood, supervised, and accomplished* - Communication is the key to this responsibility.

10. *Train as a team* - Although many so called leaders call their organization, department, section, etc. a team; they are not really teams...they are just a group of people doing their jobs.

11. *Use the full capabilities of your organization* - By developing a team spirit, you will be able to employ your organization, department, section, etc. to its fullest capabilities.

Factors of Leadership

There are four major factors in leadership:

1. *Follower:* Different people require different styles of leadership. For example, a new hire requires more supervision than an experienced employee. A person who lacks motivation requires a different approach than one with a high degree of motivation. You must know your people! The fundamental starting point is having a good understanding of human nature, such as needs, emotions, and motivation. You must become to know your employees' be, know, and do attributes.

2. *Leader:* You must have a honest understanding of who you are, what you know, and what you can do. Also, note that it is the followers, not the leader who determines if a leader is successful. If they do not trust or lack confidence in their leader, then they will be uninspired. To be successful you have to convince your followers, not yourself or your superiors, that you are worthy of being followed.

3. *Communication:* You lead through two-way communication. Much of it is nonverbal. For instance, when you "set the example," that communicates to your people that you would not ask them to perform anything that you would not be willing to do. What and how you communicate either builds or harms the relationship between you and your employees.

4. *Situation:* All are different. What you do in one situation will not always work in another. You must use your judgment to decide the best course of action and the leadership style needed for each situation. For example, you may need to confront an employee for inappropriate behaviour, but if the confrontation is too late or too early, too harsh or too weak, then the results may prove ineffective.

Leadership Models

Leadership models help us to understand what makes leaders act the way they do. The ideal is not to lock yourself in to a type of behaviour discussed in the model, but to realize that every situation calls for a different approach or behaviour to be taken. Two models will be discussed, the Four Framework Approach and the Managerial Grid.

Four Framework Approach

In the Four Framework Approach, Bolman and Deal (1991) suggest that leaders display leadership behaviours in one of four types of frameworks: Structural, Human Resource, Political, or Symbolic. The style can either be effective or ineffective, depending upon the chosen behaviour in certain situations.

1. *Structural Framework:* In an effective leadership situation, the leader is a social architect whose leadership style is analysis and design. While in an ineffective leadership situation, the leader is a petty tyrant whose leadership style is details. Structural Leaders focus on structure, strategy, environment, implementation, experimentation, and adaptation.

2. *Human Resource Framework:* In an effective leadership situation, the leader is a catalyst and servant whose leadership style is support, advocate, and empowerment. while in an ineffective leadership situation, the leader is a pushover, whose leadership style is abdication and fraud. Human Resource Leaders believe in people and communicate that belief; they are visible and accessible; they empower, increase participation, support, share

information, and move decision making down into the organization.

3. *Political Framework:* In an effective leadership situation, the leader is an advocate, whose leadership style is coalition and building. While in an ineffective leadership situation, the leader is a hustler, whose leadership style is manipulation. Political leaders clarify what they want and what they can get; they assess the distribution of power and interests; they build linkages to other stakeholders, use persuasion first, then use negotiation and coercion only if necessary.

4. *Symbolic Framework:* In an effective leadership situation, the leader is a prophet, whose leadership style is inspiration. While in an ineffective leadership situation, the leader is a fanatic or fool, whose leadership style is smoke and mirrors. Symbolic leaders view organizations as a stage or theater to play certain roles and give impressions; these leaders use symbols to capture attention; they try to frame experience by providing plausible interpretations of experiences; they discover and communicate a vision.

Leadership Theories

Earliest theories assumed that the primary source of leadership effectiveness lay in the personal traits of the leaders themselves. Yet, traits alone cannot explain leadership effectiveness. Thus, later research focused on what the leader actually did when dealing with employees. These behavioural theories of leadership sought to explain the relationship between what the leader did and how the employees reacted, both emotionally and behaviorally. Yet, behaviour can't always account for leadership in different situations. Thus, contingency theories of leadership studied leadership style in different environments. Transactional leaders, such as those identified in contingency theories, clarify role and task requirements for employees. Yet, contingency can't account for the inspiration and innovation that leaders need to compete in today's global marketplace. Newer transformational leadership studies have shown that leaders, who are charismatic and visionary, can inspire followers to transcend their own self-interest for the good of the organization. Figure 5.1 reflects the scope of the leadership studies.

Trait Theories

In the 1920s and 1930s, leadership research focused on trying to identify the traits that differentiated leaders from non-leaders. These early leadership theories were content theories, focusing on "what" an effective leader is, not on 'how' to effectively lead. The trait approach to understanding leadership assumes that certain physical, social, and personal characteristics are inherent in leaders. Sets of traits and characteristics were identified to assist in selecting the right people to become leaders. Physical traits include being young to middle-aged, energetic, tall, and handsome. Social background traits include being educated at the "right" schools and being socially prominent or upwardly mobile. Social characteristics include being charismatic, charming, tactful, popular, cooperative, and diplomatic. Personality traits include being self-confident, adaptable, assertive, and emotionally stable. Task-related characteristics include being driven to excel, accepting of responsibility, having initiative, and being results-oriented.Trait theories intended to identify traits to assist in selecting leaders since traits are related to leadership effectiveness in many situations. The trait approach to understanding leadership supports the use of tests and interviews in the selection of managers. The interviewer is typically attempting to match the traits and characteristics of the applicant to the position. For example, most interviewers attempt to evaluate how well the applicant can work with people.

Trait theory has not been able to identify a set of traits that will consistently distinguish leaders from followers. Trait theory posits key traits for successful leadership (drive, desire to lead, integrity, self-confidence, intelligence, and job-relevant knowledge) yet does not make a judgement as to whether these traits are inherent to individuals or whether they can be developed through training and education. No two leaders are alike. Furthermore, no leader possesses all of the traits. Comparing leaders in different situations suggests that the traits of leaders depend on the

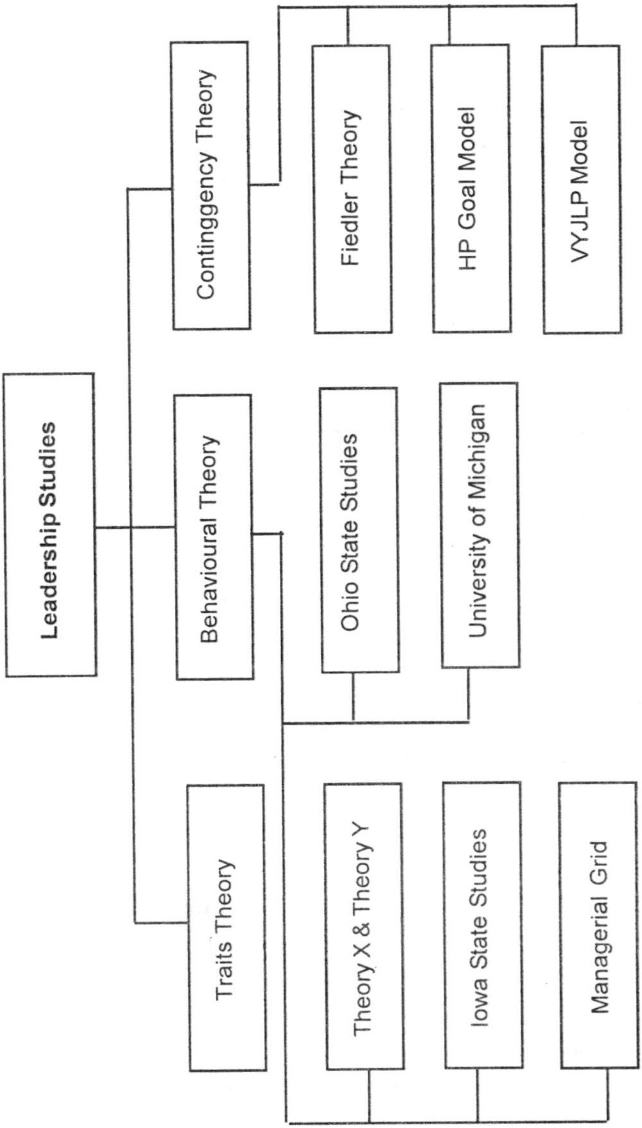

Fig. 5.1: Scope of Leadership Studies

situation. Thus, traits were deemphasized to take into account situational conditions (contingency perspective).

Behavioural Theories

The behavioural theorists identified determinants of leadership so that people could be trained to be leaders. They developed training programmes to change managers' leadership behaviours and assumed that the best styles of leadership could be learned.

Theory X and Theory Y

Douglas McGregor described Theory X and Theory Y in his book, *The Human Side of Enterprise*. Theory X and Theory Y each represent different ways in which leaders view employees. Theory X managers believe that employees are motivated mainly by money, are lazy, uncooperative, and have poor work habits. Theory Y managers believe that subordinates work hard, are cooperative, and have positive attitudes.

Theory X is the traditional view of direction and control by managers.

- The average human being has an inherent dislike of work and will avoid if he can.
- Because of this human characteristic of dislike of work, most people must be controlled, directed, and threatened with punishment to get them to put forth adequate effort toward the achievement of organizational objectives.
- The average human being prefers to be directed, wishes to avoid responsibility, has relatively little ambition, wants security above all.

Theory X leads naturally to an emphasis on the tactics of control - to procedures and techniques for telling people what to do, for determining whether they are doing it, and for administering rewards and punishment. Theory X explains the consequences of a particular managerial strategy. Because its assumptions are so unnecessarily limiting, it prevents managers from seeing the possibilities inherent in other managerial strategies.

As long as the assumptions of Theory X influence managerial strategy, organizations will fail to discover, let alone utilize, the potentialities of the average human being.

Theory Y is the view that individual and organizational goals can be integrated.

- The expenditures of physical and mental effort in work are as natural as play or rest.
- External control and the threat of punishment are not the only means for bringing out effort toward organizational objectives.
- Commitment to objectives is a function of the rewards associated with their achievement.
- The average human being learns, under proper conditions, not only to accept but also to seek responsibility.
- The capacity to exercise a relatively high degree of imagination, ingenuity, and creativity in the solution of organizational problems in widely, not narrowly, distributed in the population.
- Under the condition of modern industrial life, the intellectual potentialities of the average human being are only partially utilized.

Theory Y's purpose is to encourage integration, to create a situation in which an employee can achieve his or her own goals best by directing his or her efforts toward the objectives of the organization. It is a deliberate attempt to link improvement in managerial competence with the satisfaction of higher-level ego and self-actualization needs. Theory Y leads to a preoccupation with the nature of relationships, with the creation of an environment which will encourage commitment to organizational objectives and which will provide opportunities for the maximum exercise of initiative, ingenuity, and self-direction in achieving them.

Ohio State

The Studies conducted at the Ohio State University and the University of Michigan identified two leadership styles and two

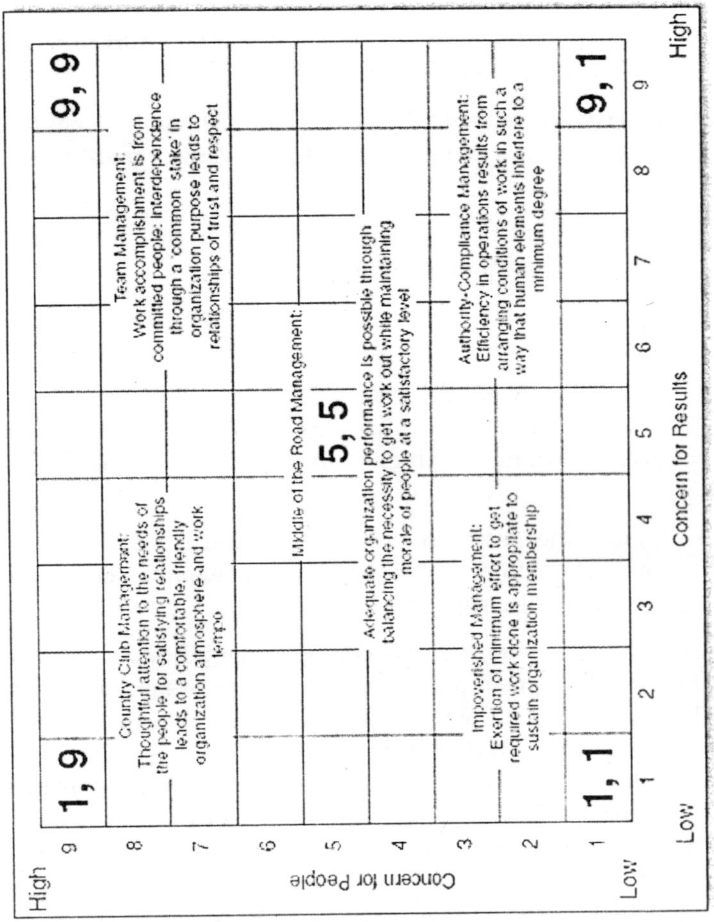

Fig. 5.2: The Managerial Grid

types of leader behaviours. The Ohio State study identified two leadership styles: *considerate* and *initiating* structure.

University of Michigan

The University of Michigan study classified leaders' behaviours as being production- or employee-centred. The primary concern of leaders with considerate and employee-centered style is the employee's welfare. The primary concern of leaders with initiating-structure and production-centred styles is achieving goals. Research findings on which dimension is most important for satisfaction and productivity are inconclusive. However, employee-oriented leaders appear to be associated with high group productivity and job satisfaction.

University of Iowa

Another approach to leader behaviour focused on identifying the best leadership styles. Work at the University of Iowa identified democratic (participation and delegation), autocratic (dictating and centralized) and laissez-faire styles (group freedom in decision-making). Research findings were also inconclusive.

The Managerial Grid

The dimensions identified at the University of Michigan provided the basis for the development of the managerial grid model developed by Robert Blake and Jane Mouton. It identifies five various leadership styles that represent different combinations of concern for people and concern for production. Managers who scored high on both these dimensions simultaneously (labeled team management) performed best. The five leadership styles of the managerial grid include impoverished, country club, produce or perish, middle-of-the road, and team (See Fig. 5.2). The impoverished style is located at the lower left-hand corner of the grid, point (1, 1). It is characterized by low concern for both people and production. The primary objective of the impoverished style is for managers to stay out of trouble.

The country club style is located at the upper left-hand corner of the grid, point (1, 9). It is characterized as a high concern for people and a low concern for production. The primary objective of the country club style is to create a secure and comfortable atmosphere and trust that subordinates will respond positively.

The produce or perish style is located at the lower right-hand corner of the grid, point (9, 1). A high concern for production and a low concern for people characterize it. The primary objective of the produce or perish style is to achieve the organization's goals. To accomplish the organization's goals, it is not necessary to consider employees' needs.

The middle-of-the-road style is located at the middle of the grid, point (5, 5). A balance between workers' needs and the organization's productivity goals characterize it. The primary objective of the middle-of-the-road style is to maintain employee morale at a level sufficient to get the organization's work done.

The team style is located at the upper right-hand of the grid, point (9, 9). It is characterized by a high concern for people and production. The primary objective of the team style is to establish cohesion and foster a feeling of commitment among workers.

Contingency Theories

Successful leaders must be able to identify clues in an environment and adapt their leader behaviour to meet the needs of their followers and of the particular situation. Even with good diagnostic skills, leaders may not be effective unless they can adapt their leadership style to meet the demands of their environment.

Fiedler's Contingency Model

Fred E. Fiedler's contingency theory postulates that there is no best way for managers to lead. Situations will create different leadership style requirements for a manager. The solution to a managerial situation is contingent on the factors that impinge on the situation. For example, in a highly routinized (mechanistic) environment where repetitive tasks are the norm, a certain leadership style may result in the best performance. The same leadership style may not work in a very dynamic environment. Fiedler looked at three situations that could define the condition of a managerial task (Fig. 5.3):

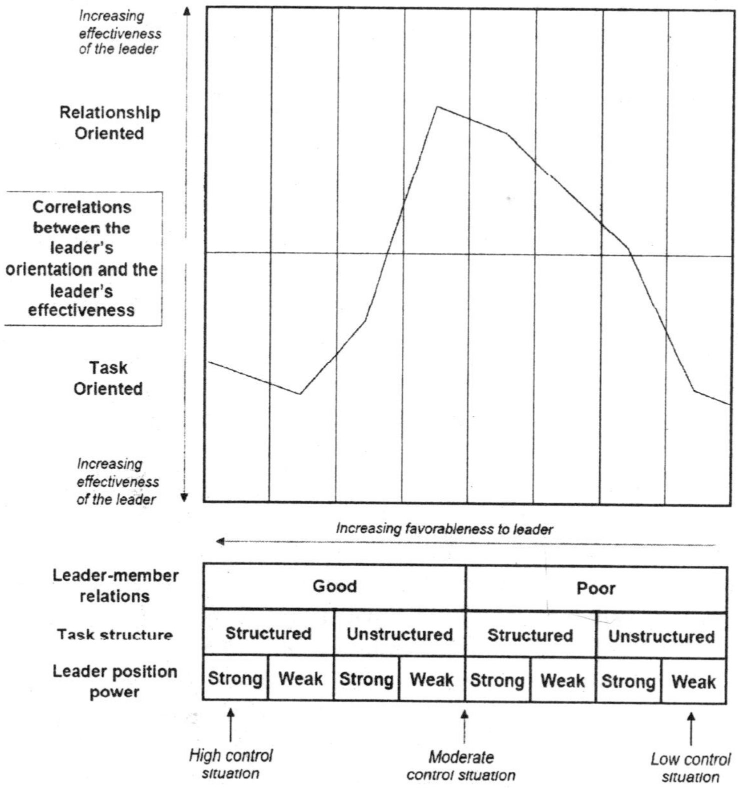

Fig. 5.3: Condition of a Managerial Task

- *Leader-member relations*: How well do the manager and the employees get along?
- *The task structure*: Is the job highly structured, fairly unstructured, or somewhere in between?
- *Position power*: How much authority does the manager possess?

Managers were rated as to whether they were relationship-oriented or task oriented. Task-oriented managers tend to do better in situations that have good leader-member relationships, structured tasks, and either weak or strong position power. They do well when the task is unstructured but position power is strong. Also, they did well at the other end of the spectrum when the leader member relations were moderate to poor and the task was unstructured. Relationship-oriented managers do better in all other situations. Thus, a given situation might call for a manager with a different style or a manager who could take on a different style for a different situation. These environmental variables are combined in a weighted sum that is termed "Favorable" at one end and "unfavourable" at the other. Task-oriented style is preferable at the clearly defined extremes of "favorable" and "unfavourable" environments, but relationship orientation excels in the middle ground. Managers could attempt to reshape the environment variables to match their style.

Another aspect of the contingency model theory is that the leader-member relations, task structure, and position power dictate a leader's situational control. Leader-member relations are the amount of loyalty, dependability, and support that the leader receives from employees. It is a measure of how the manager perceives him or her and the group of employees is getting along together. In a favourable relationship the manager has a high task structure and is able to reward and or punish employees without any problems. In an unfavourable relationship the task is usually unstructured and the leader possesses limited authority. The spelling out in detail (favourable) of what is required of subordinates affects task structure.

Positioning power measures the amount of power or authority the manager perceives the organization has given him or her for the purpose of directing, rewarding, and punishing subordinates. Positioning power of managers depends on the taking away (favourable) or increasing (unfavourable) the decision-making power of employees.

The task-motivated style leader experiences pride and satisfaction in the task accomplishment for the organization, while the relationship-motivated style seeks to build interpersonal relations and extend extra help for the team development in the organization. There is no good or bad leadership style. Each person has his or her own preferences for leadership. Task-motivated leaders are at their best when the group performs successfully such as achieving a new sales record or outperforming the major competitor. Relationship-oriented leaders are at their best when greater customer satisfaction is gained and a positive company image is established.

Hersey-Blanchard Situational Leadership

The Hersey-Blanchard Situational Leadership theory is based on the amount of direction (task behaviour) and amount of socio-emotional support (relationship behaviour) a leader must provide given the situation and the "level of maturity" of the followers. Task behaviour is the extent to which the leader engages in spelling out the duties and responsibilities to an individual or group. This behaviour includes telling people what to do, how to do it, when to do it, where to do it, and who's to do it. In task behaviour the leader engages in one-way communication. Relationship behaviour is the extent to which the leader engages in two-way or multi-way communications. This includes listening, facilitating, and supportive behaviours. In relationship behaviour the leader engages in two-way communication by providing socio-emotional support. Maturity is the willingness and ability of a person to take responsibility for directing his or her own behaviour. People tend to have varying degrees of maturity, depending on the specific task, function, or objective that a leader is attempting to accomplish through their efforts. To determine the appropriate leadership style to use in a given situation, the leader must first determine the maturity level of the followers in relation to the specific task that the leader is attempting to accomplish through the effort of the followers. As the level of followers' maturity increases, the leader should begin to reduce his or her task behaviour and increase relationship behaviour until the followers reach a moderate level of maturity. As the followers begin to move into an above average level of maturity, the leader should decrease not only task behaviour but also relationship behaviour.

Once the maturity level is identified, the appropriate leadership style can be determined. The four leadership styles are telling, selling, participating, and delegating. High task/low relationship behaviour (S1) is referred to as "telling." The leader provides clear instructions and specific direction. Telling style is best matched with a low follower readiness level. High task/high relationship behaviour (S2) is referred to as "selling." The leader encourages two-way communication and helps build confidence and motivation on the part of the employee, although the leader still has responsibility and controls decision making. Selling style is best matched with a moderate follower readiness level. High relationship/low task behaviour (S3) is referred to as "participating." With this style, the leader and followers share decision making and no longer need or expect the relationship to be directive. Participating style is best matched with a moderate follower readiness level. Low relationship/low task behaviour (S4) is labelled "delegating." This style is appropriate for leaders whose followers are ready to accomplish a particular task and are both competent and motivated to take full responsibility. Delegating style is best matched with a high follower readiness level.

House's Path-Goal Model

The path-goal theory developed by Robert House is based on the expectancy theory of motivation. The manager's job is viewed as coaching or guiding workers to choose the best paths for reaching their goals. "Best" is judged by the accompanying achievement of organizational goals. It is based on the precepts of goal setting theory and argues that leaders will have to engage in different types of leadership behaviour depending on the nature and demands of the particular situation. It's the leader's job to assist followers in attaining goals and to provide direction and support needed to ensure that their goals are compatible with the organization's. A leader's behaviour is acceptable to subordinates when viewed as a source of satisfaction, and motivational when need satisfaction is contingent on performance, and the leader facilitates, coaches and rewards effective performance. Path goal theory identifies achievement-oriented, directive, participative and supportive leadership styles. In achievement-oriented leadership, the leader sets challenging goals for followers, expects them to perform at their highest level, and shows confidence in their ability to meet this expectation. This style is appropriate when the follower suffers from a lack of job challenge. In directive leadership, the leader lets followers know what is expected of them and tells them how to perform their tasks. This style is appropriate when the follower has an ambiguous job. Participative leadership involves leaders consulting with followers and asking for their suggestions before making a decision. This style is appropriate when the follower is using improper procedures or is making poor decisions. In supportive leadership, the leader is friendly and approachable. He or she shows concern for followers' psychological well being. This style is appropriate when the followers lack confidence (See Fig. 5.4).

Path-Goal theory assumes that leaders are flexible and that they can change their style, as situations require. The theory proposes two contingency variables (environment and follower characteristics) that moderate the leader behaviour-outcome relationship. Environment is outside the control of followers-task structure, authority system, and work group. Environmental factors determine the type of leader behaviour required if follower outcomes are to be maximized. Follower characteristics are the locus of control, experience, and perceived ability. Personal characteristics of subordinates determine how the environment and leader are interpreted. Effective leaders clarify the path to help their followers achieve their goals and make the journey easier by reducing roadblocks and pitfalls. Research demonstrates that employee performance and satisfaction are positively influenced when the leader compensates for the shortcomings in either the employee or the work setting.

Vroom, Yetton, Jago Leader-Participation Model

The Vroom, Yetton, Jago leader-participation model relates leadership behaviour and participation to decision making. The model provides a set of sequential rules to determine the form and amount of participative decision-making in different situations. It is a decision tree, requiring yes and no answers incorporating contingencies about task structure and alternative styles. The following contingency questions must be answered to determine the appropriate leadership style in the leader-participation model.

- *Quality Requirement*: How important is the technical quality of this decision?
- *Commitment Requirement*: How important is subordinate commitment to the decision?

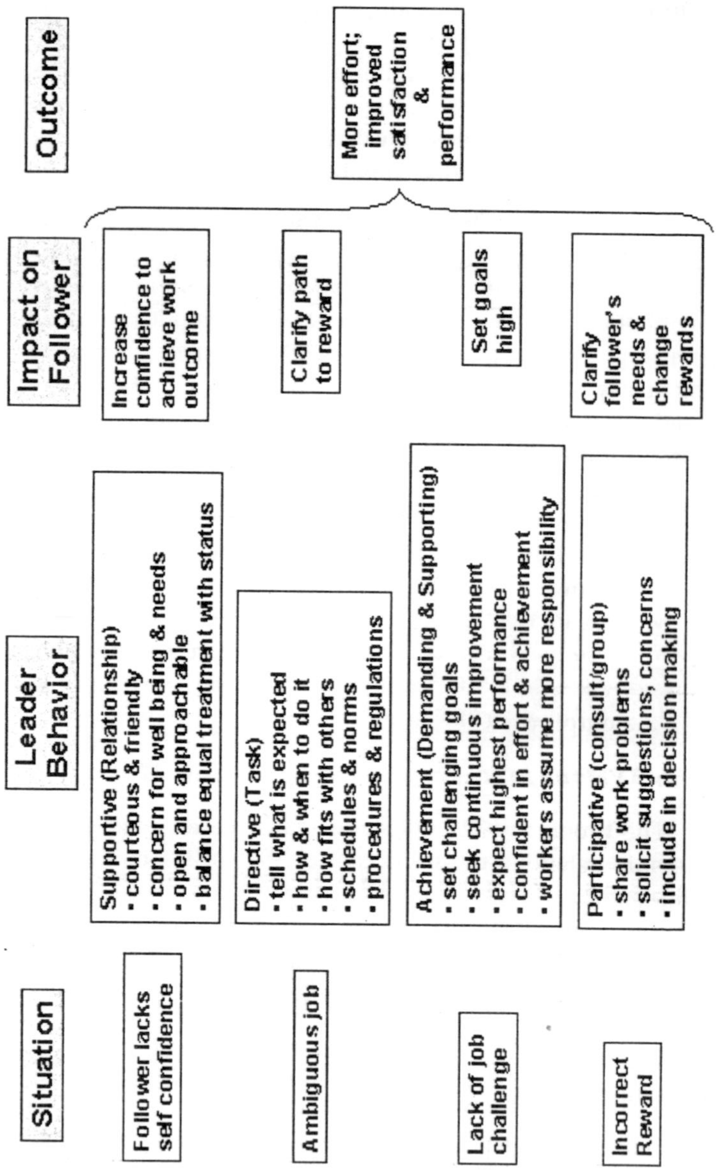

Fig. 5.4: Path-Goal Theory

- *Leader's Information*: Do you have sufficient information to make a high-quality decision?
- *Problem Structure*: Is the problem well structured?
- *Commitment Probability*: If you were to make the decision yourself, are you reasonably certain that your subordinates would be committed to the decision?
- *Goal Congruence*: Do subordinates share the organizational goals to be attained in solving this problem? Subordinate Conflict: Is conflict among subordinates over preferred solutions likely?
- *Subordinate Information*: Do subordinates have sufficient information to make a high-quality decision?

Transformational Leadership

It blends the behavioural theories with a little dab of trait theories. Transactional leaders, such as those identified in contingency theories, guide followers in the direction of established goals by clarifying role and task requirements. However, transformational leaders, who are charismatic and visionary, can inspire followers to transcend their own self-interest for the good of the organization. Transformational leaders appeal to followers' ideals and moral values and inspire them to think about problems in new or different ways. Leader behaviours used to influence followers include vision, framing, and impression management. Vision is the ability of the leader to bind people together with an idea. Framing is the process whereby leaders define the purpose of their movement in highly meaningful terms. Impression management is a leader's attempt to control the impressions that others form about the leader by practicing behaviours that make the leader more attractive and appealing to others. Research indicates that transformational, as compared to transactional, leadership is more strongly correlated with lower turnover rates, higher productivity, and higher employee satisfaction (See Fig 5.5).

A transformational leader instills feelings of confidence, admiration and commitment in the followers. He or she is charismatic, creating a special bond with followers, articulating a vision with which the followers identify and for which they

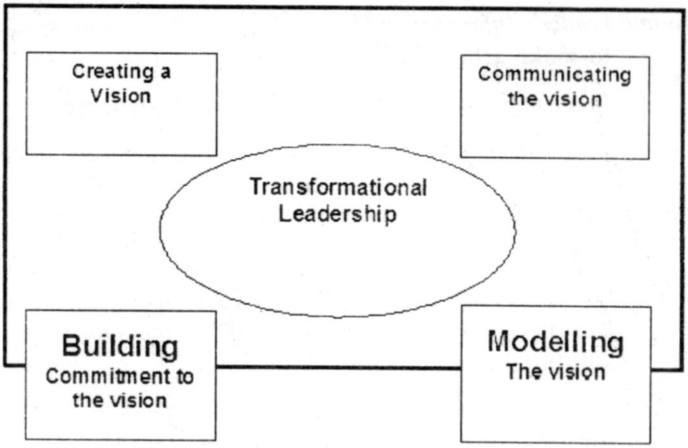

Fig. 5.5: Transformational Leadership

are willing to work. Each follower is coached, advised, and delegated some authority. The transformational leader stimulates followers intellectually, arousing them to develop new ways to think about problems. The leader uses contingent rewards to positively reinforce performances that are consistent with the leader's wishes. Management is by exception. The leader takes initiative only when there are problems and is not actively involved when things are going well. The transformational leader commits people to action and converts followers into leaders.

Transformational leaders are relevant to today's workplace because they are flexible and innovative. While it is important to have leaders with the appropriate orientation defining tasks and managing interrelationships, it is even more important to have leaders who can bring organizations into futures they have not yet imagined. Transformational leadership is the essence of creating and sustaining competitive advantage.

REFERENCES

Alexander, J. and Ciaschi, E. (2002). "Leadership Development in the Digital Age." Presented at the Human Resource Planning Society annual conference.

Barrett, A. and Beeson, J. (2002). *Developing Business Leaders for 2010.* The Conference Board, New York.

Bass, Bernard (1989). *Stogdill's Handbook of Leadership: A Survey of Theory and Research*. New York: Free Press.

Blake, Robert R. and Mouton, Janse S. (1985). *The Managerial Grid III: The Key to Leadership Excellence*. Houston: Gulf Publishing Co.

Bolman, L. and Deal, T. (1991). *Reframing Organizations*. San Francisco: Jossey-Bass.

Cacioppe, R. (1998). "An Integrated Model and Approach for the Design of Effective Leadership Development Programs." *Leadership and Organization Development Journal*, 19(1): 44-53.

Collier, J. and Esteban, R. (2000). "Systemic Leadership: Ethical and Effective." *Leadership and Organization Development Journal*, 21(4): 207-215.

Day, D.V. (2001). "Leadership Development: A Review in Context." *Leadership Quarterly*, 11(4): 581-613.

Fulmer, R.M. (1997). "The Evolving Paradigm of Leadership Development." *Organizational Dynamics*, 25(4).

Goleman, D., Boyatzis, R., and McKee, A. (2002). *Primal Leadership*. Boston: Harvard Business School Press.

Hersey, Paul, Kenneth H. Blanchard, Dewy E.Johson, (2004), *Management of Organizaitonal Behaviour – Leading Human Resources*, Prentice-Hall of India Private Limited, New Delhi,

Intagliata, J., Ulrich, D. and Smallwood, N. (2000). "Leveraging Leadership Competencies to Produce Leadership Brand: Creating Distinctiveness by Focusing on Strategy and Results." *Human Resource Planning*, 23(3).

Kincaid, S.B. and Gordick, D. (2003). "The Return on Investment of Leadership Development: Differentiating Our Discipline." *Consulting Psychology Journal: Practice and Research*, 55(1): 47-57.

Kouzes, James M. and Posner, Barry Z. (1987). *The Leadership Challenge*. San Francisco: Jossey-Bass.

Moxley, R.S. and O'Connnor Wison, P. (1998). "A Systems Approach to Leadership Development." In C.D. McCauley, R.S. Moxley, and E. Van Velsor (eds.), *Handbook of Leadership Development*. San Francisco: Jossey-Bass, 217-241.

Nevins, M., and Stumpf, S. (1999). "21st-Century Leadership:Redefining Management Education," *Strategy, Management,Competition*,3rd Quarter: 41-51.

Prahalad, C K (2004). *The Fortune at the Bottom of the Pyramid: Eradicating Poverty through Profit*, Wharton Business Publishing.

Prahalad, C K and Ramaswamy, Venkatram (2004). *The Future of Competition: Co-creating Value with Customers*, Harvard Business School Press.

Spiro, L.N. (2003). "In Search of Leaders." *CEO Magazine*, October: 25-30.

Tichy, N.M., DeRose, C. (1996). "The Pepsi Challenge: Building a Leader-Driven Organization." *Training and Development*, 50(5): 58-66.

Vicere, A.A. (2002). "Leadership and the Networked Economy." *Human Resource Planning*, 25(2): 26-33.

6 Communicating

The art of communication is the language of leadership
– James Humes

Meaning of Communication

Communication is the process of sharing our ideas, thoughts, and feelings with other people and having those ideas, thoughts, and feelings understood by the people we are talking with. When we communicate we speak, listen, and observe. The way we communicate is a learned style. As children we learn from watching our parents and other adults communicate. As an adult we can learn to improve the way we communicate by observing others who communicate effectively, learning new skills, and practicing those skills.

Communication is the process of exchanging information. Information is conveyed as words, tone of voice, and body language. Studies have shown that words account for 7 percent of the information communicated. Vocal tone accounts for 55 percent and body language accounts for 38 percent. To be effective communicators, team members must be aware of these forms, how to use them effectively, and barriers to the communications process.

Communication establishes relationships and makes organizing possible. Every message has a purpose or objective. The sender intends – whether consciously or unconsciously – to accomplish something by communicating. In organizational contexts, messages typically have a definite objective: to motivate, to inform, to teach, to persuade, to entertain, or to inspire. This definite purpose is, in fact, one of the principal differences between casual conversation and managerial communication. Effective communication in the organization centers on well-defined objectives that support the organization's goals and mission. Managers strive to achieve understanding among parties to their communications.

Organizational Communication

Organizational communication establishes a pattern of formal communication channels to carry information vertically and horizontally. (The organization chart displays these channels.) To ensure efficient and effective accomplishment of objectives, information is exchanged. Information is passed *upward* from employees to managers and *laterally* to adjacent departments. Instructions relating to the performance of the department and policies for conducting business are conveyed *downward* from managers to employees. The organization carries information from within the department back up to top management. Management furnishes information about how things are going, notifies the manager of what the problems are, and provides requests for clarification and help. Managers, in turn, keep their employees informed and render assistance. Managers continually facilitate the process of gaining necessary clarification and problem solving; both up and down the organization. Also, managers communicate with sources *outside* the organization, such as vendors and customers.

The Communication Process

Communication is the process of passing information and understanding from one person to another. The communication process involves six basic elements: sender (encoder), message, channel, receiver (decoder), noise, and feedback. Managers can improve communication skills by becoming aware of these elements and how they contribute to successful communication. Communication can break down at any one of these elements (See Fig. 6.1).

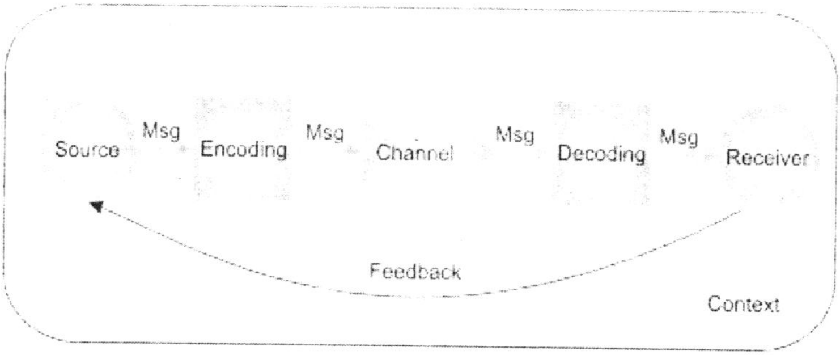

Fig. 6.1: The Communication Process

Sender Encodes

The *sender* initiates the communication process. When the sender has decided on a meaning, he or she *encodes* a message, and selects a channel for transmitting the message to a receiver. To encode is to put a message into words or images. The *message* is the information that the sender wants to transmit. The medium is the means of communication, such as print, mass, electrical, and digital. As a sender, the manager should define the purpose of the message, construct each message with the receiver in mind, select the best medium, time each transmission thoughtfully, and seek feedback. Words can be verbal - written and spoken. Words are used to create pictures and stories (scenarios) are used to create involvement.

Sender transmits the message

In order for the sender to transmit the encoded message, the sender has to choose a channel, a medium through which to send the message. Senders can send information verbally or nonverbally.

Receiver gets the message

Unless he or she has a hearing problem or he or she is affected by noises distorting the reception of the message, the receiver receives the signal sent by the sender.

Receiver Decodes

Information technology is revolutionizing the way organizational members communicate. Network systems, electronic links among an organization's computer hardware and software, enable members to communicate instantaneously, to retrieve and share information from anyplace, at anytime. The receiver is the person or group for whom the communication effort is intended. Noise is anything that interferes with the communication. Feedback ensures that mutual understanding has taken place in a communication. It is the transfer of information from the receiver back to the sender. The receiver decodes or makes out the meaning of the message. Thus, in the feedback loop, the receiver becomes the sender and the sender becomes the receiver.

Receiver send feedback to the sender

Using the same phases as the sender, the receiver sends a message back to the sender providing information on his or her level of comprehension of the message.

Written communication

It is used when the situation is formal, official, or long term; or when the situation affects several people in related ways. Interoffice memos are used for recording informal inquiries or replies. Letters are formal in tone and addressed to an individual. They are used for official notices, formally recorded statements, and lengthy communications. Reports are more impersonal and more formal than a letter. They are used to convey information, analyses, and recommendations. Written communications to groups include bulletin-board notices, posters, exhibits, displays, and audio and visual aids. Communication and the need to exchange information are no longer constrained by place and time. Email, voice mail, and facsimile have facilitated communications and the sharing of sharing of knowledge. Email is the computer transmission and storage of written messages. Voice mail is the transmission and storage of digitized spoken messages. Facsimile (fax) is the transmission of documents.

Verbal or Spoken Communication

It includes informal staff meetings, planned conferences, and mass meetings. Voice and delivery are important. Informal talks are suitable for day-to-day liaison, directions, exchange or information, progress reviews, and the maintenance of effective interpersonal relations. Planned appointments are appropriate for regular appraisal review and recurring joint work sessions. Planning for an appointment includes preparing, bringing adequate information, and limiting interruptions. Telephone calls are used for quick checkups and for imparting or receiving information. Teams using information technology have access to information, share knowledge, and construct documents. Meetings take place electronically from multiple locations, saving the organization's resources in both the expenses of physically bringing people from different locations together, and the time lost by employees traveling. Teleconferencing is simultaneous group verbal exchanges. Videoconferencing is group verbal and visual exchanges.

Non-verbal Communication

Non-verbal messages include images, actions and behaviors used to communicate. Images include photographs, film, charts, tables, graphs, and video. Nonverbal behaviors include actions, body language, and active listening. Actions and body language include eye contact, gestures, facial expressions, posture, and appearance. The effective communicator maintains eye contact for four to five seconds before looking away. Gestures should be natural and well timed. Grooming and dress should be appropriate for the situation. Listening requires good eye contact, alert body posture, and the frequent use of verbal encouragement.

Channel

It is the path a message follows from the sender to the receiver. Managers use *downward* channels to send messages to employees. Employees use *upward* channels to send messages to managers. *Horizontal* channels are used when communicating across departmental lines, with suppliers, or with customers. An informal channel is the grapevine. It exists outside the formal channels and is used by people to transmit casual, personal, and social interchanges at work. The grapevine consists of rumors, gossip, and truthful information. The manager should pay attention to the grapevine, but should not depend on it for accurate information.

Interpersonal Communication

Not all communication should be considered interpersonal communication. Frequently, you are engaged in impersonal interactions. When you ask for directions, pay for a purchase, or call for a doctor's appointment, you are not automatically involved in interpersonal communication. If you ask a teacher for clarification, discuss a project with a boss, or plan a family reunion with a distant cousin, you may be involved in necessary, functional interactions but you do not share a strong, significant relationship.

Interpersonal communication occurs when two or more people engage in voluntary, ongoing, interdependent interactions that involve meaningful interpretation of their verbal and nonverbal behaviors. In short, this implies a perception of the relationship as positive, reflecting a choice to continue to relate to each other over time in order to deepen the relationship and make it increasingly unique. There may be exceptions to this description, such as when you interact involuntarily with particular teachers or managers for a long period of time, learn how to communicate effectively with them, and eventually develop a voluntary interpersonal relationship. In the case of involuntary but required relationships, it is likely that the person with the less power is adapting to the person with greater power, setting up a one-up/one-down interaction pattern. Such relationships tend to remain impersonal, although, on occasion, these persons develop a friendship.

REFERENCES

Bahl, Sushil (2009). *Business Communication Today*, Response Books, Reprint.

Bailey, E.P. (1996). *Plain English at Work: a guide to business writing and speaking*, Oxford University Press, UK.

Baugh, L.S., Fryar, M., Thomas, D.A. (1999). *How to Write First-Class Business Correspondence*, NTC Publishing Group, USA.

Beatty, R.H. (1986). *The Five-Minute Interview*, John Wiley and Sons, USA.

Chambers, R. (2002). *Participatory Workshops: A Sourcebook of 21 Sets of Ideas and Activities*, Earthscan, UK.

Courtland L. Bovee (2008). *Business Communication Today*, 9th edition.

Dance, Frank E. X., and Larson, Carl (1976). *The Functions of Human Communication: A Theoretical Approach*. New York: Holt, Rinehart and Winston.

Dance, Frank E. X., and Zak-Dance, Carol (1986). *Public Speaking*. New York: Harper and Row.

Foster, T., 2001. *101 Ways to Better Business Writing*, Kogan Page, India

Galvin, Kathleen M. and Charles A.Wilkinson, (2006). *The Communication Process: Impersonal and Interpersonal*, Roxbury Publishing Company.

Gilsdorf, J.W., (1989). *Business Correspondence for Today*, John Wiley and Sons, USA.

Hager, P. and Scheiber, H., (1997). *Designing and Delivering Scientific, Technical, and Managerial Presentations*, John Wiley and Sons, USA.

Kaul, Asha (2009). *Business Communication*, Prentice Hall of Indian Publications, New Delhi. 2nd edition.

Madhukar, (2008). *Business Communication*, Vikas Publishing House.

Markham, R., (1998). *Excellence in Public Speaking*, Simon and Schuster, USA.

Mort, S. (1997). *Professional Report Writing*, Gower Publishing, USA.

Murphy, H.A. and Hilderbrandt, H.W. (1997). *Effective Business Communication*, McGraw-Hill, Singapore.

Poe, R.W. (1994). *The McGraw-Hill Handbook of Business Letters*, 3rd edition, McGraw-Hill, USA.

Pretty, J., *et al.* (1995). *Participatory Learning and Action: a trainers guide*, IIED, UK.

Rai, Urmila and S.M. Rai (2008). *Business Communication*, Himalaya Publishing House, Mumbai.

Raman, Meenakshi and Prakash Singh, (2006). *Business Communication*, Oxford Higher Education.

Reiser, Paul (1994). *Couplehood*. New York: Bantam Books.

Tierney, E.P. (1996). *How to make Effective Presentations*, Sage Publications, UK

Vilanilam, J.V. (2000). *More Effective Communication: A Manual for Professionals*, Response Books, India.

Wilder, L. (1986). *Professionally Speaking*, Simon and Schuster, USA.

Wood, Julia (2000). *Relational Communication*. 2nd ed. Belmont, CA: Wadsworth.

Wright, C. (ed.) (1995). *Communication Skills: A Practical Handbook*, The Industrial Society, UK.

7 Motivating

Our greatest glory is not in never falling but in rising every. time we fall.

– *Confucius*

The word *'motivation'* is common in everyday language, but is not easy to define rigorously in a scientific context. The concept of motivation is related to, but distinct from other concepts, such as *instincts, drives,* and *reflexes.* Motivated behaviour is usually goal-oriented; the goal may be associated with a drive such as hunger or thirst (called *primary motivation*). However, motivation is also closely tied to sensory stimuli: an animal will not usually exhibit eating behaviour unless food is presented. Unlike instinctive behaviour, motivation depends on *affect* (emotional state). Finally, motivation can be learned (in which case it is called *secondary motivation*) and typically elicits more complex behaviours than simple reflexes.

Definitions of Motivation

- *The psychological meaning of motivation:* It is the internal mental state of a person which relates to the initiation, direction, persistence, intensity, and termination of behaviour.
- *The managerial meaning of motivation:* It is the activity of managers to induce others to produce results desired by the organization or, perhaps, by the manager.
- *Work Motivation* is a set of energetic forces that originate both within as well as beyond an individual's being, to initiate work-related behaviour, and to determine its form, direction, intensity and duration.

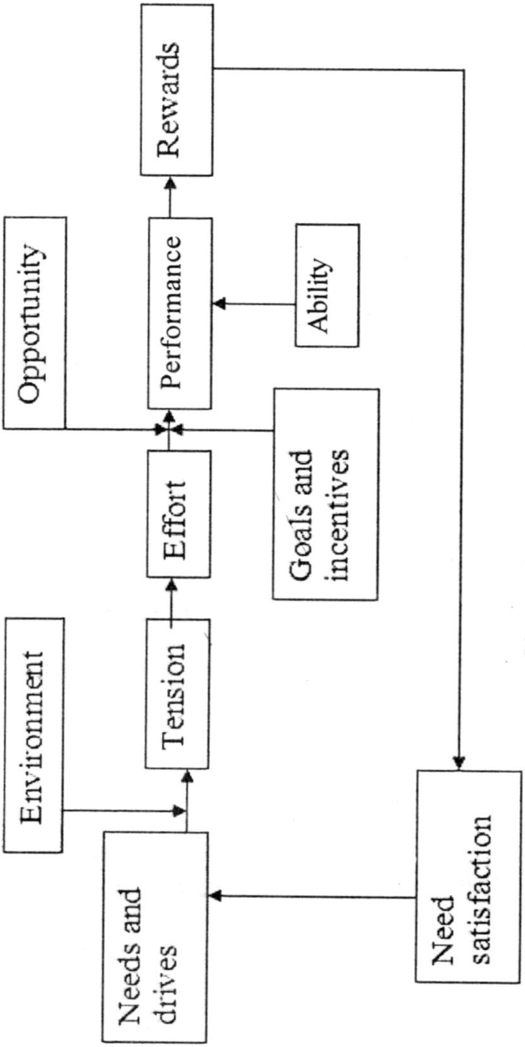

Fig. 7.1: Process of Motivation

Since motivation influences productivity, managers need to understand what motivates employees to reach peak performance. It is not an easy task to increase employee motivation because employees respond in different ways to their jobs and their organization's practices. Motivation is the set of processes that moves a person toward a goal. Thus, motivated behaviours are voluntary choices controlled by the individual employee. The manager (motivator) wants to influence the factors that motivate employees to higher levels of productivity.

Factors that affect work motivation include individual differences, job characteristics, and organizational practices. Individual differences are the personal needs, values, and attitudes, interests and abilities that people bring to their jobs. Job characteristics are the aspects of the position that determine its limitations and challenges. Organizational practices are the rules, human resources policies, managerial practices, and rewards systems of an organization. Managers must consider how these factors interact to affect employee job performance.

Simple Model of Motivation

The purpose of behaviour is to satisfy needs. A *need* is anything that is required, desired, or useful. A *want* is a conscious recognition of a need. A need arises when there is a difference in self-concept (the way I see myself) and perception (the way I see the world around me). The presence of an active need is expressed as an inner state of tension from which the individual seeks relief.

Theories of Motivation

Many methods of employee motivation have been developed. The study of work motivation has focused on the motivator (manager) as well as the motivatee (employee). Motivation theories are important to managers attempting to be effective leaders. Two primary approaches to motivation are content and process. The content approach to motivation focuses on the assumption that individuals are motivated by the desire to fulfil inner needs. Content theories focus on the needs that motivate people (See Fig. 7.2).

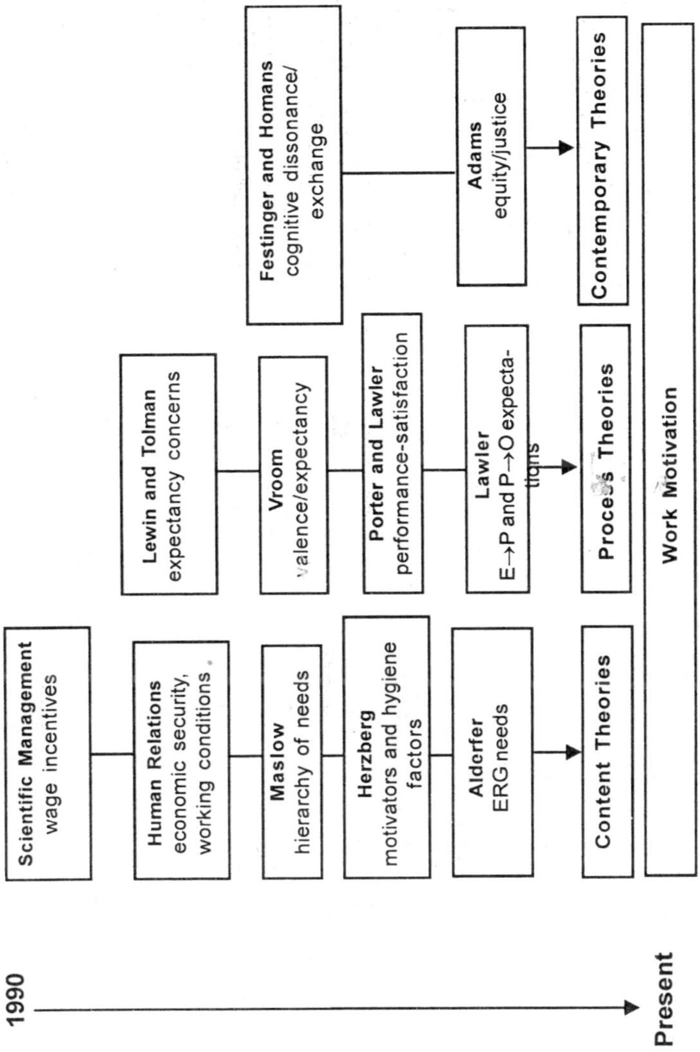

Fig. 7.2: The Theoretical Development of Work Motivation

Maslow's Hierarchy of Needs

Maslow's Hierarchy of Needs identifies five levels of needs, which are best seen as a hierarchy with the most basic need emerging first and the most sophisticated need last. People move up the hierarchy one level at a time. Gratified needs lose their strength and the next level of needs is activated. As basic or lower-level needs are satisfied, higher-level needs become operative. A satisfied need is not a motivator. The most powerful employee need is the one that has not been satisfied. Abraham Maslow first presented the five-tier hierarchy in 1942 to a psychoanalytic society and published it in 1954 in *Motivation and Personality* (New York: Harper and Row). The five levels of needsare as follows (Fig. 7.3):

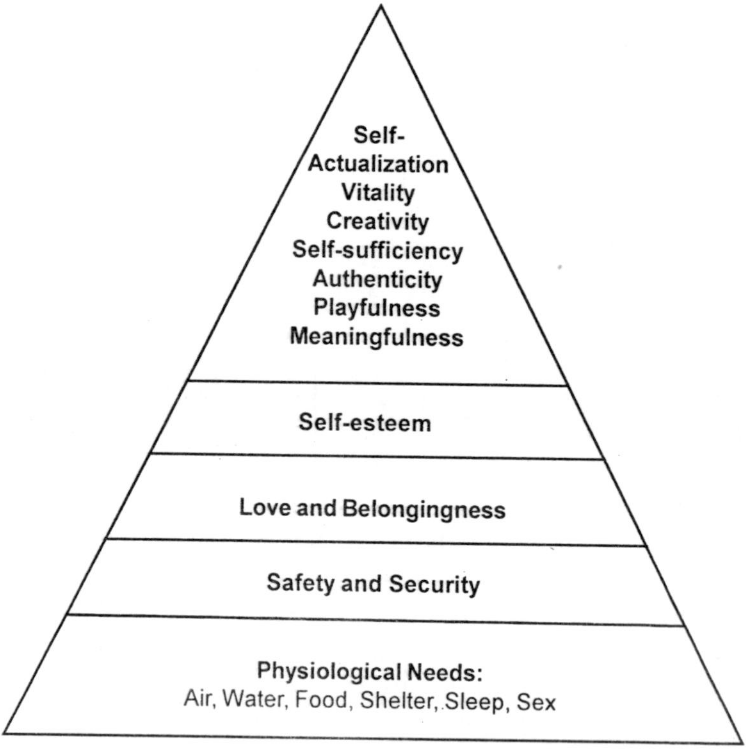

Fig. 7.2: Maslow's Five-tier Hierarchy Model

I. *Physiological needs* are the most basic human needs. They include food, water, and comfort. The organization helps to satisfy employees' physiological needs by a paycheck.

II. *Safety needs* are the desires for security and stability, to feel safe from harm. The organization helps to satisfy employees' safety needs by benefits.

III. *Social needs* are the desires for affiliation. They include friendship and belonging. The organization helps to satisfy employees' social needs through sports teams, parties, and celebrations. The manager can help fulfil social needs by showing direct care and concern for employees.

IV. *Esteem needs* are the desires for self-respect and respect or recognition from others. The organization helps to satisfy employees' esteem needs by matching the skills and abilities of the employee to the job. The manager can help fulfil esteem needs by showing workers that their work is appreciated.

V. *Self-actualization needs* are the desires for self-fulfilment and the realization of the individual's full potential. The manager can help fulfil self-actualization needs by assigning tasks that challenge employees' minds while drawing on their aptitude and training.

Alderfer's ERG (Existence, Relatedness and Growth)

He identified three categories of needs. The most important contribution of the ERG model is the addition of the frustration-regression hypothesis, which holds that when individuals are frustrated in meeting higher level needs, the next lower level needs reemerge (Fig. 7.4).

- *Existence* needs are the desires for material and physical well-being. These needs are satisfied with food, water, air, shelter, working conditions, pay, and fringe benefits.
- *Relatedness* needs are the desires to establish and maintain interpersonal relationships. These needs are satisfied with relationships with family, friends, managers, subordinates, and co-workers.

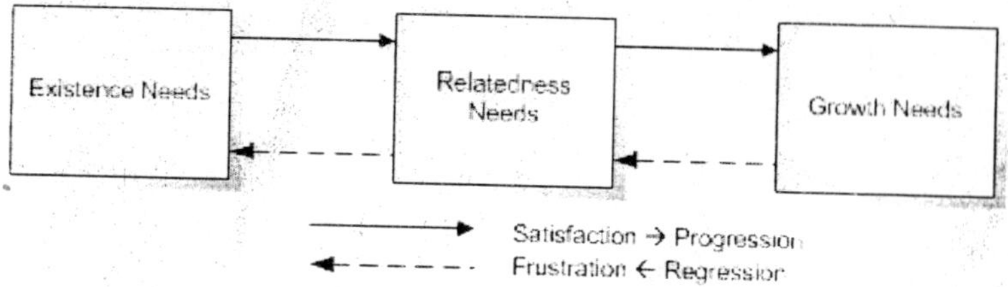

Fig. 7.4: Clayton Alderfer's ERG Theory

- *Growth* needs are the desires to be creative, to make useful and productive contributions and to have opportunities for personal development.

McClelland's Learned Needs

McClelland's Learned Needs divide motivation into needs for power, affiliation, and achievement.

- *Achievement* motivated people thrive on pursuing and attaining goals. They like to be able to control the situations in which they are involved. They take moderate risks. They like to get immediate feedback on how they have done. They tend to be preoccupied with a task-orientation towards the job to be done.
- *Power* motivated individuals see almost every situation as an opportunity to seize control or dominate others. They love to influence others. They like to change situations whether or not it is needed. They are willing to assert themselves when a decision needs to be made.
- *Affiliation* motivated people are usually friendly and like to socialize with others. This may distract them from their performance requirements. They will usually respond to an appeal for cooperation.

Herzberg's Two-Factor Theory

The Two-Factor Theory of Herzberg describes needs in terms of satisfaction and dissatisfaction (Fig. 7.5). Frederick Herzberg examined motivation in the light of job content and contest. (See

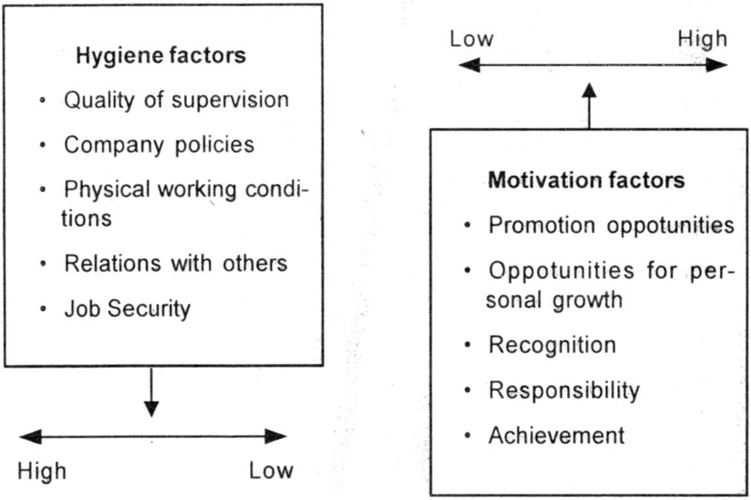

Fig. 7.5: Herzberg's Two-Factor Theory

Work an the Nature of Man, Crowell Publications, 1966.) Motivating employees is a two-step process. First provide hygienes and then motivators. One continuum ranges from no satisfaction to satisfaction. The other continuum ranges from dissatisfaction to no dissatisfaction.

Satisfaction comes from motivators that are intrinsic or job content, such as achievement, recognition, advancement, responsibility, the work itself, and growth possibilities. Herzberg uses the term motivators for job satisfiers since they involve job content and the satisfaction that results from them. Motivators are considered job turn-ons. They are necessary for substantial improvements in work performance and move the employee beyond satisfaction to superior performance. Motivators correspond to Maslow's higher-level needs of esteem and self-actualization.

Dissatisfaction occurs when the following hygiene factors, extrinsic or job context, are not present on the job: pay, status, job security, working conditions, company policy, peer relations, and supervision. Herzberg uses the term *hygiene* for these factors because they are preventive in nature. They will not produce motivation, but they can prevent motivation from occurring.

Hygiene factors can be considered job stay-ons because they encourage an employee to stay on a job. Once these factors are provided, they do not necessarily promote motivation; but their absence can create employee dissatisfaction. Hygiene factors correspond to Maslow's physiological, safety, and social needs in that they are extrinsic, or peripheral, to the job. They are present in the work environment of job context (Fig. 7.6).

Motivation comes from the employee's feelings of accomplishment or job content rather than from the environmental factors or job context. Motivators encourage an employee to strive to do his or her best. Job enrichment can be used to meet higher-level needs. To enrich a job, a manager can introduce new or more difficult tasks, assign individuals specialized tasks that enable them to become experts, or grant additional authority to employees. The process approach emphasizes how and why people choose certain behaviours in order to meet their personal goals. Process theories focus on external influences or behaviours that people choose to meet their needs. External influences are often readily accessible to managers.

Vroom's Expectancy Model

The Model of Vroom's Expectancy suggests that people choose among alternative behaviours because they anticipate that particular behaviours will lead to one or more desired outcomes and that other behaviours will lead to undesirable outcomes. Expectancy is the belief that effort will lead to first-order outcomes, any work-related behaviour that is the direct result of the effort an employee expends on a job. *Equity* is the perception of fairness involved in rewards given (See Fig. 7.7). A fair or equitable situation is one in which people with similar inputs experience similar outcomes. Employees will compare their rewards with the rewards received by others for their efforts. If employees perceive that an inequity exists, they are likely to withhold some of their contributions, either consciously or unconsciously, to bring a situation into better balance.

For example, if someone thinks he or she is not getting enough pay (output) for his or her work (input), he or she will try to get that pay increased or reduce the amount of work he

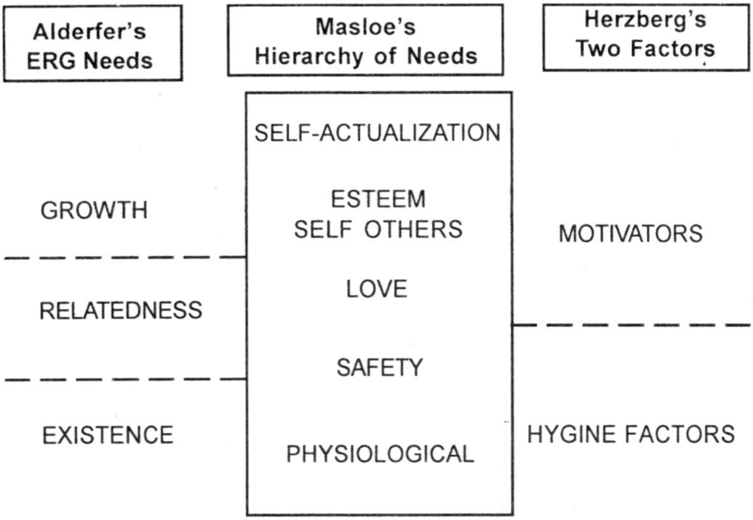

Fig. 7.6: The Relationships between Alderfer's ERG needs, Maslow's five-level hierarchy, and Herzberg's two-factor theory.

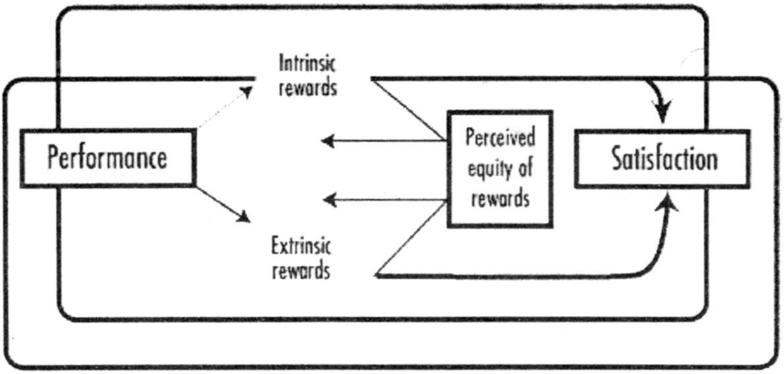

Fig. 7.7: Equity Theory

or she is doing. On the other hand, when a worker thinks he or she is being paid too much for the work he or she is doing, he or she tends to increase the amount of work. Not only do workers compare their own inputs and outputs; they compare their input/output ratio with the input/output ratio of other workers. If one work team believes they are doing more work than a similar team for the same pay, their sense of fairness will be violated and they will tend to reduce the amount of work they are doing. It is a normal human inclination to want things to be fair.

Bowditch and Buono note that while equity theory was originally concerned with differences in pay, it may be applied to other forms of tangible and intangible rewards in the workplace. That is, if any input is not balanced with some fair output, the motivation process will be difficult. Managers must manage the perception of fairness in the mind of each employee. If subordinates think they are not being treated fairly, it is difficult to motivate them.

Reinforcement involves four types of consequence. Positive reinforcement creates a pleasant consequence by using rewards to increase the likelihood that a behaviour will be repeated. Negative reinforcement occurs when a person engages in behaviour to avoid unpleasant consequences or to escape from existing unpleasant consequences. Punishment is an attempt to discourage a target behaviour by the application of negative outcomes whenever it is possible. Extinction is the absence of any reinforcement, either positive or negative, following the occurrence of a target behaviour. Employees have questions about their jobs. Can I do what management is asking me to do? If I do the job, will I be rewarded? Will the reward I receive be satisfactory to me?

REFERENCES

Amabile, T.M. (1988). A model of creativity and innovation in organizations. In: B.M. Staw and L.L. Cummings (Eds.), *Research in Organizational Behaviour:* Vol. 10, pp. 123-167, JAI Press.

Deci, E.L. and Ryan, R.M. (2000). The "What" and the "Why" of goal pursuits: Human needs and the self-determination of behaviour. *Psychological Inquiry*, 11: 227-268.

Edwards, J.R. (1996). "An examination of competing versions of the person-environment fit approach to stress." *Academy of Management Journal*, 39: 292-339.

Eisenberger, R., Rhoades, L., and Carmeron, J. (1999). Does pay for performance increase or decrease perceived self-determination and intrinsic motivation? *Journal of Personality and Social Psychology*, 77: 1026-1040.

Floyd, F. J. and Widaman, K. F. (1995). Factor analysis in the development and refinement of clinical assessment instruments. *Psychological Assessement*, 7: 286-299.

Hersey, P. and K.H. Blanchard (1982) *Management of Organisational Behaviour: Utilizing Human Resources*. 4th Edition. Prentice-Hall of India Pvt. Ltd., New Delhi, p. 343.

Hertzberg, F. (1966). *Work and the Nature of Man*. Cleveland: World Publishing.

Kolb, D.A., I.M.. Rubin and J.M. McIntyre (1979) *Organizational Psychology – An Experiential Approach*. Third edition, Prentice-Hall, Inc., Englewood Cliffs, New Jersey, p. 496.

Komaki, J. (1982). Managerial effectiveness: Potential contributions of the behavioral approach. *Journal of Organizational Behavior Management*, 3: 71-83.

Locke, E.A. (1976). The nature and causes of job satisfaction. In: M.D. Dunette (Ed.), *Handbook of Industrial and Organizational Psychology*: 1297-1350. Chicago: Rand McNally.

Maslow, A.H. (1943). A theory of human motivation. *Psychological Review*, 50: 370-396.

Sansone, C., and Harackiewicz, J.M. (2000). *Intrinsic and extrinsic motivation: The search for optimal motivation and performance*. San Diego: Academic Press.

Seashore, S. E., Lawler, E. E., Mirvis, P., and Cammann, C. (eds.) (1982). *Observing and Measuring Organizational Change: A Guide to Field Practice*. Wiley, New York.

Sims, H. P., Szilagyi, A. D., and McKemey, D. R. (1976). Antecedents of work-related expectancies. *Academy of Management Journal*, 19: 547-559.

Staw, B.M., and Ross, J. (1978). Commitment to a Policy Decision: A multi-theoretical perspective. *Administrative Science Quarterly*, 23: 40-64.

Van Vianen, A.E.M. (2000). Person-organization fit: The match between newcomers' and recruiters' preferences for organizational cultures. *Personnel Psychology*, 53: 113-149.

8 Controlling Process

Effective managers live in the present but concentrate on the future.

– James L. Hayes

Controlling

Controlling is directly related to planning. The controlling process ensures that plans are being implemented properly. In the functions of management cycle - planning, organizing, directing, and controlling - planning moves forward into all the other functions, and controlling reaches back. Controlling is the final link in the functional chain of management activities and brings the functions of management cycle full circle. Control is the process through which standards for performance of people and processes are set, communicated, and applied. Effective control systems use mechanisms to monitor activities and take corrective action, if necessary. The manager observes what happens and compares that with what was supposed to happen. He or she must correct below-standard conditions and bring results up to expectations. Effective control systems allow managers to know how well implementation is going. Control facilitates delegating activities to employees. Since managers are ultimately held accountable for their employees' performance, timely feedback on employee activity is necessary.

Controlling Process

The control process is a continuous flow between measuring, comparing and action. There are four steps in the control process: establishing performance standards, measuring actual performance, comparing measured performance against established standards, and taking corrective action.

Step 1. Establish Performance Standards

Standards are created when objectives are set during the planning process. A standard is any guideline established as the basis for measurement. It is a precise, explicit statement of expected results from a product, service, machine, individual, or organizational unit. It is usually expressed numerically and is set for quality, quantity, and time. Tolerance is permissible deviation from the standard. What is expected? How much deviation can be tolerated? Time controls relate to deadlines and time constraints. Material controls relate to inventory and material-yield controls. Equipment controls are built into the machinery, imposed on the operator to protect the equipment or the process. Cost controls help ensure cost standards are met. Employee performance controls focus on actions and behaviours of individuals and groups of employees. Examples include absences, tardiness, accidents, quality and quantity of work. Budgets control cost or expense related standards. They identify quantity of materials used and units to be produced.

Financial controls facilitate achieving the organization's profit motive. One method of financial controls is budgets. Budgets allocate resources to important activities and provide managers with quantitative standards against which to compare resource consumption. They become control tools by pointing out deviations between the standard and actual consumption.

Operations control methods assess how efficiently and effectively an organization's transformation processes create goods and services. Methods of transformation controls include Total Quality Management (TQM) statistical process control and the inventory management control. Statistical process control is the use of statistical methods and procedures to determine whether production operations are being performed correctly, to detect any deviations, and to find and eliminate their causes. A control chart displays the results of measurements over time and provides a visual means of determining whether a specific process is staying within predefined limits. As long as the process variables fall

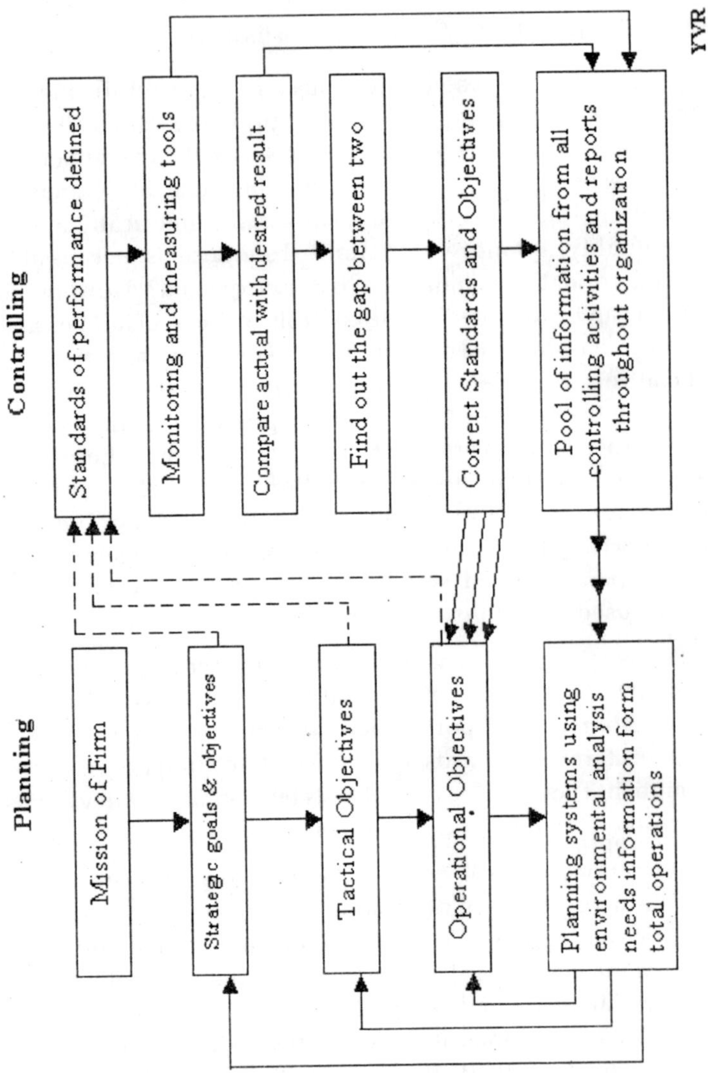

Fig. 8.1: Planning and Controlling

within the acceptable range, the system is in control. Measurements outside the limits are unacceptable or out of control. Improvements in quality eliminate common causes of variation by adjusting the system or redesigning the system. (See Fig. 8.1).

Inventory is a large cost for many organizations. The appropriate amount to order and how often to order impact the firm's bottom line. The economic order quantity model (EOQ) is a mathematical model for deriving the optimal purchase quantity. The EOQ model seeks to minimize total carrying and ordering costs by balancing *purchase costs, ordering costs, carrying costs* and *stockout costs*. In order to compute the economic order quantity, the manager needs the following information: forecasted demand during a period cost of placing the order, that value of the purchase price, and the carrying cost for maintaining the total inventory.

The just-in-time (JIT) system is the delivery of finished goods just in time to be sold, subassemblies just in time to be assembled into finished goods, parts just in time to go into subassemblies, and purchased materials just in time to be transformed into parts. Communication, coordination, and cooperation are required from managers and employees to deliver the smallest possible quantities at the latest possible date at all stages of the transformation process in order to minimize inventory costs.

Step 2. Measure Actual Performance:

Managers collect data to measure actual performance to determine variation from standard. Written data might include time cards, production tallies, inspection reports, and sales tickets. Personal observation, statistical reports, oral reports and written reports can be used to measure performance. Management by walking around, or observation of employees working, provides unfiltered information, extensive coverage, and the ability to read between the lines. While providing insight, this method might be misinterpreted by employees as mistrust. Oral reports allow for fast and extensive feedback.

Computers give managers direct access to real time, unaltered data, and information. On line systems enable managers to identify problems as they occur. Database programmes allow managers to query, spend less time gathering facts, and be less dependent on other people. Managers have access to information at their fingertips. Employees can supply progress reports through the use of networks and electronic mail. Statistical reports are easy to visualize and effective at demonstrating relationships. Written reports provide comprehensive feedback that can be easily filed and referenced. Computers are important tools for measuring performance. In fact, many operating processes depend on automatic or computer-driven control systems. Impersonal measurements can count, time, and record employee performance.

Step 3. Compare Measured Performance Against Established Standards:

Comparing results with standards determines variation. Some variation can be expected in all activities and the range of variation - the acceptable variance - has to be established. Management by exception lets operations continue as long as they fall within the prescribed control limits. Deviations or differences that exceed this range would alert the manager to a problem.

Step 4. Take Corrective Action:

The manager must find the cause of deviation from standard. Then, he or she takes action to remove or minimize the cause. If the source of variation in work performance is from a deficit in activity, then a manager can take immediate corrective action and get performance back on track. Also, the managers can opt to take basic corrective action, which would determine how and why performance has deviated and correct the source of the deviation. Immediate corrective action is more efficient, however basic corrective action is the more effective.

An *example* of the control process is a *thermostat.*

- *Standard:* The room thermostat is set at 68 degrees.
- *Measurement:* The temperature is measured.
- *Corrective Action:* If the room is too cold, the heat comes on. If the room is too hot, the heat goes off.

Types of Control

Controls are most effective when they are applied at key places. Managers can implement controls before the process begins (feedforward), during the process (concurrent), or after it ceases (feedback).

Feed forward controls focus on operations before they begin. Their goal is to prevent anticipated problems. An example of feed forward control is scheduled maintenance on automobiles and machinery. Regular maintenance feeds forward to prevent problems. Other examples include safety systems, training programmes, and budgets.

Concurrent controls apply to processes as they are happening. Concurrent controls enacted while work is being performed include any type of steering or guiding mechanism such as direct supervision, automated systems (such as computers programmed to inform the user when they have issued the wrong command), and organizational quality programmes.

Feedback controls focus on the results of operations. They guide future planning, inputs, and process designs. Examples of feedback controls include timely (weekly, monthly, quarterly, annual) reports so that almost instantaneous adjustments can be made.

Characteristics of Effective Controls

Control systems must be designed properly to be effective. When control standards are inflexible or unrealistic, employees cannot focus on the organization's goals. Control systems must prevent, not cause, the problems they were designed to detect.

Performance variance can also be the result of an unrealistic standard. The natural response for employees whose performance falls short is to blame the standard or the manager. If the standard is appropriate, then it is up to the manager to stand his or her ground and take the necessary corrective action.

An *example* of effective controls is the *dashboard on a car.* There are many things that can go wrong with a car. Only the most critical items to the car's operation are the focus on the dashboard (oil level, engine heat, fuel gauge, etc.). Variations in these items are most likely to inflict the most damage to the car. The critical items on the dashboard are easily understood and used by drivers. They point out a problem and specify a solution.

They are accurate and timely. They call the driver's attention to variations in time to prevent serious damage. Yet, there is not so much information on the dashboard that the driver is overwhelmed.

REFERENCES

Blake and Mouton (n.d.), *The Versatile Manager: A Grid Profile*, pp. 239-161.

Bowditch, James L. and Anthony F. Buono (1997), *A Primer on Organizational Behavior*, 4th, John Wiley and Sons.

Burns, Tom and G. M. Stalker (1961), *Management of Innovation*, London: Tavistock Publications, p. 19.

Davies, Keith (1969), *Management Communication and the Grapevine, Harvard Business Review*, 31.

Drucker, Peter F. (1988), "The Coming of the New Organizations," *Harvard Business Review*, 88(1): 45–53.

Freiberg, Kevin and Jackie Freiberg (1996), *NUTS! Southwest Airlines' Crazy Recipe for Business and Personal Success*, Bard Press, p. 298.

Holt, David H. (n.d), *Personal Communication And Consulting Withy Falcooner Glass Industries*, Inc,. Jamestown, New York

John P. Kotter, (1990), *A Force for Change: How Leadership Differs From Management*, The Free Press.

Robbins, Stephen P. (1980), *The Administrative Process*, 2nd ed. Englewood Cliffs, NJ, Prentice-Hall, pp. 194-195.

Taber, Mark (1992), Systems Management Beyond the Glass House, *Datamation*, March 15: 63-67.

PART - II
ORGANIZATIONAL BEHAVIOUR

9 Introduction to Organizational Behaviour

If you command wisely, you'll be obeyed cheerfully.
– *Thomas Fuller*

Ideas of human beings form organizations. The organization as a mechanism is used to bring the ideas into reality. The existence of organization, therefore, cannot be seen without the people as its members. The members who are associated with the organizations are not static in their totality, but change takes place in every spare of their life. The changes in member's behaviour naturally affect the organizational activities. The success of an organization is very much depended on understand, prediction, and control of organizational members behaviour. Hence, the study of organizational behaviour is an essential part of every person who responsible for organizational activities at managerial level. In this connection let us understand the basic terms of organization, behaviour and organizational behaviour.

Organization

E.H. Schein defined organization as the rational coordination of the activities of a number of people for the achievement of some common explicit purpose or goals, through division of labor and function, and through a hierarchy of authority and responsibility. In the words of Stephen P. Robbins (1998), organization is a consciously coordinated social entity, with a relatively identifiable boundary, that functions on a relatively continuous basis to achieve a common goals or set of goals.

Organizations are undergoing profound transformation brought about by the changing nature of competition, which requires increasingly flexible and proactive responses, and by cultural and social change which has led on the one hand to a scaling down of the hierarchical organization as an instrument of coordination and control, and on the other, to growing demand for autonomy, innovation, commitment and learning. It is increasingly evident that an ability to handle these changes and expectations is essential for the survival and success of companies. The challenge raised by today's business environment for managements concerns a set of crucial factors: *leadership, integration,* and *continuing learning.*

Leadership is the ability to construct the meaning of organizational action, communicate it to persons and groups, and lead them towards a shared goal, generating cohesion and responsibilization but also assuming that care for the individual is a core value. Integration is the ability to bind people together and tie them to the organization and its goals, to foster participation, sharing, and communication between people and the parts of the system. Continuing learning is today the most crucial task for managers. They must seek to learn constantly from experience, taking personal responsibility for their own development while fostering that of subordinates and colleagues, acting as coaches, trainers, consultants and mentors.

This is a demanding challenge: firstly because professional behaviour is the complex outcome of individual and organizational histories, of the development of the personality, and of individual choices; secondly, because the development of relational skills requires commitment, motivation and adequate processes, regardless of the misleading promises sometimes made by management training organizations.

Behaviour

The term behaviour is taken in its totality connoting a wide and comprehensive meaning. Woodworth says that 'any manifestation of life is activity' and behaviour is a collective name for these activities. Therefore the term behaviour includes all the motor or cognitive activities like walking, swimming, dancing and so on. The cognitive activities like thinking, reasoning, imagining and also affective activities like feeling, happy, sad and angry and so on. It includes not only the conscious behaviour and activities of the human mind but also the sub-conscious and unconscious. Consequently, it covers not only the overt behaviour but also the covert behaviour involving all the inner experiences and mental processes.

Human Behaviour

Behaviour has origins and evolves in the crucible of our life's experiences. Behaviour is shaped by our early parental relationships, as well as the many others who impact our sense of self, our degree of trust or lack thereof. We are molded by our victories and our defeats and how those most important to us react to those different outcomes. Establishing causality of undesirable behaviour is an odyssey where various factors are reviewed, including upbringing and formative socialization experiences, chemical imbalances, and displaced responses.

Human behaviour and its existence can be more fully understood by viewing ourselves as biological, psychological, sociological, humanistical, and spiritual entities. By understanding ourselves and our existence we may also live to fully experience what it is to be human. In one regard, we may view a human as a biological organism consisting of a complex structure of chemical components while possessing thoughts and feelings through integrated electrical-chemical reactions. Furthermore, the human organism has evolved through time to reflect the environmental and social obstacles placed on it through the process of evolutionary selection. We can also distinguish ourselves as psychological and social entities. From a very early age we learn from those around us and develop particular comfort zones in which we develop our personality. From our personality and our place in life we develop our identity of ourselves. Recognizing an individual in a humanistic light has been a major step toward understanding the total being. The humanistic system of thought centers on the person and their values, capacities, and worth. In addition, it is concerned with the interests, needs, and welfare of human beings.

Development of Maladaptive Behaviour

The holistic health concept includes developing and maintaining physical, mental, emotional, mental, social, and spiritual growth. Although it is optimal to develop all components of holistic health equally, sometimes the development a just few of these components may be enough to bring about the degree of self-worth or happiness necessary for a seemingly normal life. Often, a weak development of one or more of these components may adversely effect other components of holistic health. Sometimes this weak link may be felt as a void or unquenchable thirst in ones life. Conversely, discontent is experienced when what occurs does not match with what was expected This void or discontentment may bring about several exaggerated needs that may stagnate the development of holistic health.

Individuals may futilely attempt to satisfy these exaggerated needs by implementing particular behaviours. A perception of at least temporary satisfaction is sometimes enough to reinforce this behaviour for a life long pattern. In most cases, we can implement this behaviour within socially acceptable boundaries. In some cases, though, this behaviour may be socially unacceptable or self-destructive. Modern values have compromised our being. We rationalize day care, divorce, and the materialistic world in which we live with no real understanding of our selfishness, insecurities, and the consequences of our behaviours. We have alienated our lives, our children lives, and ultimately our society. This has threatened all aspects of our individual holistic health: physical, mental, emotional, mental, social, and spiritual.

Organizational Behaviour

Organizational behaviour is related with the study and analysis of human behaviour at work. It strives to identify ways in which people can act more effectively. It is the newly designed field of study, which focuses on the application of knowledge about how people as individuals and as groups behave or act in organizations. Different behavioral scientists have offered variety of definitions for this field of discipline.

The renowned management thinker *Fred Luthans* described in very simplest way. According to him the organizational behaviour is 'directly concerned with the understanding, prediction, and control of human behaviour in organizations'. As per *Stephen P. Robbins*, OB is 'a field of study that investigates the impact that individuals, group, and structure have on behaviour within organizing for the purpose of applying such knowledge toward improving an organization's effectiveness'.

Organizational behaviour is concerned with the study of what people do in an organization and how that behaviour affects the performance of the organization. It is specifically concerned with employment related situations and emphasizes behaviour as related to jobs, work, absenteeism, employment turnover, productivity, human performance, and management.

Essence of Organizational Behaviour

Do people really matter? Our understanding of the role of people and the management of this vital resource is undergoing a fundamental reassessment. Advances in technology and communication are causing many organization to radically change their structures and, as a consequence, the processes and techniques of managing people. This section is about some of the issues and debates which characterise these management dilemmas.

Management Competence

Here we consider the increasing attention paid to defining the characteristics and capabilities of managers, and how those might be changing now we have moved into the 21st Century.

Culture and Values

Organizations are fragmenting and re-forming under many different guises. The social 'glue' which was culture and values may need to be re-considered in today's continually transitional structures.

Leadership and Teams

Management literature is filled with stories of leaders as heroes and of teams pulling together to achieve outstanding successes. But what is the impact of change on organizational working practices and the techniques of those who need to deliver results?

Change Management

We are on the look out for an organization that can genuinely claim to be able to resist change. For the rest of us, the role and purpose of managers is to lead change. This implies that everything is, to some extent, transient and cloaked in uncertainty. However, we need to enhance our understanding of successful change and learn how to adapt these techniques to our own, evolving, circumstances.

Organizational culture

It is the shared beliefs, values and norms of a business. It could be said it is a general view throughout the organization of how the employees should behave, their general attitudes and the nature of working relationships. The understanding of a company's culture is being seen as increasingly important as organizations realise the positive benefits of placing great emphasis on employees' understanding of the company's culture. Japanese companies are a good example of this.

REFERENCES

Adam-Smith, D. and Peacock, A. (1994) *Cases in Orgasational Behaviour.* London: Pitman.

Bennett, R. (1991) *Organisational Behaviour.* London: Pitman.

Cohen, A. et al. (1995) *Effective Behaviour in Organisations: Cases, Concepts, and Student Experiences.* 6th ed. Irwin/McGraw-Hill.

Cowling, A., Stanworth, M., Bennett, R., Curran, J. and Lyons, P. (1993) *Behavioral Sciences for Managers.* 2nd ed. London: Edward Arnold.

Fincham, R. and Rhodes, P. (2005) *Principles of Organizational Behavior.* 4th ed. Oxford: Oxford University Press.

French, W. and Bell, C. (1984) *Organization Development: Behavioral Science Interventions for Organization Improvement.* 3rd ed. New Jersey: Prentice-Hall.

Gibson, J., Ivanchevich, J., Donnelly, J. and Konopaske, R. (2006) *Organizations: Behaviour, Structure, Processes.* 12th ed. McGraw-Hill

Gordon, J. (1993) *A Diagnostic Approach to Organizational Behavior.* 4th ed. Boston: Allyn and Bacon.

Greenberg, J. and Baron, R. (1993) *Behavior in organizations: understanding and managing the human side of work.* 4th ed. Boston: Allyn and Bacon.

Hilgard, Ernest R., Richard C. Atkinson and Rital L. Atkinson (1975) *Introduction to Psychology,* Oxford and IBH Publication Co. Pvt. Ltd.

Hodge, B. and Anthony, W. (1984) *Organization Theory.* 2nd ed. Boston: Allyn and Bacon.

Huczynski, A. and Buchanan, D. (1991) *Organisational Behaviour: An Introductory Text,* 2nd ed., Harlow: FT/Prentice-Hall.

Luthans, Fred (1995) *Organizational Behaviour,* Tata McGraw-Hill Publications, Delhi.

Mullins, L. (2007) *Management and Organizational Behaviour.* 8th ed. FT/Prentice-Hall.

Nelson, D. and Quick, J. (2006) *Organizational Behaviour: Foundations, Realities and Challenges.* 5th ed. Thomson South-Western.

Robbins, S. (1993) *Organisational Behaviour: Concepts, Controversies and Applications.* 6th ed. New Jersey: Prentice-Hall.

Robbins, S. and Judge, T. (2008) *Essentials of Organizational Behaviour.* 9th ed. New Jersey: Pearson/Prentice-Hall.

Robbins, Stephen P. (2003) *Organizational Behaviour,* 10th ed., Printice-Hall of India Private Limited, New Delhi.

Schein ,Hdgar H. (1997) *Organizational Culture and Leadership,* 2nd ed. San Francisco, CA: Jossey Bass Publishers.

Smith, M. *et al.* (1982) *Introducing Organizational Behaviour.* London: Macmillan.

Tyson, S. and Jackson, T. (1992) *The Essence of Organizational Behaviour.* New York: Prentice-Hall.

Vecchio, R. (1995) *Organisational Behaviour.* 3rd ed. The Dryden Press

Weiss, J. (1996), *Organisational Behaviour and Change: Managing Diversity, Cross-cultural Dynamics, and Ethics.* New York: West Publishing Co.

10 Background to Organizational Behaviour

If you command wisely, you'll be obeyed cheerfully

– Thomas Fuller

Background of Organization Behaviour

Organization behaviour, as a management discipline, is relatively new compared to marketing or even to human resource management. The concept as we understand it today, that business organizations had their own specific forms of behaviour and action, and that the examination of these constitute a legitimate field of study in its own right, did not emerge until the late 1930s and was not fully formed until after the World War II. But 'organizations' have been a subject of study and enquiry by scholars in management and related fields since the late nineteenth century, and even a cursory study of this literature shows that modern organization behaviour emerged from a body of literature and thought which was strikingly rich and diverse.

The growth of the large-scale business organization in Europe, the USA and parts of Asia has been well described by many business historians. By 1890, corporations, trusts and other large business forms were becoming increasingly prominent and were coming under scrutiny from many quarters, some favourable, some hostile. There were those social commentators who thought that the growth of big business was ushering in a new era of prosperity and civilization; there were those who believed that big business was the enemy of civilization and freedom. Many of those engaged in the debate were motivated by ideology, and often had only a hazy idea of the concepts they were discussing.

Others, however, began to cut through the ideological mists and to examine, as if under a microscope, the organizations they had been so vigorously discussing and to consider them on their own merits. These early works fall into several categories: historical and legal studies, historical and military studies, sociological and economic studies, psychological studies, natural scientific and biological studies, and studies based on technical needs for managerial efficiency.

Historical and Legal Studies

One of the earliest approaches to the study of the modern business organization was that which looked at it in evolutionary terms and considered its roots in other previous forms of organization, particularly as defined by law. The representative scholar in this field is John Patterson Davis, an American lawyer and historian who completed a major two-volume work, *Corporations*, shortly before his untimely death in 1905. Although almost unknown today, this is a work of some importance. In it, Davis defines the corporation as being first and foremost a social entity generated by cultures and societies in response to certain needs. A general characteristic of human society is to generate structured responses to needs, and these structured responses take the form of corporations. Davis's idea of modern business corporations as evolving out of earlier corporate forms is a powerful one, and its influence can be seen in much later work, notably James Mooney and Alan Reiley's *Onward Industry!* Which is regarded as one of the foundation texts of organization study. Of equal importance, however, is his description of the corporation as a social entity. Although Davis used this idea to generate a description of how corporations have evolved - and there are important implications here for business ethics as well; a corporation which is a social entity must perforce behave according to the ethical norms of the society that created it - there is also a further implication: if corporations are social entities, then they are presumably themselves social in nature, and their behaviour and governance will have something in common with forms of behaviour and governance found elsewhere in society. Davis confirms this view when he speaks of corporations as 'artificial personalities'. His final definition of what a corporation is remains valid in terms of organizational thinking today.

A corporation is a body of persons upon whom the state has conferred such voluntarily accepted but compulsorily maintained relations to one another and to all others that, as an autonomous, self-sufficient and self-renewing body, they may determine and enforce their common will; and in the pursuit of their private interest may exercise more efficiently social functions both specially conducive to public welfare and most appropriately exercised by associated persons.

Sociological and Economic Studies

The reason for grouping these writers together will be clear from the samples of works provided. Both economists such as Alfred Marshall and Thorstein Veblen and sociologists such as Lucy Larcom were interested, from their various standpoints, in the impact that business organizations were having on their workers. Although human nature is nearly the same now as of old time, while the plant and processes of almost every industry have changed fundamentally more than once during the last five generations; yet the problems which the head of a business has to solve in relation to its personnel have changed and are changing their character much more completely than those which he has to solve in relation to its plant and processes, except in a few industries.

Whereas the historical and legal writers noted above were asking questions about why organizations exist and how they came to be, economists and writers on worker welfare were interested in looking *inside* the organization and examining its behaviour and function internally. Many of these writers were highly critical of what they saw as a tendency by organizations to be internally focused. Veblen famously criticizes commercial organizations for focusing on their own goals and making no attempt to guide the course of industry, and notes, *pace* Marx, the fundamentally antagonistic relations between workers and their managers, the organizational-level manifestation of the broader struggle of capital and labour. Larcom, who has fewer ideological axes to grind than Veblen, wonders nonetheless about the impact which business organization as a whole has on its individual members: 'Work, the mere use of the hands, as we all know, has in it no moral or progressive quality. Work is only great through the impulse that guides it, the motive in the worker's mind. The laborer must be greater than his occupation, or it will crush him'.

Studies based on Psychology

Lillian Gilbreth's *Psychology of Management* is one of the most important of the early texts that influenced organization behaviour, and the first full-length application of psychological concepts to management. Gilbreth, one of the first women in the USA to be awarded a degree in psychology, returned to university to study the subject after working with her husband Frank Bunker Gilbreth on motion studies. The observation of what people did in the workplace prompted Gilbreth to question why they behaved as they did.

It has been demonstrated that the emphasis in successful management lies on the man, not on the *work*; that efficiency is best secure by placing the emphasis on the man, and modifying the equipment, materials and methods to make the most of the man. It has, further, been recognized that the man's mind is a controlling factor in his efficiency, and has, by teaching, enabled the man to make the most of his powers. The effect of Gilbreth's work, and of other psychologically based studies that followed it, was to begin to turn the focus of organization thinking away from structure and control and towards the individual as the primary element that composed the organization. Many of the subsequent studies belong more properly to the related field of human resource management, but one work in particular, Mary Parker Follett's *Creative Experience*, had an important impact on thinking about organization as well.

Follett's view of organizations is one where people at all levels should be motivated to work and participate. They should gather their own information, make their own decisions, define their own roles and shape their own lives. She also rejects empiricism: experience should not be used to create theories and concepts, but to inform the mind and liberate the spirit, in a process that she calls 'evocation'. In this way, experience can become truly creative, a powerful force that creates advancement and progress. As she sums up:

"We seek reality in experience. Let us reject the realm of the compensatory; it is fair, but a prison. Experience may be hard but we claim its gifts because they are real, even though our feet bleed on its stones. We seek progressive advancement through the transformation of daily experience. Into what, conceptual pictures? No, daily experience must be translated not into conceptual pictures but into spiritual conviction. Experience can both guide and guard us. Foolish indeed are those who do not bring oil to its burning. *Creative Experience*, which launched Follett into a late career as a management guru, also led her to consider more deeply the problems of organization. She saw organizations as being based fundamentally on cooperation and coordination, and believed this to be the single unifying principle which held them together. In a later lecture at the London School of Economics, reprinted in 1937 in *Papers on the Science of Administration*, she speaks of 'the correlation of many controls rather than a superimposed control'."

The ramifications of modern industry are too wide-spread, its organization too complex, its problems too intricate for it to be possible for industry to be managed by commands from the top alone. This being so, we find that when central control is spoken of, that does not mean a point of radiation, but the gathering of many controls existing throughout the enterprise.

Follett's views were taken up later by Thomas North Whitehead, one of the researchers in the famous programme at the Hawthorne Works in the 1930s. His *Leadership in a Free Society* draws on both Follett and the Australian psychologist Elton Mayo to describe in detail the psychological connections that go on both within organizations and between organizations and their environments.

Studies based on Natural Science and Biology

By the middle of the second decade of the twentieth century, much in the fashion described by Thomas Kuhn in his theory of the development of scientific paradigms, writers on organization were beginning to search for a single model that would allow them to link historical, psychological, sociological and economic views to create a holistic view of organization. One model that began to develop was a biological one, using the natural world and more especially the human body as a metaphor. Veblen had already begun discussing economic activity in terms of biological evolution as early as 1904, and Emerson in his later work began to consider the business organization as an evolving biological entity. The foremost proponent of this view, however, was one of the first writers to write specifically on the problems of organization and thus one of the founders of the modern discipline, the management consultant Charles Knoeppel. Chapter 5 of his *Organization and Administration* (1918) is an extended account of the biological metaphor, drawn in part on the work of his colleagues Emerson and Herbert Casson, but here greatly expanded.

A close study of the foregoing conclusively indicates the wisdom of following the human body as closely as we can in determining the correct type of man building organization. First in order of importance is the executive, or director of activities, or guide, or co-ordinator, or whatever you choose to call him. Then comes the staff, the counselors who advise, criticise, prescribe and assist the executive in directing and coordinating. Now comes the question of adjusting the remaining two classes of organs, the organs of growth and upkeep and of creation and achievement as Mr. Emerson defined them, or the involuntary and voluntary organs as I had come to consider them, to the staff and the executive.

The biological metaphor, says Knoeppel, is fully compatible with the line and staff model. The brain functions as the staff, providing guidance and control; the limbs and organs execute commands and carry out functions. Borrowing a concept from Casson, he adds that the heart plays the role of the organizational will and purpose, setting the goals towards which the brain and other components work. As a guiding concept, today this metaphor looks at best naive. Yet it is a vitally important step in the history of thinking about organization, because here we see for the first time a concept that can unite the rational and technical aspects of organization with the emotional, social and psychological aspects. The idea that we ourselves are organizations and that the larger organizations we create are in some way images of ourselves remains a powerful one.

Studies-based on Technical Needs for Management Efficiency

The last group of writers to make an impact were those whose attitude was more pragmatic in nature. Engineers and managers themselves, they sought not to answer grand questions about organizations, but to understand how they can be made efficient. Thinking about organization began in a highly technical-rational mode, as exemplified in the work of Davis, Jones, Mason and Kimball. From an early period, however, economists and sociologists questioned the nature of the organization's relationship with its human elements, and this brought about the introduction of psychological thinking, led by Lillian Gilbreth. The emergence of many new approaches to organization led to the search for an overarching model of organization, a search which led Emerson and Knoeppel to develop the biological metaphor. This metaphor was only partially successful, but it did create awareness of a need to consider organizations holistically. Through the late 1920s and 1930s, writers like Follett, Luther Gulick, James Mooney and John Lee struggled to develop more fully on the nature, purpose, motivation and behaviour of organizations.

That struggle, of course, is still going on. In some ways, we are no nearer to a complete model of organization than we were in 1918. More recently, Gareth Morgan has described no less than eight different models for or metaphors of organization. His conclusion is that each of the eight is, in some way, valid; each has some special insight into organizations, and each views the subject from a different aspect. The greatest benefit can be achieved in studying not one model in isolation but all together, looking for the insights that each can give and so achieving a view of organization in the round. Much the same approach motivated this collection of works by earlier scholars and practitioners. The roots of organization theory are many; the disciplines that influenced organization thinkers range from military administration to economics to biology to sociology and psychology. By putting together a representative sample of all these views, we hope not only to shed light on the origins of organization theory but also to provide food for thought for those considering the ongoing problems of organization today.

Construction of Organizational Behaviour Field

Organizational behaviour is an applied behaviour science that is built up on contributions from a number of behavioral disciplines. The predominant areas are psychology, sociology, social psychology anthropology, and political science. Psychology's contributions have been mainly at the individual or micro level of analsysis; the other four disciplines have contributed to our understanding of macro concepts such as group processes and organization. The diagram presents an overview of the major contributions to the study of organizational behaviour (Fig. 10.1)

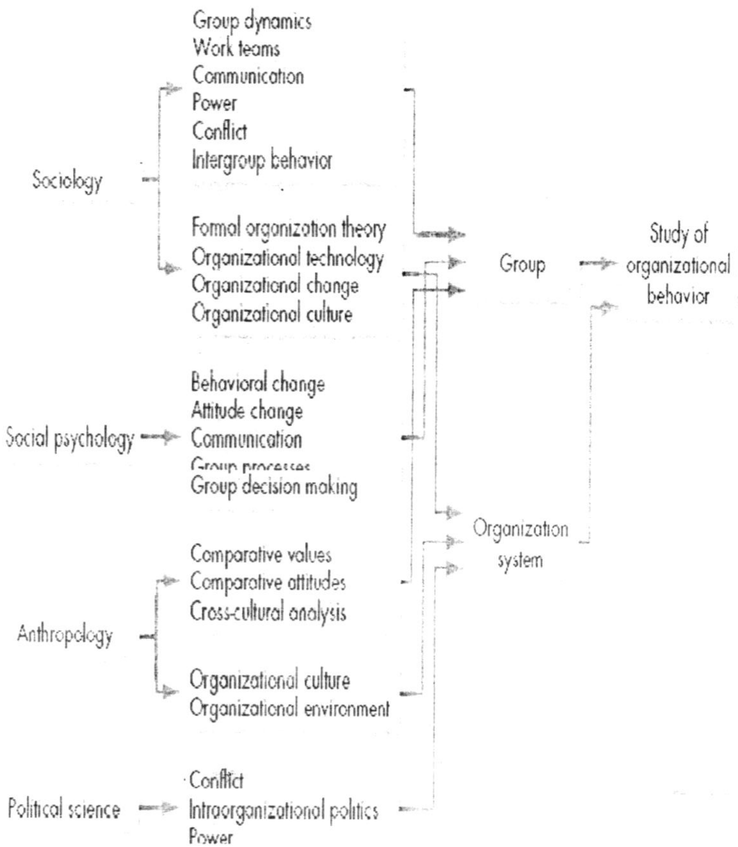

Fig. 10.1: Major Contributions to the Study of Organizational Behaviour

Psychology

It is the science that seeks to measure, explain and sometimes change the behaviour of humans. Psychologists concern themselves with studying and attempting to understand individual behaviour. As mentioned in the diagram good number of concepts has been barrowed to add to the knowledge of OB. The early industrial and organizational psychologist concern themselves with problems of fatigue, boredom, and other factors relevant to working conditions that could impede efficient work performance. More recently, their contributions have been expanded to include learning, perception, personality training and so on.

Sociology

It is the study of people in relation to their fellow human beings. The filed of sociology has make valuable contributions to understanding of group dynamics within organization. The topics derived from sociology include group dynamics, formation of groups, communications, formal and informal organizations.

Anthropology

It is the study of societies to learn about human beings and their activities. Anthropologists work on cultures and environment, values, attitudes, and behaviour between people in different countries and within different organizations. Culture dictates what people learn and how they behave. Organizations crate a unique culture that influences the way organizational members think about the organization and behave.

Political Science

It studies the behaviour of individuals and groups within a political environment. Specific topics of concerns include structuring of conflict, allocation of power, and how people manipulate power for individual self-interest.

Impact of Changing Environment On Human Behaviour

Global Environmental Change and Food Systems:

Human activity is leading to globally important

environmental changes - such as climate change, supplies of freshwater, the cycling of nitrogen and carbon, and biodiversity. The impact of these biophysical changes will complicate the task of providing sufficient food of the right quality to many sections of society. Not all individuals and sections of society are equally vulnerable to the effects of global environmental change on the provision of food. The capacity to cope with existing and anticipated changes in biophysical conditions, and the ability to perceive global environmental change and adapt accordingly, is highly variable. Vulnerability of food provision is a consequence of the interaction of biophysical conditions and socio-economic factors. Understanding the link between global environmental change and societal well being, and promoting effective intervention strategies requires an innovative interdisciplinary approach.

Rapid Climate Change - Vulnerability, Adaptability and Resilience

Many natural scientists suggest that changes in global thermohaline circulation in the North Atlantic have been the source of past rapid climatic fluctuations. Ocean circulation has been shown to be highly sensitive to changes in freshwater discharge - even small changes in the amount of freshwater entering the North Atlantic (as a result of melting polar ice from global warming, for example) could force a large and rapid shift in patterns of circulation. The impact of changes in ocean circulation could be catastrophic, leading to rapid cooling in the climate. The socio-economic implications of such events would be enormous, impacting on: fuel poverty, the location of industrial activities; agriculture, levels of energy demand and supply; transport systems; and indeed lifestyles and culture.

Sustainable Mobility and Human Behaviour

Historically, transport improvements have offered new opportunities and choices, not merely reductions in the time and monetary costs of established journeys. As a result, the spatial patterning of human activity has been increasingly dynamic. Car ownership has become a central feature of our lives in the West, and further increases in the volume of car traffic have been projected. This is not simply due to increasing levels of affluence, but the result of successive generations growing up within a culture characterised by greater mobility in general, and personal car use in particular. In a period in which mass car ownership has dominated mobility, there have been significant changes in other economic and social factors, such as the nature and terms of employment, the economic participation of women, leisure activities, and the composition of social networks.

Urban Systems, Long-term Climate Change

Urban environments are particularly important when considering climate change; they account for a large proportion of carbon emissions; they are the locations of the wealth-creating enterprises that would be affected by climate change; and they include large proportions of the population that would be vulnerable to climate change. A co-evolutionary perspective is beginning to emerge in which the interactions between social patterns, cultures, local economics and the physical conditions of climatic variability and climate change are considered.

REFERENCES

Bennett, R. (1997) *Organizational Behaviour.* 3rd ed. London: M&E Pitman.

Buchanan, D. and Huczynski, A. (2004) *Organisational Behaviour: An Introductory Text*, 5th ed., Harlow: FT/Prentice-Hall.

Davis, 'The Nature of Corporations', which appeared in *Political Science Quarterly* in 1897, are to be found in Volume 7 of this set.

Luthans, Fred (1995) *Organizational Behaviour*, McGraw-Hill, New York, (Eight Edition).

Gulick, L and Urwick. L. (1937) 'The Process of Control', *Papers on the Science of Administration*, pp. 161–169. Volume 8, pp. 236–247.

Hersey and Blanchard (2002) *Management of Organisational Behaviour*,8th Edition, Prentice-Hall of India, New Delhi.

Hurzynski, A. and Buchanan, D. (2001) *Organisational Behaviour: An Introductory Text*, 4th ed., Harlow: FT/Prentice-Hall.

John W. Newstrom and Keith Davis (1999) Organizational Behaviour-Human Behaviour at Work, Tata McGraw-Hill Edition, (Tenth Edition), New Delhi.

Luthans, F. (2001) Organisational Behaviour. 9th ed. McGraw Hill

Macionis, J. and Plummer, K. (1997) Sociology: a global introduction. New York: Prentice hall

Morgen Witzel (ed.) (2001) 'Introduction', *Organization Behaviour, 1890-1940* (Bristol: Thoemmes Press), pp. v- xvii.

Morgen Witzel, (2000) *Human Resource Management*, ed., 8 vols. (Bristol: Thoemmes Press.

Mullins, L. (2002) *Management and Organizational Behaviour*. 6th ed. FT/Prentice-Hall.

Munn.N.L, *Introduction to Psychology , Oxford and IBH,* (Indian Ed.), New Delhi, 1967.

Plender, J. (1997) A Stake in the future: the Stakeholding Solution, Nicholas Breadley Publishing.

Pugh, D. (1997) *Organization theory: Selected Readings*. 4th ed. London: Penguin books.

Rollinson, , D. and Edwards, D. and Broadfield, A. (1998) *Organisational Behaviour Analysis: An Integrated Approach*. Harlow: Addison Wesley

Scott, P. (2005) *Divisions of Labour*. A Pearson Custom Publications

Staw, B.M. (1995) *Psychological Dimensions of Organizational Behaviour*, 2nd Edition, Engle Wood Cliffs, Prentice-Hall.

Stephen P. Robbins, (2002) *Organizational Behaviour, 9th Edition, Pearson Education*, New Delhi.

Stephen P.Robbins (1998) *Organizational Behaviour, Concepts, Controversies and Applications,* Printice Hall of India Private Limited, New Delhi, (Eight Edition).

Thompson, P. and McHugh, D. (2002) *Work Organisations: A Critical Introduction*. 3rd ed. Palgrave.

Thompson, P. and Warhurst, C. (ed) (2003) *Workplaces of the Future*. Palgrave Macmillan.

Woodworth,R.S, (1984) *Contemporary Schools of Psychology*, Londaon, Methuen.

11 Perception

"We see things not as they are, but as we are."
– *H.M. Tomlinson*

We always remain surrounded by the forces of our environment. Our sensory receptors are bombarded continuously by the various stimuli present in this environment. As a result we become aware of some light, sound or chemical stimuli by experiencing some typical sensations. This awareness or information about the stimuli is then relayed by our sensory transmitter to the centers of the nervous system. Our eyes for instance, only make us aware of some light stimuli – it does not see the book or the pen. Our ears are aware of some auditory stimulation but cannot tell that the train is whistling or birds are twittering.

Leaders make decisions based on how they perceive, that is sense and understand, the events, people, and things around them. Yet most of us have experienced instances where our perceptions were clearly erroneous and the events, people and things around us were not what they appeared to be. While more accurate perceptions should obviously provide a stronger base for decision-making, some leaders may argue that problems resulting from inaccurate perceptions are infrequent and often minor. Of course, most of us do perceive reasonably accurately most of the time, but effective executives know that, as in sports or any other professional field, the difference between top and mediocre performance is often measured in millimetres and microseconds. Since most leaders strive to be that little bit better than their peers, they must seek to understand the perceptual process better in order to develop the skill to perceive events and people more accurately and thus have a better base for making decisions.

Definition of Perception

Perception refers to the way we try to understand the world around us. We gather information through our five sense organs, but perception adds meaning to these sensory inputs. The process of perception is essentially subjective in nature, as it is never an exact recording of the event or the situation.

Perception is the process by which we organize and interpret our sensory impressions in order to give meaning to the environment. As pointed out, a situation may be the same but the interpretation of that situation by two individuals may be immensely different.

Perception is defined as the set of processes by which an individual becomes aware of and interprets information about the environment.

The model of perceptionprocess helps one understand the basic processes involved in human perception in a rather simplistic way. At a point of time, we are flooded with a myriad of stimuli impinging on our sense organs, like now as you are reading this particular page in front of you, light rays from the page are reaching your eyes. But these are, by no means, all. Light rays from every possible direction are also impinging on your retina as well. At the same time you are also receiving a host of auditory stimuli – the humming of the air conditioner, somebody talking out aloud outside, the rustling of the papers on your table, etc. Similarly, every sense organs of your body are bombarded with a number of different stimuli simultaneously. But our brain and the nervous system are not capable of processing so many pieces of information all together. As it is now happening with you, you are, in all probability, hardly aware of all these sensory inputs reaching you. Thus what happens is that we only *selectively* choose from among a host of stimuli and process only those. If we examine the model above we will find that only those stimuli are given entry to the process of 'registration' which have got adequate attention or have aroused our interest.

Factors affecting Perception

Internal Factors

Sensory Limits and Thresholds

Our sensory organs have specialized nerves which respond differently to the various forms of energy they receive. For instance, our eyes receive and convert light waves into electrical energy which are transmitted to the visual cortex of the brain to create the sensation of vision and subsequently leading to perception. But each sense receptor requires a minimum level of energy to excite it before perception can take place. The minimum level is called the *absolute threshold* - a point below which we do not perceive energy. The *differential threshold* is the smallest amount by which two similar stimuli must be different in order to be perceived as different.

Psychological Factors

Psychological factors such as personality, past experiences and learning and motives affect an individual's perceptual process to considerable extent. The internal *set* or the inclination to perceive certain stimuli in a particular way also influences one's perception. These largely determine why people select and attend to a particular stimulus or situation over other. Things compatible to one's learning, interest, attitude and personality are likely to get more attention than others. As you must have noticed, a person who is sitting aloof from your group in a far away corner, automatically turn to your direction the moment you utter his name. Similarly, if you happen to hear the word 'management' or 'organizational behaviour' while traveling in a public transport, your attention is surely going to the conversation. This happens because of one's strong association (with one's own name) or the current interest in the topics. Likewise, one's expectancy can affect and even distort one's perception. We hardly rely too much on pure sensory inputs and perceive the reality in our own subjective way.

External Factors

The Target

The characteristics of the target that is being observed can affect perception. We have earlier noted (refer to Fig 11.1) that

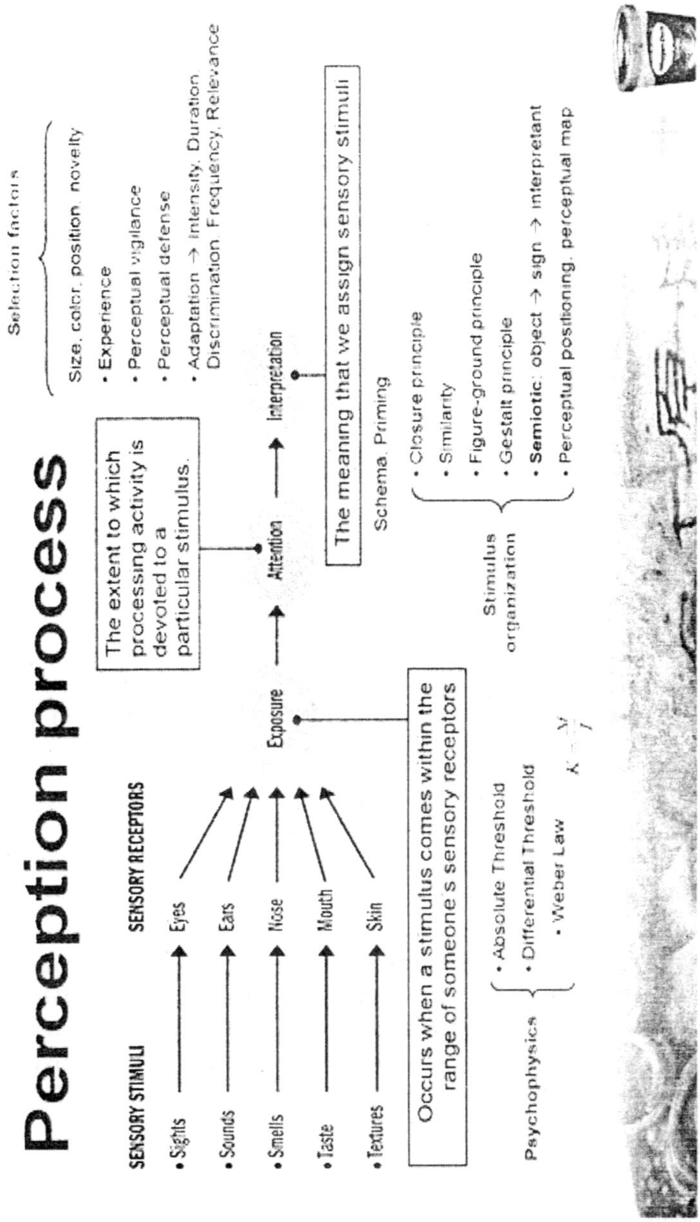

Fig. 11.1: The model of perceptionprocess

a prerequisite of perception is attention. It has been found that there is a tendency to give more attention to stimuli which are:

- Large in size
- Moving
- Intense
- Loud
- Bright
- Contrasted
- Novel
- Repeated
- Stand out from the background.

The Situation

The situation or the context in which we see objects or events is important to shape our perception. The presence of a policeman near the police station hardly draws any attention, but if one is found in your classroom will certainly be the topic of the day. The word 'terminal' can be perceived quite differently in the context of say, the ICU of a hospital, an airport or the computer lab.

Person Perception

Our perceptions of people differ from the perceptions of inanimate objects like tables, chairs, books, pencil, etc. mainly because we are prone to make inferences regarding the intentions of people and thus form judgment about them. The perceptions and judgments regarding a person's actions are often significantly influenced by the assumptions we make about the person's internal state. Attribution theory refers to the ways in which we judge people differently, depending on what meaning we attribute to a given behaviour. Whenever we observe the behaviour of an individual, we attempt to determine whether it was internally or externally caused. Internally caused behaviours are those that are believed to be under the personal control of the individual or have been done deliberately by him. Externally caused behaviour is seen as resulting from outside causes, that is the person is seen as having been compelled to behave in a particular way by the force of the situation, and not because of his own choice. When after repeated requests your friend failed to turn up at the special old school boys' meet you might ascribe his absence as a deliberate move on his part, and you will feel hurt since it appeared that he is quite unconcerned and careless about your feeling.

The determination of internally or externally caused behaviour depends chiefly on the following three factors:

- Distinctiveness which refers to whether an individual displays different behaviour at different situations. If the behaviour (say being late in the class on a particular day) is unusual, we tend to give the behaviour an external attribution; and if it usual, the reverse.
- Consensus refers to the uniformity of the behaviour shown by all the concerned people. If everyone reports late on a particular morning, it is easily assumed that there must be a severe traffic disruption in the city and thus the behaviour is externally attributed. But if the consensus is low, it is internally attributed.
- Consistency is the reverse of distinctiveness. Thus in judging the behaviour of an individual, the person looks at his past record. If the present behaviour is consistently found to occur in the past as well (that is being late at least three times a week), it is attributed as internally caused. In other words, the more consistent the behaviour, the more the observer is inclined to attribute it to external causes

Attributions

Attributions are found to strongly affect various functions in an organization, e.g. the process of employee performance evaluations, nature of supervision or guidance or the general attitude towards the organization in general. As mentioned earlier, we also tend to make various types of errors while judging others (Fig. 11.2).

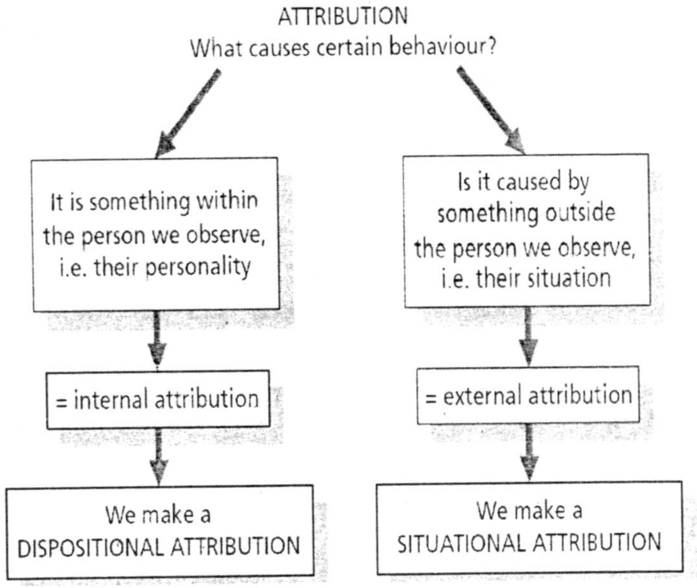

Fig. 11.2: Attributions

A few of the frequently committed mistakes are given below:

- **Selective Perception:** People have a tendency to selectively interpret what they see on the basis of their interests, background, experiences and attitudes. We hardly have either time or inclination to process all the relevant inputs and we automatically select a few. Naturally chances are there to miss some important cues in the process.
- **Halo Effect:** It refers to the tendency of forming a general impression about an individual on the basis of a single characteristic. The smartly dressed guy who is very fluent in English often tends to create a favorable impression on the interviewer even when the job is of an accountant or engineer, requiring little or no verbal fluency.
- **Contrast Effect:** It refers to the process of rating individuals in the light of other people's performance which are close in time frame. You might be rated excellent in your project presentation if your predecessor makes a mess in his presentation.

- **Stereotyping:** It is the process of judging someone on the basis of one's perception of the group to which that perception belongs to. Common examples include the debate regarding the effectiveness of a lady doctor or manager or MBA'S from prestigious B'schools.

Perceptual Difficulties

Leaders have a better view of reality because they tend to recognize that:

- Everyone is biased by their life experiences both positively and negatively.
- Everyone constructs their perceptions to meet their needs and assumptions about the world.
- Perceptions serve the purpose of explaining the world, and also defending ourselves (self-image) from other explanations.
- Perceptions often serve the function of reducing uncertainties and may become "reality", rather than possibility, in the eyes of the individual concerned. "If something is perceived as real, it is real in its consequences.
- Untested perceptions create self-fulfilling or circular perceptual processes. We continue to selectively perceive what we want to perceive to prove our hypotheses; we will ourselves off from competing information.
- Our assumption(s)/belief(s) lead to behaviour on our part that will be congruent with thes perceptions. We create a self-fulfilling prophecy.

REFERENCES

Adam-Smith, D. and Peacock, A. (1994) *Cases in Orgasational Behaviour.* London: Pitman.

Bartunek, Jean M. (1981) "Why Did You Do That? Attribution Theory in Organizations", *Business Horizons,* September-October.

Combs, Arthur W. and Donald Snygg (1949) *Individual Behaviour: A Perceptual Approach to Behaviour,* Harper and Row: NY 1949.

Cowling, A., Stanworth, M., Bennett, R., Curran, J. and Lyons, P. (1993) *Behavioural Sciences for Managers*. 2nd ed. London: Edward Arnold.

Fincham, R. and Rhodes, P. (1999) *Principles of Organizational Behaviour*. 3rd ed. Oxford: Oxford University Press.

Gallagher, K. *et al.* (1999) *People in Organisations: An Active Learning Approach*. Blackwell.

Gibson, J., Ivanchevich, J., Donnelly, J. and Konopaske, R. (2006) *Organizations: Behaviour, Structure, Processes*. 12th ed. McGraw-Hill.

Gordon, J. (1993) *A Diagnostic Approach to Organizational Behaviour*. 4th ed. Boston: Allyn and Bacon.

Greenberg, J. and Baron, R. (1993) *Behaviour in Organizations: Understanding and Managing the Human Side of Work*. 4th ed. Boston: Allyn and Bacon.

Huczynski, A. and Buchanan, D. (2007) *Organisational Behaviour: An Introductory Text*, 6th ed., Harlow: FT/Prentice-Hall.

Kelley, Harold H. (1973) "The Processes of Casual Attribution", *American Psychologist*, February.

Leavitt, Harold J., (1964) *Managerial Psychology*, University of Chicago Press: Chicago (2nd Ed.).

Leighton, Alexander H. (1949) *Human Relations in a Changing World*, New York: E. P. Dutton and Co. Inc., pp 156-161.

Levine, Michael W., and Jeremy M. Shefner (1991) *Fundamentals of Sensation and Perception*, (2nd Ed), Brooks/Cole, Pacific Grove CA.

Livingston, J. Sterling (1969) "Pygmalion in Management", *Harvard Business Review*, July/August.

London, Manuel (Ed.) (2001) *How People Evaluate Others in Orgnizations*, Mahwah NJ: Erlbaum.

Matteson, M. and Ivancevich, J. (1999) *Management and Organisational Behaviour Classics*. 7th ed. Irwin/McGraw-Hill.

Nicholson, Nigel, (2003) "How to Motivate Your Problem People", *Harvard Business Review*, January, p. 62.

Robbins, S. (1993) *Organisational Behaviour: Concepts, Controversies and Applications*. 6th ed. New Jersey: Prentice-Hall.

Robbins, S. and Judge, T. (2008) *Essentials of Organizational Behaviour.* 9th ed. New Jersey: Pearson/Prentice-Hall.

Rosenfeld, R. and Wilson, D. (1999) Managing Organisations: text, readings and cases. 2nd ed. London: McGraw-Hill.

Tronpenaars, F. and Hampden-Turner, C. (2001) *Twenty-one Leaders for the 21st Century: How Innovative Leaders Manage in the Digital Age.* Capstone.

Tyson, S. and Jackson, T. (1992) *The Essence of Organizational Behaviour.* New York: Prentice-Hall.

Zaleznik, Abraham, and Manfred F. R. Kets de Vries, (1985) *Power and the Corporate Mind,* Bonus Books, Chicago (2nd Ed.).

12 Learning

Knowing is not enough; we must apply. Willing is not enough; we must do.

– Johann von Goethe

Learning

Learning is the process by which we receive and process sensory data, encode such data as memories within the neural structures of our brain, and retrieve those memories for subsequent use. The variety of information stored within such memories is enormous. All learning takes place within the brain, and as our understanding of the underlying structures and processes of the brain increases we can begin to apply that knowledge to improve our construction of learning environments. Learning environments should not be construed simply as the traditional formal classroom within the context of institutionalized public education. Such environments occur within the workplace, the home, and other social institutions as communication and information technology continues to penetrate Western society. We should also be aware that the use of multimedia will have an impact upon the development of the human brain, particularly when such techniques are used with children and adolescents whose brains are still developing and maturing.

Learning and Neuron System

Our ability to describe and understand the basic processes by which our brain learns has been enhanced by recent technological developments and by the accumulation of long-term studies in human and animal populations. Of particular benefit has been the development of brain-imaging techniques that allow us to observe the operation of normal human brains during the performance of a variety of tasks. Magnetic Resonance Imaging (MRI) and similar technologies have allowed researchers to map neural activity during sensory data processing and monitor the transfer of information into long-term memory. Researchers have also made great strides in determining the basic mechanisms that underlie the transmission of information within the brain. Such research on brain structure, neural transmitters, and the process by which memories are stored and retrieved have allowed the development of neuro-physiological models of learning.

Neuroscience

Neuroscience is the study of the human nervous system, the brain, and the biological basis of consciousness, perception, memory, and learning. The nervous system and the brain are the physical foundation of the human learning process. Neuroscience links our observations about cognitive behaviour with the actual physical processes that support such behaviour.

Structure of Neurons

While there are as many as 10,000 specific types of neurons in the human CNS, generally speaking, neurons come in three flavors: motor neurons (for conveying motor information), sensory neurons (for conveying sensory information), and interneurons (which convey information between different types of neurons). The following image identifies how neurons come in various shapes and sizes. (It is based on drawings made by Cajal.)

Don't worry. You are not responsible for being able to recognize any of these neurons or to know what, say, the reticular formation is or does. After all, this is your *introduction* to neurons. And by way of introduction, you should know that a "typical" neuron has four physically distinct parts (or more accurately, morphologically defined regions). The first part is the cell body (or soma). This is not only the metabolic "control center" of the neuron, it is also its "manufacturing and recycling plant." (For instance, it is within the cell body that neuronal proteins are

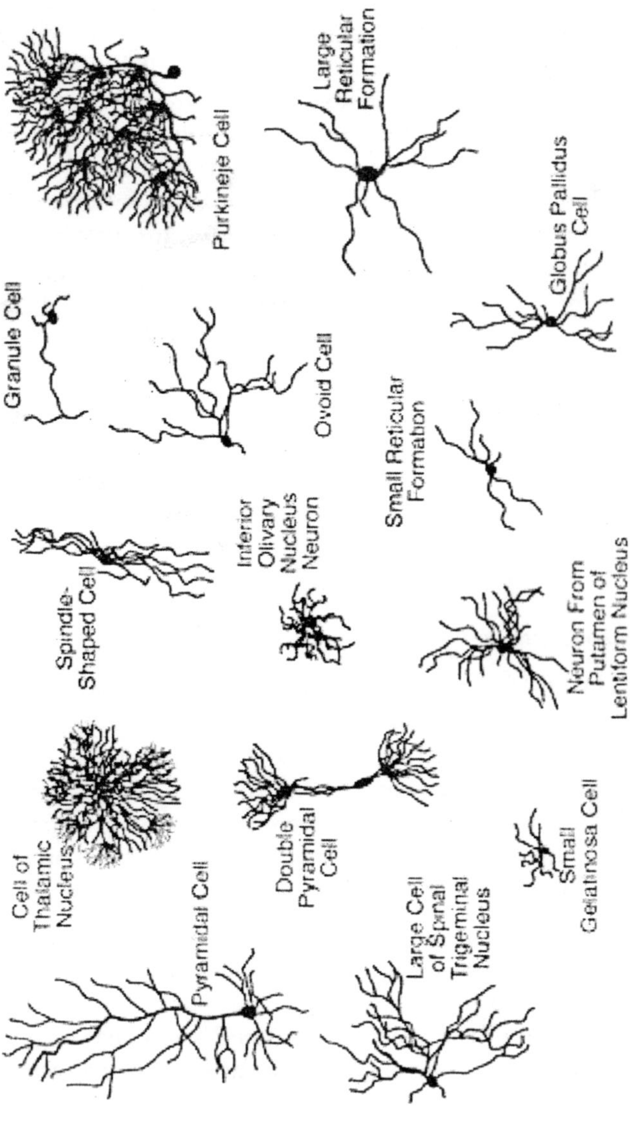

Fig. 12.1: Structure of Neurons

synthesized.) The second and third parts are *processes* – structures that extend away from the cell body. Generally speaking, the function of processes is to be conduits through which information flows to the cell body and away from the cell body. Incoming information from other neurons is (typically) received through its dendrites. The outgoing information to other neurons flows along its axon. A neuron may have many thousands of dendrites, but it will have only one axon. The fourth distinct part of a neuron lies at the end of the axon, the axon terminals. These are the structures that contain neurotransmitters. Because we shall explore what neurotransmitters are shortly, for now you need to know only that neurotransmitters are the chemical medium through which "information" flows from one neuron to the next. You also need to know that information flows from one neuron to another only at a synapse. Before we turn our attention to how information is processed within a neuron, the following image summarizes the story so far.

Neurons Process

Once again, the function of a neuron is to receive Input "information," to process that information, then to send "information" as Output. This is true regardless of whether the neuron a sensory neuron, a motor neuron, or an interneuron. But since the Input information to a sensory neuron will be a physical stimulus (such as light on the retina, pressure on the skin, etc.), it is not the case that that the only way a neuron can receive Input information is through synapses with other neurons. And since the Output of motor neuron will be a signal sent to a muscle, neither is it the case that every neuron sends its Output information to other neurons. Nevertheless, since the aim of this section is to introduce you to how a "typical" neuron does what it does, for now, let's ignore questions about how the transduction of a physical stimulus occurs. Let's also ignore questions about how the Output of a neuron can affect a muscle. Hence, let's consider only how a typical interneuron processes information.

For any interneuron, its function is to receive Input "information" *from other neurons through synapses*, to process that information, then to send "information" as Output *to other neurons through synapses at its axon terminals.* Consequently, an interneuron cannot fulfil its function if it is not connected to other neurons in a network. A network of neurons (or neural network) is merely a group of neurons through which information flows from one neuron to another. The image below represents a neural network. To explore what neurons do, we are going to focus on the blue neuron (**B**). And the first thing you need to understand is that information flows from left to right. So, **B** will receive its Input from **A** through a synapse at its dendrite. After processing this information, **B** will send its Output information through its axon terminal at the synapse with pink neuron (**C**).

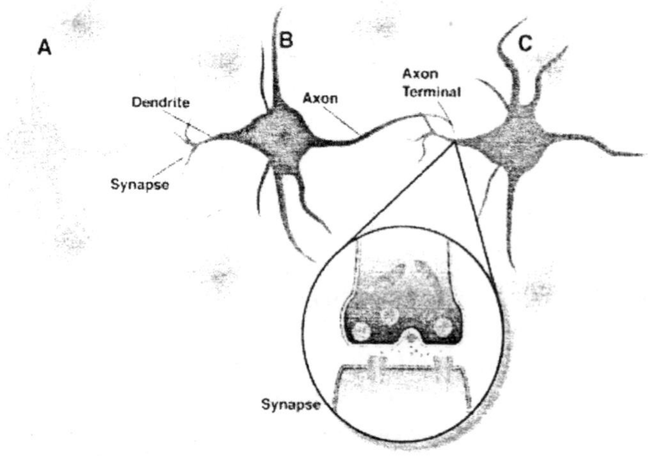

Fig. 12.2: Neurons Process

Although it is reasonable to think of dendrites and axons as conduits through which information flows *within* a neuron, a neuron's dendrites and axon are part of its structure. Synapses are not. Synapses are where information "flows" from one neuron to another. And since the function of a neuron is to receive Input information, to process it, then to send Output information, it would be impossible for a neuron to do what it does without synapses. And before we explore exactly what it is that neurons do, you should know that a neuron never receives Input information from just one synapse. Remember, a typical neuron receives Input from thousands of synapses. And Input synapses can occur anywhere, not just at dendrites.

Learning and Brain

The three-pound universe that is our brain consists of more than 100 billion neurons and the associated structures that organize, nourish, and protect their functioning. Each neuron may have between 5,000 and 50,000 connections to other neurons, forming a dense connective mat that allows the storage of enormous amounts of information. It is important to remember that structures within the brain continue to develop until late adolescence and that neurons will continue to grow connections to other neurons throughout adult life.

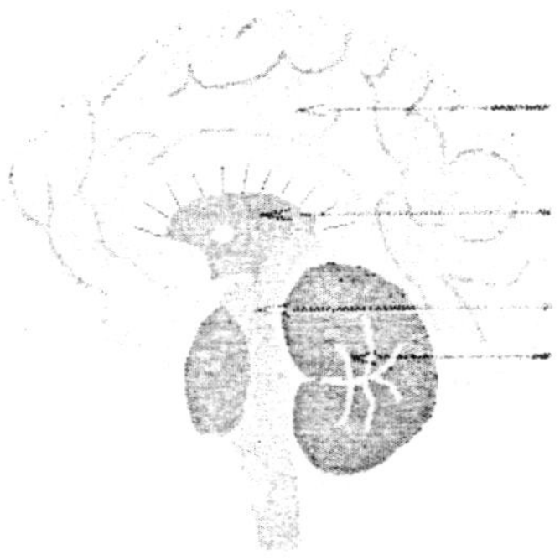

Fig. 12.3:

Brain Structures

The diagram above shows four basic structures in the brain those are important for bodily functions and for learning and memory. The *brain stem* is primarily concerned with basic survival functions and the regulation of body systems. The *cerebellum* is involved in the performance of automatic movement patterns (walking, running, touch-typing, and other physical skills that can become part of automatic procedural memory). The *limbic system* is responsible for the processing of short-term memory into long-term memory as well as the generation and regulation of emotions. The *cerebral cortex* is the area of the brain in which sensory data is received and analyzed, decisions are made, and behavioral responses are activated. Information is received from the major sensory organs of the body: eyes, ears, nose, tongue, and skin; and is held briefly in sensory memory. The further processing of that information appears to be dependent upon the state of emotional arousal of the brain and the utility of such information for potential survival. Long-term memories are generated through the growth and spread of neural connections between those modular structures that contain the memory. The more often such structures are activated and the stronger the connections become to associated structures, the more easily such memories are retrieved and used by the brain in decision-making and conscious thought.

Our brain actually contains three brains: the lower or reptilian brain that controls basic sensory motor functions; the mammalian or limbic brain that controls emotions, memory, and biorhythms; and the neocortex or thinking brain that controls cognition, reasoning, language, and higher intelligence. Mental concentration and effort alters the physical structure of the brain. Our nerve cells (neurons) are connected by branches called dendrites. There are about 10 billion neurons in the brain and about 1,000 trillion connections. The possible combination of connections is about ten to the one-millionth power. As we use the brain, we strengthen certain patterns of connection, making each connection easier to create next time. This is how memory develops.

Nature of Learning

Learning occupies a very important place in our life. Most of what we do or do not do is influenced by what we learn and how we have learned it. Learning therefore provides a key or structure to one's personality and behaviour. An individual starts learning immediately after his birth or in a strict sense even earlier when in the womb of the mother. Experiences –direct or indirect is found to play a dominant role in molding and shaping the behaviour of the individual from the very beginning. In this way the term learning broadly speaking, stands for all those changes and modifications in the behaviour of the individual which he undergoes from his birth till death.

The term learning covers every modification in behaviour to meet environmental requirements'. The term also described as 'the acquisition of new behaviour of the strengthening or weakening of old behaviour as the result of experience'. A generally accepted definition of learning is, therefore, any relatively permanent change in behaviour that occurs as a result of experience'.

Types of Learning

Learning, defined as a process of bringing relatively permanent changes in behaviour of an organism, may be classified in a number of categories depending upon the domain or specific area of the behaviour in which changes are introduced or in terms of the methods or techniques that are employed of the introduction of behavioral changes. The types of learning are follows:

Verbal learning

Learning of this type helps in the acquisition of verbal behaviour. The languages we speak, the communication devices we use, are the result of such learning.

Motor learning

The learning of all types of motor skills may be included in such type of learning. Learning how to swim, riding a horse, driving a car, flying a plane, playing the piano, hitting a moving targets drawing a geometrical design etc.

Concept Learning

A concept in the form of a mental image denotes a generalized idea about the things, person or events.

Problem Solving

in the ladder of learning and acquisition of behaviour, problem-solving denotes a higher type of learning. Such type of learning requires the use of the cognitive abilities like reasoning, thinking, power of observation, discrimination generalization imagination, ability to infer and drew conclusions, trying out novel ways and experimenting etc.

Theories of Learning

Learning Theory is a discipline of psychology that attempts to explain how an organism learns. It consists of many different theories of learning, including instincts, social facilitation, observation, formal teaching, memory, mimicry, and classical and operant conditioning. It is these last two that are of most interest to animal trainers.

Ivan Pavlov's (1849-1936): Classical Conditioning Theory

Ivan Pavlov was born in a small village in central Russia. His family hoped that he would become a priest, and he went to a theological seminary. After reading Charles Darwin, he found that he cared more for scientific pursuits and left the seminary for the University of St. Petersburg. There he studied chemistry and physiology, and he received his doctorate in 1879. He continued his studies and began doing his own research in topics that interested him most: digestion and blood circulation. His work became well known, and he was appointed professor of physiology at the Imperial Medical Academy.

Pavlov was much more interested in physiology than psychology. He looked upon the young science of psychiatry a little dubiously. But he did think that conditioned reflexes could explain the behaviour of psychotic people. His ideas played a large role in the behaviorist theory of psychology, introduced by John Watson around 1913. Pavlov was held in extremely high regard in his country both as Russia and the Soviet Union and around the world. In 1904, he won the Nobel Prize in physiology/medicine for his research on digestion. He was outspoken and often at odds with the Soviet government later in his life, but his world renown, and work that his nation was proud of, kept him free from persecution. He worked actively in the lab until his death at age 87.

Theory

Classical Conditioning is the type of learning made famous by Pavlov's experiments with dogs. The gist of the experiment is this: Pavlov presented dogs with food, and measured their salivary response (how much they drooled). Then he began ringing a bell just before presenting the food. At first, the dogs did not begin salivating until the food was presented. After a while, however, the dogs began to salivate when the sound of the bell was presented. They learned to associate the sound of the bell with the presentation of the food. As far as their immediate physiological responses were concerned, the sound of the bell became equivalent to the presentation of the food (Fig. 12.4).

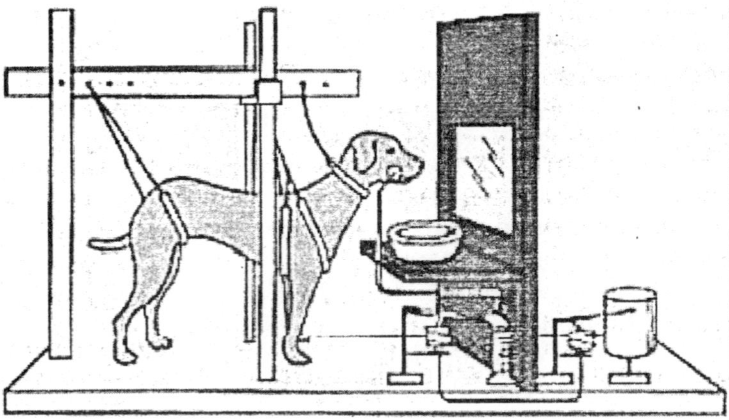

Fig. 12.4

Classical conditioning is used by trainers for two purposes: To condition (train) autonomic responses, such as the drooling, producing adrenaline, or reducing adrenaline (calming) without using the stimuli that would naturally create such a response; and, to create an association between a stimulus that normally would not have any effect on the animal and a stimulus that would.

Stimuli that animals react to without training are called *primary* or *unconditioned stimuli* (US). They include food, pain, have to learn to react to an electric shock, for example. Pavlov's dogs did not need to learn about food.

Stimuli that animals react to only after learning about them are called *secondary* or *conditioned stimuli* (CS). These are stimuli that have been associated with a primary stimulus. In Pavlov's experiment, the sound of the bell meant nothing to the dogs at first. After its sound was associated with the presentation of food, it became a conditioned stimulus. If a warning buzzer is associated with the shock, the animals will learn to fear it.

Secondary stimuli are things that the trainee has to learn to like or dislike. Examples include school grades and money. A slip of paper with an "A" or an "F" written on it has no meaning to a person who has never learned the meaning of the grade. Yet students work hard to gain "A's" and avoid "F's". A coin or piece of paper money has no meaning to a person who doesn't use that sort of system. Yet people have been known to work hard to gain this secondary reinforcer.

The theory of Classical conditioning can be used to describe many events in peoples' lives. For example, the amount a person likes another person may be associated with how much the other person has come to represent positive stimuli or gratification. People may develop certain fears due to negative stimuli that occurred at the same time as another event. Freud's interpretation of little Hans, who developed fear of horses after seeing one horse fall and bleed, is an example of phobia development by classical conditioning. Another example is in Watson's experiment where a boy was exposed simultaneously to rats and a loud noise. The boy subsequently developed a strong aversion to rats, and eventually, all fuzzy things. Many of the reasons people avoid certain situations may stem from classical conditioning.

Operant Conditioning

Theory

Classical conditioning forms an association between two stimuli. *Operant* conditioning forms an association between a behaviour and a consequence. (It is also called *response-stimulus* or RS conditioning because it forms an association between the animal's response [behaviour] and the stimulus that follows [consequence]).

Four Possible Consequences

There are four possible consequences to any behaviour. They are:

- Something Good can start or be presented;
- Something Good can end or be taken away;
- Something Bad can start or be presented;
- Something Bad can end or be taken away.

Consequences have to be immediate, or clearly linked to the behaviour. With verbal humans, we can explain the connection between the consequence and the behaviour, even if they are separated in time. For example, you might tell a friend that you'll buy dinner for them since they helped you move, or a parent might explain that the child can't go to summer camp because of her bad grades. With very young children, humans who don't have verbal skills, and animals, you can't explain the connection between the consequence and the behaviour. For the animal, the consequence has to be immediate. The way to work around this is to use a bridge (see above).

The technical terms for tart or be presented is *positive,* since it's something that's *added* to the animal's environment. The technical terms for end or be taken away is *negative,* since it's something that's *subtracted* from the animal's environment.

Anything that *increases* a behaviour - makes it occur more frequently, makes it stronger, or makes it more likely to occur— is termed a *reinforcer.* Often, an animal (or person) will perceive "starting Something Good" or "ending Something Bad" as something worth pursuing and they will repeat the behaviours that seem to cause these consequences. These consequences will increase the behaviours that lead to them they are *reinforcers.* These are consequences the animal will work to attain, so they strengthen the behaviour.

Anything that *decreases* a behaviour - makes it occur less frequently, makes it weaker, or makes it less likely to occur - is termed a *punisher*. Often, an animal (or person) will perceive "ending something Good" or "starting Something Bad" as something worth avoiding, and they will not repeat the behaviours that seem to cause these consequences. These consequences will decrease the behaviours that lead to them they are *punishers*.

Applying these terms to the Four Possible Consequences, you get:

- Something good can start or be presented, so behaviour increases = positive reinforcement (R+)
- Something good can end or be taken away, so behavoir decreases = negative punishment (P-)
- Something bad can start or be presented, so behaviour decreases = positive punishment (P+)
- Something bad can end or be taken away, so behaviour increases = negative reinforcement (R-)

or:

	Reinforcement (behaviour increases)	*Punishment (behaviour decreases)*
Positive (something added)	Positive Reinforcement: Something added increases behaviour	Positive Punishment Something added decreases behaviour
Negative (something removed)	Negative Reinforcement Something removed increases behaviour	Negative Punishment Something removed decreases behaviour

Remember that these definitions are based on their actual effect on the behaviour in question: they must reduce or strengthen the behaviour to be considered a consequence and be defined as a punishment or reinforcement. Pleasures meant as rewards but that do not strengthen a behaviour are indulgences, not reinforcement; aversives meant as a behaviour weakener but which do not weaken a behaviour are abuse, not punishment.

Observational Learning or Social Learning

Observational learning, also called social learning theory, occurs when an observer's behaviour changes after viewing the behaviour of a model. An observer's behaviour can be affected by the positive or negative consequences called vicarious reinforcement or vicarious punishment of a model's behaviour. Learning by observation involves four separate processes: attention, retention, production and motivation.

Attention

Observers cannot learn unless they pay attention to what's happening around them. This process is influenced by characteristics of the model, such as how much one likes or identifies with the model, and by characteristics of the observer, such as the observer's expectations or level of emotional arousal.

Retention

Observers must not only recognize the observed behaviour but also remember it at some later time. This process depends on the observer's ability to code or structure the information in an easily remembered form or to mentally or physically rehearse the model's actions.

Production

Observers must be physically and/intellectually capable of producing the act. In many cases the observer possesses the necessary responses. But sometimes, reproducing the model's actions may involve skills the observer has not yet acquired. It is one thing to carefully watch a circus juggler, but it is quite another to go home and repeat those acts.

REFERENCES

Adam-Smith, D. and Peacock, A. (1994) *Cases in Orgasational Behaviour.* London: Pitman.

Barker, L. M. (1994). *Learning and Behaviour: A Psychobiological Perspective.* Macmillan, New York.

Cohen, A. *et al.* (1995) *Effective Behaviour in Organisations: Cases, Concepts, and student Experiences.* 6th ed. Irwin/McGraw-Hill

Cowling, A., Stanworth, M., Bennett, R., Curran, J. and Lyons, P. (1993) Behavioural Sciences for Managers. 2nd ed. London: Edward Arnold

Edelman, Gerald (1992) *Bright Air, Brilliant Fire: On the Matter of the Mind.* Basic Books.

Fincham, R. and Rhodes, P. (1996) *The individual, work and organization: behavioral studies for business and management.* 2nd ed. Oxford: Oxford University Press

Hilgard, Ernest R., Richard C. Atkinson and, Rita L. Atkinson (1975) *Introduction to Psychology,* Oxford and IBM Publishing Co. Pvt. Ltd.

Hull, C. L. (1943). Principles of Behaviour. Appleton-Century, New York.

Kakabadse, A. (1991) *The Wealth Creations: Top Peoples, Top Teams and Executive Best Practice.* Kogan Page.

Kandel, E. R., Schwartz, J. H., and Jessell, T. M. (Eds.). (1991). *Principles of Neural Science* (Third edition). Elsevier, New York.

Klein, S. B. (1991). Learning: *Principles and Applications* (second edition). McGraw-Hill, New York.

Luthans, F. (1992) *Organisational Behaviour.* 6th ed. McGraw Hill

Morris, C.G., and Maisto, A.A. (1999). *Understanding Psychology.* 4th ed. New Jersey: Prentice Hall, Inc

Mowrer, O. H. (1960). *Learning Theory and Behaviour.* Wiley, New York.

Robbins, S. (1993) Organisational Behaviour: Concepts, Controversies and Applications. 6th ed. New Jersey: Prentice Hall

Robert Sylwester, (1993) "What the Biology of the Brain Tells Us About Learning," *Education Leadership,* December.

Schwartz,M.D. (1973) *Physiological Psychology,* Englewood Cliffs, N.J. Prentice-Hall.

Sutton, R. S., and Barto, A. G. (1990). Time-derivative models of Pavlovian reinforcement. In Moore, J. W., and Gabriel, M. (Eds.), Learning and Computational Neuroscience. MIT Press.

Thompson, R.F. (1967) *Foundations of Physiological Psychology,* N.Y. Harper and Row.

Tyson, S. and Jackson, T. (1992) *The Essence of Organizational Behaviour.* New York: Prentice Hall.

Vecchio, R. (1995) *Organisational Behaviour.* 3rd ed. The Dryden Press

Weiss, J. (1996) *Organisational Behaviour and Change: Managing Diversity, Cross-cultural Dynamics, and Ethics.* New York: West Publishing

13 Attitude

A smile is a curve that sets everything straight.

– Phyllis Diller

Meaning of Attitude

The attitude is the evaluative statements or judgments concerning objects, people, or events. More precisely attitudes can be defined as a persistent tendency to feel and behave in a particular way toward some object which may include events or individuals as well.

Attitude can be characterized in three ways:

- First, they tend to persist unless something is done to change them.
- Second, attitudes can fall anywhere along a continuum from very favorable to very unfavorable.
- Third, attitudes are directed toward some object about which a person has feelings (sometimes called "affect") and beliefs.

Components of Attitude

Attitude positions are the summary aggregation of four components:

- Affective responses,
- cognitions,
- behaviours, and

- behavioural intentions.

Affective Component of Attitude

The affective component of attitude is said to consist of a person's evaluation of, liking of, or emotional response to some situation, object, or person. Affective responses reflect one's attitude with sensations of pleasure, sadness, or other levels of physical arousal. For example, for the attitude construct of computer anxiety, a topic of current interest, the affective component would be a person's liking of the computer and his feeling of excitement, or dread, when she or he used one.

Cognitive Component

The *cognitive* component of an attitude is conceptualized as a person's factual knowledge of the situation, object, or person, including oneself. In other words, the cognitive component refers to how much a person knows about a topic, such as computers. The cognitive component of computer anxiety would be based on how much a person knows about computers and her level of understanding of computer operation.

Behavioural Component

The behavioural component of an attitude involves the person's overt behavior directed toward a situation, object, or person. For example, the behavioural component of computer anxiety would be related to how often a person had used a computer, and what kind of experience he had. Persons, who routinely use computers, especially if they choose to use them freely, would be more likely to have positive attitudes toward computers, and be less anxious, than would others who have fewer experiences with computers.

Behavioural Intention

Finally, the behavioural intention component involves the person's plans to perform in a certain way, even if sometimes these plans are never acted upon. An example, once again, is the construct of computer anxiety. Computer anxiety is defined by Maurer and Simonson as "the fear or apprehension felt by an individual when considering the implications of utilizing computer technology, or when actually using computer technology." The behavioural intention component of this attitude construct would be the "apprehension felt by an individual when considering the implications of utilizing computer technology." In other words, if people knew that they were going to have to use computers in an upcoming class, this would partially shape their level of computer anxiety. If the class were to be a difficult one, say in statistics, then computer anxiety would be likely to be increased.

These four components of attitude form an attitude system. The components are not isolated but are interrelated and produce an organizing framework or mental representation of the attitude construct. Cognitive schemata provide structure to interrelated attitudes and guide the information processes of attending, interpreting, and reconstructing. Behavioural research supports the idea that actions lead to the formation of cognitive schemata, which lead to the creation of attitudes. It would seem that the opposite is also true. Attitudes help form cognitive relationships, which in turn predispose behaviours.

Attitude Formation

Situational stimuli or events in the environment directly influence behaviour and the formation of attitudes. Strict behaviorists would argue that internal events that form attitudes are the result of observable actions. A change in attitude or beliefs occurs as a result of actions that have been influenced by reinforcers. Social-learning theory expands this principle. According to social-learning theorists, it is not essential to learn behaviours directly through action and reinforcement, as traditional behavioural psychologists would propose. Indirect learning through observing a model and receiving verbal instruction has a powerful impact on behaviour and attitude formation.

Situations that include a change in the behavioural component of attitude lead to changes in attitudes. But there is also a reciprocal action. Since the components of attitude systems are interrelated, a change in liking (affect) may result in a change in behaviour. For example, the currently popular concept of the cognitive apprenticeship is based on the idea of learners

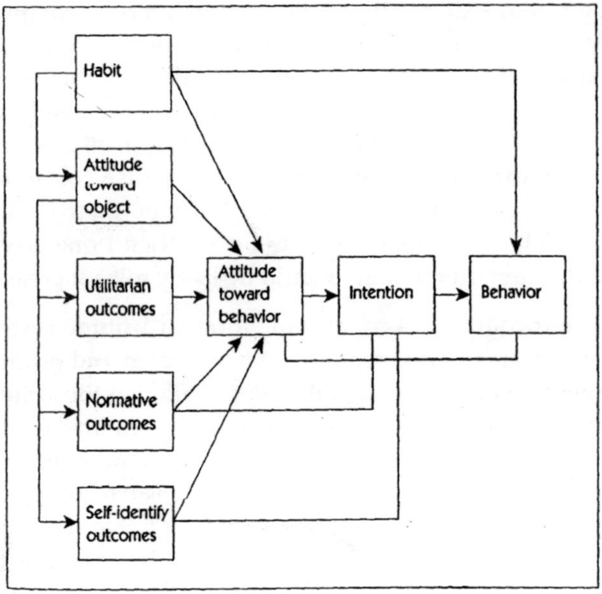

Fig. 13.1

participating as apprentices in real-world activities with those who are more knowledgeable than they. If designed correctly, these situations are perceived by learners as important and realistic, and learners come to value them. The overt activities of cognitive apprenticeships produce in students favorable dispositions (i.e., affects), which in turn promote a sense of value and often a desire to learn more.

Importance of Attitudes

Traditionally when instruction is designed, there are two categories of outcomes in mind: those directed toward cognitive goals, and those related to the attitudes of the learner. There is little necessity to argue the importance of the acquisition of knowledge by a student as a result of instruction. Achievement is the paramount objective of most instructional activities; however, it may also be important to recognize the need for establishing attitudinal goals and for planning activities designed to facilitate affective outcomes in learners as a consequence of an instructional situation. As a matter of fact, it has become increasingly apparent to those involved in educational technology research that one of the major, and possibly unique, consequences of instructional situations involving media is the likelihood of the development of positive attitudinal positions in students.

In summary, attitudes, as shall be discussed later, are complex phenomena. They have been studied for decades by social scientists and educators and are beginning to be understood as organizers related to learning processes and outcomes. Attitudes are learned "predispositions to respond" held by individuals that make them likely to act in certain ways. Attitudes are not observable, but they do serve to help produce observable actions in people.

Functions of Attitude

According to Katz, attitudes serve four important functions from the viewpoint of organizational behaviour. These are as follows.

The Adjustment Function

Attitudes often help people to adjust to their work environment. Well-treated employees tend to develop a positive attitude towards their job, management and the organization in general while berated and ill-treated organizational members develop a negative attitude. In other words, attitudes help employees adjust to their environment and form a basis for future behaviour.

Ego-Defensive Function

Attitudes help people to retain their dignity and self-image. When a young faculty member who is full of fresh ideas and enthusiasm, joins the organization, the older members might feel somewhat threatened by him. But they tend to disapprove his creative ideas as 'crazy' and 'impractical' and dismiss him altogether.

The Value-Expressive Function

Attitudes provide individuals with a basis for expressing their values. For example, a manager who values hard and sincere work will be more vocal against an employee who is having a very casual approach towards work.

The Knowledge Function

Attitudes provide standards and frames of reference that allow people to understand and perceive the world around him. If one has a strong negative attitude towards the management, whatever the management does, even employee welfare programmes can be perceived as something 'bad' and as actually against them.

Changing Attitudes

Employees' attitudes can be changed and sometimes it is in the best interests of managements to try to do so. For example, if employees believe that their employer does not look after their welfare, the management should try to change their attitude and help develop a more positive attitude in them. However, the process of changing the attitude is not always easy. There are some barriers which have to be overcome if one strives to change somebody's attitude. There are two major categories of barriers that come in the way of changing attitudes:

- Prior commitment when people feel a commitment towards a particular course of action that have already been agreed upon and thus it becomes difficult for them to change or accept the new ways of functioning.
- Insufficient information also acts as a major barrier to change attitudes. Sometimes people simply see any reason to change their attitude due to unavailability of adequate information.

Some of the possible ways of changing attitudes are described below:

Providing New Information

Sometimes a dramatic change in attitude is possible only by providing relevant and adequate information to the person concerned. Scanty and incomplete information can be a major reason for brewing negative feeling and attitudes.

Use of Fear

Attitudes can be changed through the use of fear. People might resort to change their work habit for the fear of fear of unpleasant consequences. However, the degree of the arousal of fear will have to be taken into consideration as well.

Resolving Discrepancies

Whenever people face a dilemma or conflicting situation they feel confused in choosing a particular course of action. Like in the case where one is to choose from between two alternative courses of action, it is often become difficult for him to decide which is right for him. Even when he chooses one over the other, he might still feel confused. If some one helps him in pointing out the positive points in favour of the chosen course of action, he person might resolve the his dilemma.

Influence of Friends and Peers

A very effective way of changing one's attitude is through his friends and colleagues. Their opinion and recommendation for something often proves to be more important. If for example, they are all praise for a particular policy introduced in the work place, chances are high that an individual will slowly accept that even when he had initial reservations for that.

Co-opting

If you want to change the attitude of some body who belongs to a different group, it is often becomes very effective if you can include him in your own group. Like in the case of the union leader who are all the time vehemently against any management decision, can be the person who takes active initiative in implementing a new policy when he had participated in that decision making process himself.

REFERENCES

Ajzen, I., and Fishbein, M. (1980). *Understanding Attitudes and Predicting Social Behavior*. Englewood Cliffs, NJ: Prentice-Hall.

Arvey, R.D., Bouchard, T.J., Jr., Segal, N.L. and Abraham, L.M. (1989). "Job satisfaction: Environmental and genetic components." *Journal of Applied Psychology*, 74: 187-192.

Atkinson, J.W. and Birch, D. (1970). *The Dynamics of Action*. New York: Wiley.

Barnard, C. (1938). *The Functions of the Executive*. Cambridge, MA: Harvard University Press.

Becker, T.E. (1992). Foci and bases of commitment: Are they distinctions worth making? *Academy of Management Journal*, 35: 232-244.

Bowers, K. S. (1973). Situationism in psychology: An analysis and a critique. *Psychological Review*, 80: 307-336.

Brief, A.P. and Aldag, R.J. (1981). The self in organizations: A conceptual review. *Academy of Management Review*, 6: 75-88.

Cantor, N. and Kihlstrom, J.F. (1985). Social intelligence: The cognitive basis of personality. *Review of Personality and Social Psychology*, 6: 15-33.

DeCharms, R. (1968). *Personal causation: The internal affective determinants of behaviour*. New York: Academic Press.

Eagly, A. and Chaiken, S. (1993). *The psychology of attitudes*. Fort Worth, TX: Harcourt, Brace.

Etzioni, A. (1975). *Comparative Analysis of Complex Organizations*. New York: Macmillan Publishing Co.

Etzioni, A. (1988). *The Moral Dimension: Toward a New Economics*. New York: Free Press.

Festinger, L. (1957) *A Theory of Cognitive Dissonance*. Stanford, CA: Stanford University Press.

Foote, N.N. (1951). Identification as the Basis for a Theory of Motivation. *American Sociological Review*, 16: 14-21.

Gecas, V. (1982). The self-concept. *Annual Review of Sociology*, 8: 1-33.

Gerhardt, B. (1987). How important are dispositional factors as determinants of job satisfaction – Implications for job design and other personnel programs. *Journal of Applied Psychology*, 72: 366-373.

Gottfredson, L.S. (1981). Circumscription and compromise: A developmental theory of occupational aspirations. *Journal of Counseling Psychology*, 28: 545-579.

Graesser, A.C., Woll, S.B., Kowalski, D.J. and Smith, D.A. (1980). Memory for typical and atypical actions in scripted activities. *Journal of Experimental Psychology*, 6, 503-515.

Greenwald, A.G. and Pratkanis, A.R. (1984) The self. In R.S. Wyer and T.S. Srull (Eds), *Handbook of Social Cognition*. Hillsdale, NH: Earlbaum.

Katz, D. (1960). The functional approach to the study of attitudes. Public *Opinion Quarterly*, 24: 163-204.

Smith, M.J. (1982). *Persuasion and Human Action*. Belmont, CA: Wadsworth.

Zimbardo, P. and Leippe, M. (1991). *The Psychology of Attitude Change and Social Influence*. Philadelphia, PA: Temple University Press.

14 Personality

Don't think you are, know you are.

Personality is the whole person, his/her external appearance and behavior, his/her inner awareness of self, and his/her unique pattern of measurable traits that are fairly permanent. Therefore, characteristics of personality includes physique, intellect, skills, interests and values, attitudes and expressive styles that determine how others person to that personality. Personality is the sum total of an individual's psychophysical systems that determine behavior in a given environment/situation. Personality differs from person to person depending on their varying psychophysical aspects.

Concept of Personality

The term 'personality' stems from the Latin work *'persona'*, which was the name given to the masks actors wore and the characters they portrayed. It means 'to speak through'. The meaning of the word personality in practice has changed little since classical time. It is still quite common to hear the comments such as "I do not know what he sees in her, she has a very poor personality", or look at that young man, what a fine personality the has".

Watson (1930) the father of behaviorism, taking clues from his behavioral studies, tried to conclude "personality is the sum of activities that can be discovered by actual observations over a long enough period of time to give reliable information." In this way he tried tomake the word personality synonymous to the consistent behaviour paterns of an individual.

Morton Prince (1929) tried to give personality a broad base by accepting the role of both environmental and hereditary factors in constituting what is named as personality. He remarked " personality is the sum total of all the biological innate dispositions, impulses, tendencies, appetites and instincts of the individual and the dispositions and tendencies acquired by experience" Allport (1961) after evaluating 49 definitions, the arrived at the conclusion that "personality is a dynamic organization within the individual of those psychophysical systems that determine his unique adjustment to his environment".

Eysenck (1971) defined personality as "the more or less stable and enduring organization of a person's character temperament, intellect and physique which determine his unique adjustment to the environment". The definition given by him has four strong points in its favour.

- It tries to provide personality a physiological base and gives a balanced consideration to the role of heredity and environment in building one's personality.
- It gives a complete picture of the human behavior by involving all of its aspects - conative, cognitive and affective.
- It stresses the need for integrating and organization of the behavioral characteristics.
- It aims at making personality somewhat measurable and assessable and thus givens it a scientific base.

Personality Determinants

In the early stage of the development of psychology, there were many studies conducted to establish whether personality was result of heredity or of environment. Is the personality predetermined at birth itself? Or is it the result of individual's interaction with one's environment? The various determinants of personality are broadly classified into three groups:

a) Heredity,

b) Environment, and

c) Situation.

Heredity

It is the transmission of the qualities from the parents to the children through a biological mechanism lying in the chromosomes of the germs cells. These are characteristics determined by genetics such as physical stature, attractiveness, sex temperament, muscle composition, reflexes, energy level and so on are all influenced by parents/ancestors.

Environment

It is the early stage of person's conditions including family norms, friends, and social groups influence the formation of one's personality. The birth order has also been shown to influence the personality, because the environment the first born child is exposed to , is different from that experienced by other children. The parents have more effect on the personality development of their children as compared to other members of the family.

Situation

Besides the heredity and environment, situation also determines the personality. In practice, an individual's personality does change depending on the situation. This is because the different demands of the different situations call forth different aspects of one's personality. Therefore, looking at personality patterns, the situation where a personality trait is exhibited should also be taken into consideration.

Theories of Personality

Theory

It might be nice to start off with a definition of theories of personality. First, theory: A theory is a model of reality that helps us to understand, explain, predict, and control that reality. In the study of personality, these models are usually verbal. Every now and then, someone comes up with a graphic model, with symbolic illustrations, or a mathematical model, or even a computer model. But words are the basic form.

Different approaches focus on different aspects of theory. Humanists and Existentialists tend to focus on the understanding part. They believe that much of what we are is way too complex and embedded in history and culture to "predict and control." Besides, they suggest, predicting and controlling people is, to a considerable extent, unethical. Behaviorists and Freudians, on the other hand, prefer to discuss prediction and control. If an idea is useful, if it works, go with it! Understanding, to them, is secondary.

Another definition says that a theory is a guide to action: We figure that the future will be something like the past. We figure that certain sequences and patterns of events that have occurred frequently before are likely to occur again. So we look to the first events of a sequence, or the most vivid parts of a pattern, to serve as our landmarks and warning signals. A theory is a little like a map: It isn't the same as the countryside it describes; it certainly doesn't give you every detail; it may not even be terribly accurate. But it does provide a guide to action - and gives us something to correct when it fails.

Personality

Usually when we talk about someone's personality, we are talking about what makes that person different from other people, perhaps even unique. This aspect of personality is called *individual differences*. For some theories, it is the central issue. These theories often spend considerable attention on things like types and traits and tests with which we can categorize or compare people: Some people are neurotic, others are not; some people are more introverted, others more extroverted; and so on. However, personality theorists are just as interested in the *commonalities* among people. What, for example, do the neurotic person and the healthy person have in common? Or what is the common structure in people that expresses itself as introversion in some and extroversion in others? If you place people on some dimension - such as healthy-neurotic or introversion - extroversion - you are saying that the dimension is something everyone can be placed on. Whether they are neurotic or not, all people have a capacity for health and ill-health; and whether introverted or extroverted, all are "verted" one way or the other.

Another way of saying this is that personality theorists are interested in the structure of the individual, the psychological structure in particular. How are people "put together;" how do they "work;" how do they "fall apart." Some theorists go a step further and say they are looking for the essence of being a person. Or they say they are looking for what it means to be an individual human being. The field of personality psychology stretches from a fairly simple empirical search for differences between people to a rather philosophical search for the meaning of life!

Trait Theories

Trait theories of personality are based on the assumption that a person's personality can be captured in a series of binary oppositions. My students are required when considering their performance in their practical work to take into account a variety of factors, which might have influenced their performance. They seem to like to latch on to trait theories of personality as an explanation of, for example, why they didn't complete their work by the deadlines (laziness), why they had difficulty with an interviewee (shyness) and so on. Looking back over their work as a whole, they will often be tempted to explain their success or failure in terms of their own personality characteristics, which they see as largely unvarying.

Trait theorists generally take the view that our character traits are inherited. The most famous British psychologist to take that view is Hans Eysenck. He considers that there are two major dimensions of personality, which account for the any different types of person we encounter. They are extroversion and introversion. As you can see from the graphic, personality is measured on the dimensions.

extravert < – – > *introvert* and *neurotic* < – – > *normal* (or *stable*)

Each of these dimensions is made up of several second-order factors (Fig. 14.1):

Extroversion: activity, sociability, risk-taking, impulsiveness, expressiveness, reflectiveness, and responsibility.

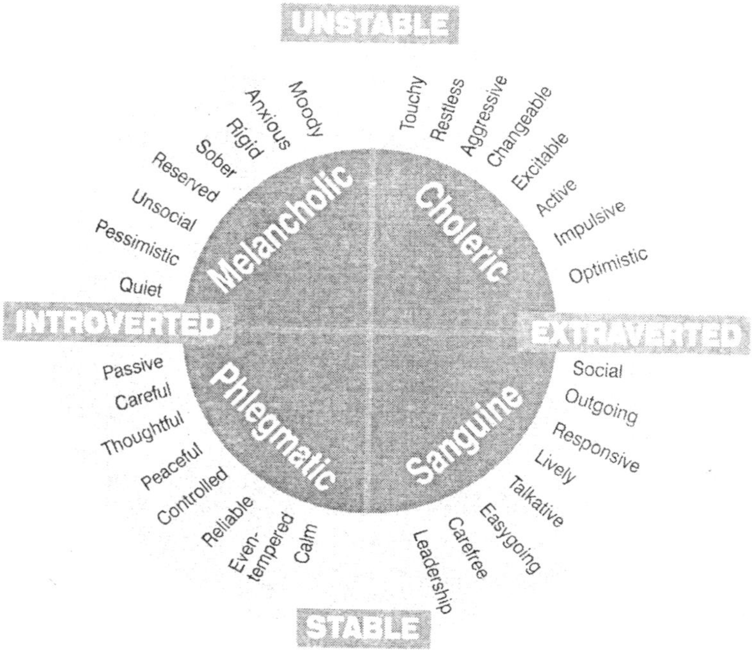

Fig. 14.1:Trait Theories

Cattell

He established his list of traits from a variety of sources and thus avoids the criticism of Eysenck's self-reporting method.

According to Cattell, there are sixteen factors of personality, all bipolar:

Reserved	Outgoing
Less intelligent	More intelligent
Affected by feelings	Emotionally stable
Submissive	Dominant
Serious	Happy-go-lucky
Expedient	Conscientious
Timid	Venturesome
Tough-minded	Sensitive

Trusting	Suspicious
Practical	Imaginative
Forthright	Shrewd
Self-assured	Apprehensive
Conservative	Experimenting
Group dependent	Self-sufficient
Uncontrolled	Controlled
Relaxed	Tense

Source: Hayes & Orrell, 1993

Cattell is often criticised for having produced an overly simplistic model. It is also objected that his system is too rigid, since certain traits may be very important for understanding some people and totally irrelevant to others. However, he himself drew attention to the variability introduced by such factors as the situation, the rôle currently being played and faking.

Types Theory

William Sheldon (1898-1977) was an American psychologist who devoted his life to observing the variety of human bodies and temperaments. He taught and did research at a number of U.S.universities and is best known for his series of books on the human constitution. He was a keen observer of animals and birds as a child, and he turned this talent to good effect by becoming an avid people-watcher, and out of his observations he gradually elaborated his typology.

The Basic Components of Physique

For his study of the human physique, Dr. Sheldon started with 4,000 photographs of college-age men, which showed front, back and side views. By carefully examining these photos he discovered that there were three fundamental elements which, when combined together, made up all these physiques or somatotypes. With great effort and ingenuity he worked out ways to measure these three components and to express them numerically so that every human body could be described in terms of three numbers, and that two independent observers could arrive at very similar results in determining a person's body type. These basic elements he named endomorphy, mesomorphy and ectomorphy, for they seemed to derive from the three layers of the human embryo, the endoderm, the mesoderm and the ectoderm.

- *Endomorphy* is centered on the abdomen, and the whole digestive system.
- *Mesomorphy* is focused on the muscles and the circulatory system.
- *Ectomorphy* is related to the brain and the nervous system.

We have all three elements in our bodily makeup, just as we all have digestive, circulatory and nervous systems. No one is simply an endomorph without having at the same time some mesomorphy and ectomorphy, but we have these components in varying degrees. Sheldon evaluated the degree a component was present on a scale ranging from one to seven, with one as the minimum and seven as the maximum.

The Extreme Endomorph - Roundness

The easiest way to get an idea of the variety of human physiques is by looking at the three extremes, even though in actual life the various combinations are much more common. According to Sheldon's system a 7-1-1 (seven-one-one) is the most extreme endomorph with minimal mesomorphy and ectomorphy. In this physique the body is round and soft, as if all the mass had been concentrated in the abdominal area. In fact, the large intestine of an extreme endomorph can be two or three times the length of that of an ectomorph. Sheldon likened this abdomen to a powerful boiler room with fine powers of assimilation. The arms and legs of the extreme endomorph are short and tapering, and the hands and feet comparatively small, with the upper arms and thighs being hammed and more developed than the lower arms and legs. The body has smooth contours without projecting bones, and a high waist. There is some development of the breast in the male and a fullness of the buttocks. The skin is soft and smooth like that of an apple, and there is a tendency towards premature baldness beginning at the top of the head and spreading in a polished circle. The hair is fine and the whole head is spherical. The head is large and the face broad and relaxed with the features blending into an over-all impression of roundness. The head is like a pumpkin sitting on a barrel, and the abdomen is like a sphere with the chest attached to it like an inverted funnel. Sheldon imagined the body of the endomorph as a balloon whose walls were thinner at the abdomen and thicker further away. When the balloon was inflated it was largest at the abdomen and smallest at the farthest extremities. Santa Claus is our society's image of the extreme endomorph.

The Extreme Mesomorph - Muscles (Fig. 14.2)

In the extremely mesomorphic physique, or 1-7-1, there is a squareness and hardness of the body due to large bones and well-defined muscles. The chest area, which Sheldon likened to an engine room, dominates over the abdominal area and tapers to a relatively narrow, low waist. The bones and muscles of the head are prominent as well, with clearly defined cheek bones and a square, heavy jaw. The face is long and broad and the head tends towards a cubical shape. The muscles on either side of the neck create a pyramid-like effect. Both the lower and upper arms and legs are well-developed and the wrists and fingers are heavy and massive. The skin is thick and tends towards coarseness. It takes and holds a tan well and can develop a leathery appearance with heavy wrinkles. Sheldon compared it to the skin of an orange. The hair is basically heavy-textured, and baldness, when it appears, usually starts at the front of the head. The extreme mesomorph is Mr. Universe or Tarzan. Sheldon's initial work with body and temperament types was based mostly on men, and it is in the description of the extreme mesomorph that we have the most need to develop a corresponding female mesomorphic description. Women on

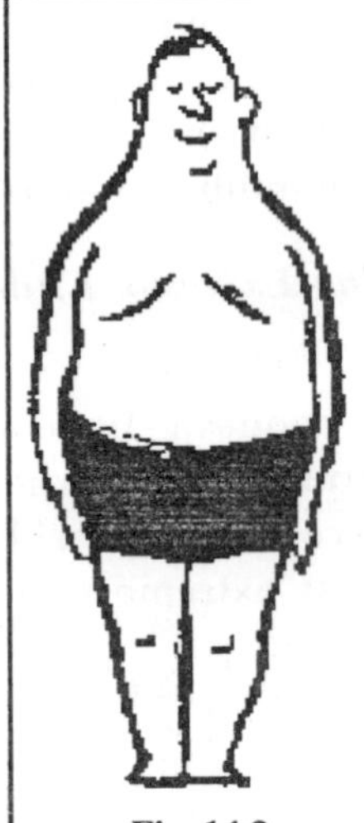

Fig. 14.2

the whole tend to have less mesomorphy than men and more endomorphy. Women who are primarily mesomorphs rarely show the same degree of sharp angularity, prominent bone structure and highly relieved muscles found in their male counterparts. Their contours are smoother, yet the chest area clearly dominates over the abdominal area and both upper and lower arms and legs are well-muscled. The skin tends to be finer than in the male mesomorph, but shows some of the same characteristics in terms of tanning and wrinkling.

The Extreme Ectomorph – Linear (Fig. 14.3)

The highly ectomorphic physique, or 1-1-7, is fragile and delicate with light bones and slight muscles. The limbs are relatively long and the shoulders droop. In contrast to the compactness of the endomorph and mesomorph, the ectomorph is extended in space and linear. The ribs are visible and delicate and the thighs and upper arms weak. The fingers, toes and neck are long. The features of the face are sharp and fragile, and the shape of the face as a whole is triangular with the point of the triangle at the chin. The teeth are of ten crowded in the lower jaw which is somewhat receding. The skin is dry and is like the outer skin of an onion. It tends to burn and peel easily and not retain a tan. The relatively great bodily area in relation to mass makes the ectomorph suffer from extreme heat or cold. The hair is fine and fast-growing and sometimes difficult to keep in place. Baldness is rare. The extreme ectomorph in our society is the absent-minded professor or Ichabod Crane.

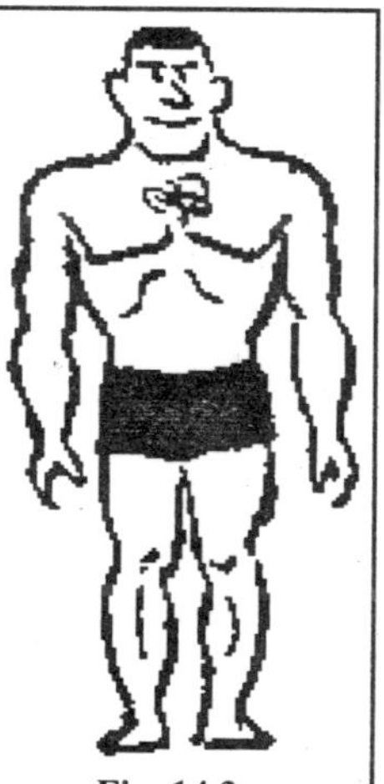

Fig. 14.3

Body Type Recognition (Fig. 14.4)

Once we had grasped these three basic elements we tried to recognize them in ourselves and our friends. We, indeed, found some people who were extreme endomorphs, or mesomorphs or ectomorphs, with little of the other components, but there were not many of them. Most of the people we knew were a bewildering variety of combinations, and we practiced mentally weighing how much of each component they had. Jim, for example, had very little endomorphy. He was one of those infuriating people who could eat and eat and never seem to gain a pound. He had some mesomorphy, but probably not as much as the average man. But he did have a lot of ectomorphy. He was tall and thin with long arms and legs, and a slight stoop to his shoulders. One friend was muscular and lean, while another was muscular and bulky. And so on. And slowly we began to recognize eight basic body types.

Fig. 14.4

	Endotonia	Mesotonia	Ectotonia
When troubled I seek out	People •	Action •	Solitude •
I prefer •	Physical Comfort	Physical adventure	Privacy
The time of my life I favour is	Childhood •	Early adulthood •	Later years •
What would bother me most would be	Being cut off from other people	Being closed off in small places	Being exposed to endless noise
When in a group I like to	Mingle •	Take charge •	Take off •
I prefer to	Let things take their course	Do things	Observe what is going on
The thing I like most is	Eating •	Exercise •	Time to myself •
The qualities that fit me best are •	Tolerance and love of people •	Love of power and leadership •	A highly developed self-awareness

Psychoanalytic Theories

Freud compared the human mind to an iceberg: we only see a little bit of it (the *conscious*) peeking out above the vast depths of the *unconscious*. Freud endeavoured to explore the unconscious by means of *free association* - a method which involves allowing the subject to talk about whatever comes into their conscious mind, however silly or trivial it may appear. Through the analysis of free associations, dreams and early childhood memories, Freud tried to figure out the basic elements of personality. He considered personality to be composed of three parts: the *id*, the *ego* and the *superego*.

The Id

The id consists of all the inherited components of personality, including sex drives and aggression. The id seeks immediate gratification of primitive impulses. It operates on the pleasure principle, seeking to avoid pain and maximise gratification. If tangible gratification of the primitive impulses are unavailable, then the id may form a mental image or hallucination to reduce the tension of ungratified desire - for example, a starving man may form a mental image of a delicious meal. That is an example of what Freud termed wish fulfillment.

The Ego

starving man might form an image of a meal, but that won't satisfy his needs. The ego emerges out of the id because we need to deal with the real world. Thus, the ego can be said to obey the reality principle, for example controlling the sex drive until conditions are right in the real world for its gratification. You can think of the ego as being the id's controller. Freud likens the ego to a man on the horseback of the id. The horse is stronger than the rider, but the rider controls it. Inevitably, however, the horse's strength will predominate and the rider will sometimes lose control or will sometimes have to content himself with guiding the horse to where it wants to go.

The Superego

The superego incorporates the values and morals of society which are learnt from one's parents and others. It develops as a result of rewards and punishments as one grows up. The superego's function is to control the id's impulses, especially those which society forbids, such as sex and aggression. It also has the function of persuading the ego to turn to moralistic goals rather than simply realistic ones and to strive for perfection. The superego consists of *conscience* - all those actions the child is reproved for doing - and the *ego-ideal* - all those things the child is praised for doing. The conscience makes the individual feel guilty and the ego-ideal makes the individual feel proud, thus directing the striving for perfection.

Anxiety and defence mechanisms

Somehow we need to satisfy the id's desires. It's all very well for the superego to control them, but that doesn't get rid of them; they are still powerfully present. When we have an urge to do something reprehensible for which we will be punished (if only by our own conscience), then we become anxious - a state of tension that we need to reduce. One way to do that is by expressing the impulse in a disguised form that society does approve of - for example becoming a racing car driver or boxer as an outlet for aggression.

Defence Mechanisms

Another method of reducing tension is to adopt methods of reduction called *defence mechanisms*, investigated more by Freud's daughter, Anna, than by Freud himself. These include:

Repression

We can force the uncomfortable desires, the painful feelings and memories into the unconscious. However, they remain there affecting our behaviour and mental states without our knowledge, perhaps sometimes emerging as 'Freudian slips'. At present, much attention is centred on the so-called 'repressed memory syndrome' of people who have been sexually abused as children. They have repressed those awful memories and have then rediscovered them through psychoanalysis and counselling. There is currently much controversy over the extent to which they constitute genuine memories or may, at least in some cases, constitute 'false memory syndrome' - memories of events that never took place.

Projection

To avoid anxiety we might attribute our unacceptable thoughts and feelings to others. You might hate someone, but your superego tells you that such hatred is unacceptable. You can 'solve' the problem by believing that they hate you.

Denial

External threats to the ego are simply cut off from consciousness. 'Assignment? What assignment?' is a fairly common example of denial. More seriously, the denial of a serious illness by a patient has just been informed of it is not uncommon.

Displacement

You redirect your unacceptable urges on to a substitute. The photocopier breaks down; you'd really love to hit the boss for being too mean to buy a decent one; instead you kick the office cat.

Sublimation

You turn the forbidden impulses into socially acceptable behaviours. The aggressive man becomes a boxer or soldier.

Freud made no substantial intellectual discoveries. He was the creator of a complex pseudo-science which should be recognized as one of the great follies of Western civilization. In creating his particular pseudo-science, Freud developed an autocratic, anti-empirical intellectual style which has contributed immeasurably to the intellectual ills of our own era.

Psychosexual Stages

According to Freud, the sex drive is the most important motivating force. In fact, Freud felt it was the primary motivating force not only for adults but for children and even infants. When he introduced his ideas about infantile sexuality to the Viennese public of his day, they were hardly prepared to talk about sexuality in adults, much less in infants! It is true that the capacity for orgasm is there neurologically from birth. But Freud was not just talking about orgasm. Sexuality meant not only intercourse, but

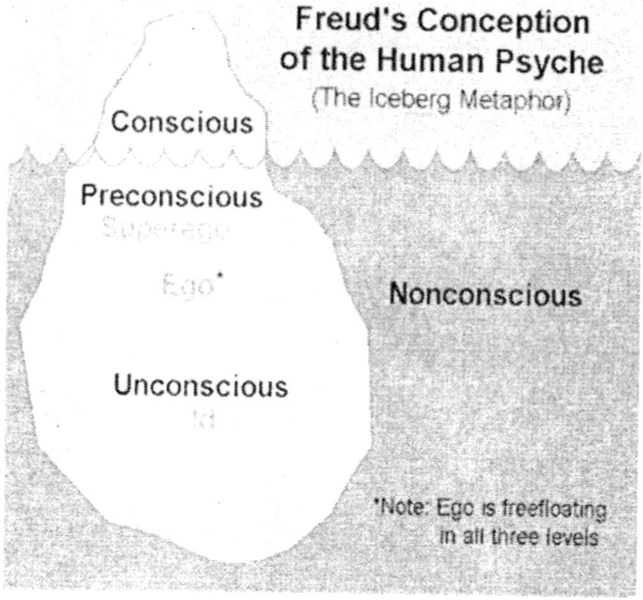

Fig. 14.5: Freud's Conception of the Human Psyche

all pleasurable sensation from the skin. It is clear even to the most prudish among us that babies, children, and, of course, adults, enjoy tactile experiences such as caresses, kisses, and so on.

Freud noted that, at different times in our lives, different parts of our skin give us greatest pleasure. Later theorists would call these areas *erogenous zones*. It appeared to Freud that the infant found its greatest pleasure in sucking, especially at the breast. In fact, babies have a penchant for bringing nearly everything in their environment into contact with their mouths. A bit later in life, the child focuses on the anal pleasures of holding it in and letting go. By three or four, the child may have discovered the pleasure of touching or rubbing against his or her genitalia. Only later, in our sexual maturity, do we find our greatest pleasure in sexual intercourse. In these observations, Freud had the makings of a psychosexual stage theory.

- The **oral stage** lasts from birth to about 18 months. The focus of pleasure is, of course, the mouth. Sucking and biting are favorite activities.
- The **anal stage** lasts from about 18 months to three or four years old. The focus of pleasure is the anus. Holding it in and letting it go are greatly enjoyed.
- The **phallic stage** lasts from three or four to five, six, or seven years old. The focus of pleasure is the genitalia. Masturbation is common.
- The **latent stage** lasts from five, six, or seven to puberty, that is, somewhere around 12 years old. During this stage, Freud believed that the sexual impulse was suppressed in the service of learning. I must note that, while most children seem to be fairly calm, sexually, during their grammar school years, perhaps up to a quarter of them are quite busy masturbating and playing "doctor." In Freud's repressive era, these children were, at least, quieter than their modern counterparts.
- The **genital stage** begins at puberty, and represents the resurgence of the sex drive in adolescence, and the more specific focusing of pleasure in sexual intercourse. Freud felt that masturbation, oral sex, homosexuality, and many other things we find acceptable in adulthood today, were immature. This is a true stage theory, meaning that Freudians believe that we all go through these stages, in this order.

The ways in which our lives intermesh are terribly complex and very frustrating to the theorist. But ignoring them is to ignore something vitally important about our development and our personalities (Table 14.1).

The first stage: The first stage, infancy or the *oral-sensory stage*, is approximately the first year or year and a half of life. The task is to develop *trust* without completely eliminating the capacity for *mistrust*. If mom and dad can give the newborn a degree of familiarity, consistency, and continuity, then the child will develop the feeling that the world – especially the social

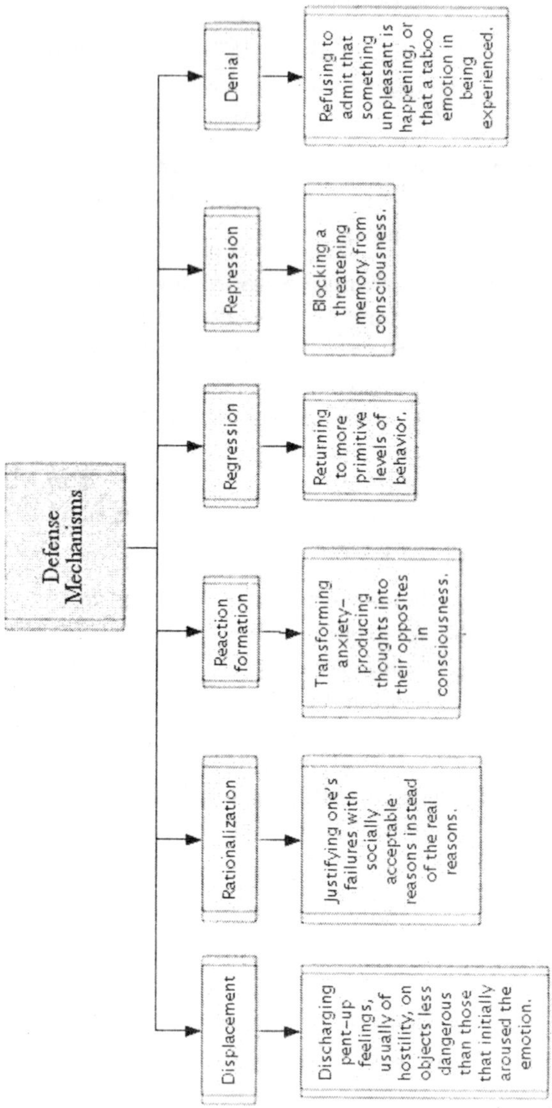
Defense Mechanisms
Displacement
Discharging pent-up feelings, usually of hostility, on objects less dangerous than those that initially aroused the emotion.
Rationalization
Justifying one's failures with socially acceptable reasons instead of the real reasons.
Reaction formation
Transforming anxiety-producing thoughts into their opposites in consciousness.
Regression
Returning to more primitive levels of behavior.
Repression
Blocking a threatening memory from consciousness.
Denial
Refusing to admit that something unpleasant is happening, or that a taboo emotion in being experienced.

Fig. 14.6

world — is a safe place to be, that people are reliable and loving. Through the parents' responses, the child also learns to trust his or her own body and the biological urges that go with it. If the parents are unreliable and inadequate, if they reject the infant or harm it, if other interests cause both parents to turn away from the infants needs to satisfy their own instead, then the infant will develop mistrust. He or she will be apprehensive and suspicious around people.

Stage two: The second stage is the *anal-muscular stage* of early childhood, from about eighteen months to three or four years old. The task is to achieve a degree of *autonomy* while minimizing *shame and doubt*. If mom and dad (and the other care-takers that often come into the picture at this point) permit the child, now a toddler, to explore and manipulate his or her environment, the child will develop a sense of autonomy or independence. The parents should not discourage the child, but neither should they push. A balance is required. People often advise new parents to be "firm but tolerant" at this stage, and the advice is good. This way, the child will develop both self-control and self-esteem.

On the other hand, it is rather easy for the child to develop instead a sense of shame and doubt. If the parents come down hard on any attempt to explore and be independent, the child will soon give up with the assumption that cannot and should not act on their own. We should keep in mind that even something as innocent as laughing at the toddler's efforts can lead the child to feel deeply ashamed, and to doubt his or her abilities. And there are other ways to lead children to shame and doubt: If you give children unrestricted freedom and no sense of limits, or if you try to help children do what they should learn to do for themselves, you will also give them the impression that they are not good for much. If you aren't patient enough to wait for your child to tie his or her shoe-laces, your child will never learn to tie them, and will assume that this is too difficult to learn!

Stage three: Stage three is the *genital-locomotor stage* or play age. From three or four to five or six, the task confronting every child is to learn *initiative* without too much *guilt*. Initiative means a positive response to the world's challenges, taking on

Table 14.1: Stage-wise Conception of the Human Psyche

Stage (age)	*Psychosocial crisis*	*Significant relations*	*Psychosocial modalities*	*Psychosocial virtues*	*Maladaptations & malignancies*
1	2	3	4	5	6
Stage I (0-1 age) Infant	Trust vs mistrust	Mother	to get, to give in return	hope, faith	sensory distortion withdrawal
Stage II (2-3) Toddler	Autonomy vs shame and doubt	Parents	to hold on, to let go	will, determination	impulsivity compulsion
Stage III (3-6) Preschooler	Initiative vs guilt	Family	to go after, to play	purpose, courage	ruthlessness inhibition
Stage IV (7-12) School child	Industry vs inferiority	neighborhood and school	to complete, to make things together	competence	narrow virtuosity inertia
Stage V (12-18) Adolescence	ego-identity vs role-confusion	peer groups, role models	to be oneself, to share oneself	fidelity, loyalty	fanaticism repudiation
Stage VI (20's) Young adult	intimacy vs isolation	partners, friends	to lose and find oneself in a another	love	promiscuity exclusivity

Stage VII (late 20s-50s) Middle adult	generativity vs self-absorption	household, workmates	to make be, to take care of	care	overextension rejectivity
Stage VIII (50's and beyond) Old adult	integrity vs despair	mankind or "my kind"	to be, through having been, to face not being	wisdom	presumption despair

responsibilities, learning new skills, feeling purposeful. Parents can encourage initiative by encouraging children to try out their ideas. We should accept and encourage fantasy and curiosity and imagination. This is a time for play, not for formal education. The child is now capable, as never before, of imagining a future situation, one that isn't a reality right now. Initiative is the attempt to make that non-reality a reality. A good balance leads to the psychosocial strength of *purpose*. A sense of purpose is something many people crave in their lives, yet many do not realize that they themselves make their purposes, through imagination and initiative. I think an even better word for this virtue would have been courage, the capacity for action despite a clear understanding of your limitations and past failings.

Stage four: Stage four is the *latency stage*, or the school-age child from about six to twelve. The task is to develop a capacity for *industry* while avoiding an excessive sense of *inferiority*. Children must "tame the imagination" and dedicate themselves to education and to learning the social skills their society requires of them. There is a much broader social sphere at work now: The parents and other family members are joined by teachers and peers and other members of the community at large. They all contribute: Parents must encourage, teachers must care, peers must accept. Children must learn that there is pleasure not only in conceiving a plan, but in carrying it out. They must learn the feeling of success, whether it is in school or on the playground, academic or social. A good way to tell the difference between a child in the third stage and one in the fourth stage is to look at the way they play games. Four-year old may love games, but they will have only a vague understanding of the rules, may change them several times during the course of the game, and be very unlikely to actually finish the game, unless it is by throwing the pieces at their opponents. A seven-year-old, on the other hand, is dedicated to the rules, considers them pretty much sacred, and is more likely to get upset if the game is not allowed to come to its required conclusion.

Stage five: Stage five *is adolescence*, beginning with puberty and ending around 18 or 20 years old. The task during adolescence is to achieve *ego identity* and avoid *role confusion*. It was adolescence that interested Erikson first and most, and the patterns he saw here were the bases for his thinking about all the other stages. Ego identity means knowing who you are and how you fit in to the rest of society. It requires that you take all you've learned about life and yourself and mold it into a unified self-image, one that your community finds meaningful. There are a number of things that make things easier: First, we should have a mainstream adult culture that is worthy of the adolescent's respect, one with good adult role models and open lines of communication.

Stage six: If you have made it this far, you are in the stage of young adulthood, which lasts from about 18 to about 30. The ages in the adult stages are much fuzzier than in the childhood stages, and people may differ dramatically. The task is to achieve some degree of *intimacy*, as opposed to remaining in *isolation*. Intimacy is the ability to be close to others, as a lover, a friend, and as a participant in society. Because you have a clear sense of who you are, you no longer need to fear "losing" yourself, as many adolescents do. The "fear of commitment" some people seem to exhibit is an example of immaturity in this stage. This fear isn't always so obvious. Many people today are always putting off the progress of their relationships: I'll get married (or have a family, or get involved in important social issues) as soon as I finish school, as soon as I have a job, as soon as I have a house, as soon as.... If you've been engaged for the last ten years, what's holding you back? Neither should the young adult need to prove him- or herself anymore. A teenage relationship is often a matter of trying to establish identity through "couple-hood." Who am I? I'm her boy-friend. The young adult relationship should be a matter of two independent egos wanting to create something larger than themselves. We intuitively recognize this when we frown on a relationship between a young adult and a teenager: We see the potential for manipulation of the younger member of the party by the older.

Stage seven: The seventh stage is that of *middle adulthood*. It is hard to pin a time to it, but it would include the period during which we are actively involved in raising children. For most people in our society, this would put it somewhere between the middle twenties and the late fifties. The task here is to cultivate the proper balance of *generativity* and *stagnation*. Generativity is an extension of love into the future. It is a concern for the next generation and all future generations. As such, it is considerably less "selfish" than the intimacy of the previous stage: Intimacy, the love between lovers or friends, is a love between equals, and it is necessarily reciprocal. Oh, of course we love each other unselfishly, but the reality is such that, if the love is not returned, we don't consider it a true love. With generativity, that implicit expectation of reciprocity isn't there, at least not as strongly. Few parents expect a "return on their investment" from their children; If they do, we don't think of them as very good parents!

Although the majority of people practice generativity by having and raising children, there are many other ways as well.

Stage eight: This last stage, referred to delicately as *late adulthood* or maturity, or less delicately as old age, begins sometime around retirement, after the kids have gone, say somewhere around 60. Some older folks will protest and say it only starts when you feel old and so on, but that's an effect of our youth-worshipping culture, which has even old people avoiding any acknowledgement of age. In Erikson's theory, reaching this stage is a good thing, and not reaching it suggests that earlier problems retarded your development. The task is to develop *ego integrity* with a minimal amount of *despair*. This stage, especially from the perspective of youth, seems like the most difficult of all. First comes a detachment from society, from a sense of usefulness, for most people in our culture. Some retire from jobs they've held for years; others find their duties as parents coming to a close; most find that their input is no longer requested or required.

Personality Assessment

Personality tests and inventories evaluate the thoughts, emotions, attitudes, and behavioral traits that comprise personality. The results of these tests determine an individual's personality strengths and weaknesses, and may identify certain disturbances in personality, or psychopathology. Personality tests are administered for a wide variety of reasons, from diagnosing psychopathology (e.g., personality disorder, depressive disorder) to screening job candidates. They may be used in an educational or vocational setting to determine personality strengths and weaknesses, or in the legal system to evaluate parolees.

Thematic Apperception Test (TAT)

The thematic apperception test (TAT) is a projective personality test that was designed at Harvard in the 1930s by Christiana D. Morgan and Henry A. Murray. Along with the MMPI and the Rorschach, the TAT is one of the most widely used psychological tests. A projective test is one in which a person's patterns of thought, attitudes, observational capacity, and emotional responses are evaluated on the basis of responses to ambiguous test materials. The TAT consists of 31 pictures that depict a variety of social and interpersonal situations. The subject is asked to tell a story about each picture to the examiner. Of the 31 pictures, 10 are gender-specific while 21 others can be used with adults of either sex and with children. As of 2001, the TAT is distributed by Harcourt Brace Educational Measurement.

Purpose

The original purpose of the Thematic Apperception Test was to reveal the underlying dynamics of the subject's personality, such as internal conflicts, dominant drives and interests, motives, etc. The specific motives that the TAT assesses include the need for achievement, need for power, the need for intimacy, and problem-solving abilities. After World War II, however, the TAT was used by psychoanalysts and clinicians from other schools of thought to evaluate emotionally disturbed patients. Another shift took place in the 1970s, when the influence of the human potential movement led many psychologists to emphasize the usefulness of the Thematic Apperception Test in assessment services— that is, using the test to help clients understand themselves better and stimulate their personal growth.

The Thematic Apperception Test is widely used to research certain topics in psychology, such as dreams and fantasies, mate selection, the factors that motivate people's choice of occupations, and similar subjects. It is sometimes used in psychiatric evaluations to assess disordered thinking and in forensic examinations to evaluate crime suspects, even though it is not a diagnostic test.

As mentioned earlier, the TAT can be used to help people understand their own personality in greater depth and build on that knowledge in making important life decisions. Lastly, it is sometimes used as a screener in psychological evaluations of candidates for high-stress occupations (law enforcement, the military, religious ministry, etc.).

Precautions

The Thematic Apperception Test has been criticized for its lack of a standardized method of administration as well as the lack of standard norms for interpretation. Studies of the interactions between examiners and test subjects have found that the race, sex, and social class of both participants influence both the stories that are told and the way the stories are interpreted by the examiner. Attempts have been made to design sets of TAT cards for African American and for elderly test subjects, but the results have not been encouraging. In addition, the 31 standard pictures have been criticized for being too gloomy or depressing, and therefore limiting the range of personality characteristics that the test can assess.

Description

There is no standardized procedure or set of cards for administering the TAT, except that it is a one-on-one test. It cannot be administered to groups. In one common method of administration, the examiner shows the subject only 10 of the 31 cards at each of two sessions. The sessions are not timed, but average about an hour in length.

Preparation

There is no specific preparation necessary before taking the TAT, although most examiners prefer to schedule sessions (if there is more than one) over two days.

Formal results

Since the Thematic Apperception Test is used primarily for personality assessment rather than diagnosis of mental disorders, it does not yield a "score" in the usual sense.

REFERENCES

Adam-Smith, D. and Peacock, A. (1994) *Cases in Organisational Behaviour*. London: Pitman.

Allpot, G.W. (1961) *Pattern and Growth in Personality*, New York, Holt.

Barker, L.M. (1994) *Learning and behavior: A Psychobiological Perspective*. Macmillan, New York.

Bennett, R. (1991) *Organisational Behaviour*. London: Pitman

Cohen, A. *et al.* (1995) *Effective Behaviour in Organisations: Cases, Concepts, and Student Experiences*. 6th ed. Irwin/McGraw-Hill

Cowling, A., Stanworth, M., Bennett, R., Curran, J. and Lyons, P. (1993) *Behavioural Sciences for Managers*. 2nd ed. London: Edward Arnold.

Eysenck, H.J., *The Structure of Human Personality* (3rd ed.), New York: Methuen, 1971.

Gordon, J. (1993) *A Diagnostic Approach to Organizational Behaviour*. 4th ed. Boston: Allyn and Bacon

Greenberg, J. and Baron, R. (1993) *Behavior in Organizations: Understanding and Managing the Human Side of Work*. 4th ed. Boston: Allyn and Bacon

Hersey and Blanchard, (2002) *Management of Organizational Behaviour*, 8th Ed. PHI.

Huczynski, A. and Buchanan, D. (1991) *Organisational Behaviour: An Introductory Text*, 2nd ed., Harlow: FT/Prentice-Hall

Hurlock, E.B. (2006) *Personality Development*, 28th Reprint. New Delhi: Tata McGraw-Hill.

Luthans, F. (1992) *Organisational Behaviour*. 6th ed. McGraw-Hill

Mullins, L. (1999) *Management and Organizational Behaviour*. 3rd ed. FT/Prentice-Hall.

Prince, Morton, (1929) *The Unconscious* (2nd ed.), New York, Macmillan.

Robbins, S. (1993) *Organisational Behaviour: Concepts, Controversies and Applications*. 6th ed. New Jersey: Prentice-Hall.

Robbins, S.B. (2005). *Organizational Behaviour*. New Delhi: Prentice-Hall of India.

Schermerhorn, Hunt and Osborn, (2001) *Organisational Behavior*, John Wiley, 7th edition, 2001.

Smith, B. (2004). Body Language. Delhi: Rohan Book Company.

Swaminathan. V.D and Kaliappan. K.V. (2001). *Psychology for Effective Living*. Chennai. The Madras Psychology Society.

Tyson, S. and Jackson, T. (1992) *The Essence of Organizational Behavior*. New York: Prentice-Hall

Vecchio, R. (1995) *Organisational Behaviour*. 3rd ed. The Dryden Press

Watson, J.B., (1930) *Behaviorism*, London, Kegan Paul.

15 Transactional Analysis

He who ask question remains fool for five minutes,
but he who does not remains a fool for life.

Transactional Analysis (TA) is a practical theory of personality, communication and organisations. Through a comprehensive set of concepts, TA serves as a guideline for effective intervention at the individual, group and organizational level. It is a powerful tool for professional and personal growth. The goal of transactional analysis is to increase awareness, spontaneity and the capacity for relationship. Transactional analysis is a kind of psychotherapy that (among other things) analyses our everyday communication - why do we say things we say, how do we say them and what made us say that.

Communication Model

Professor Albert Mehrabian has pioneered the understanding of communications since the 1960s. Aside from his many and various other fascinating works, Mehrabian established this classic statistic for the effectiveness of spoken communications:

- Seven per cent of meaning is in the words that are spoken.
- Thirty-eight per cent of meaning is paralinguistic (the way that the words are said).
- Fifty-five per cent of meaning is in facial expression.

Mehrabian's model above has become one of the most widely referenced statistics in communications. The model is particularly useful in illustrating the importance of considering factors other than words alone when trying to convey (as the speaker) or interpret (as the listener) meaning. Style, expression, tone, facial expression and body language account for 93 per cent of meaning. The understanding of how to convey (when speaking) and interpret (when listening) meaning is essential for effective communication, management and relationships. In this context, the TA would be highly useful to understand one's own transaction and analysis personality.

Meaning of Transactional Analysis

Transactional Analysis is one of the most accessible theories of modern psychology. Transactional Analysis was founded by Eric Berne, and the famous 'parent adult child' theory is still being developed today. Transactional Analysis has wide applications in clinical, therapeutic, organizational and personal development, encompassing communications, management, personality, relationships and behaviour. Whether you're in business, a parent, a social worker or interested in personal development, Eric Berne's Transactional Analysis theories, and those of his followers, will enrich your dealings with people, and your understanding of yourself. This section covers the background to Transactional Analysis, and Transactional Analysis underpinning theory.

Transactional Analysis can best be introduced by a quote from one of its most popular books, *Transactional Analysis Today* "Transactional analysis is a theory of personality and a systematic psychotherapy for personal growth and personal change. That's the definition of Transactional Analysis suggested by the International Transactional Analysis Association." In fact, TA today is all this and much more. TA is also a powerful tool in management and communications training and in organisational analysis. Among the many other applications of TA are its uses by social workers, police and probation authorities, and ministers of religion. Transactional Analysis can be used in any field where there is a need for understanding of individuals, relationships and communication.

Eric Berne

The creator of the Transactional Analysis approach was Eric Berne. He was born on May 10, 1910 in Montreal, Quebec, Canada, as Leonard Bernstein, the son of David Hiller Bernstein, MD, a general practitioner, and Sarah Gordon Bernstein, a professional writer and editor. His only sibling, his sister Grace, was born five years later. The family immigrated to Canada from Poland and Russia. Both parents graduated from McGill University, and Eric, who was close to his father, spoke fondly of how he accompanied his father, a physician, on medical rounds. Dr. Bernstein died of tuberculosis at age 38. Mrs. Bernstein then supported herself and her two children working as an editor and writer. She encouraged Eric to follow in his father's footsteps and study medicine. He received an M.D. and C.M. (Master of Surgery) from McGill University Medical School in 1935.

Roots of Transactional Analysis

Throughout history, and from all standpoints: philosophy, medical science, religion; people have believed that each man and woman has a multiple nature. In the early 20th century, Sigmund Freud first established that the human psyche is multi-faceted, and that each of us has warring factions in our subconscious. Since then, new theories continue to be put forward, all concentrating on the essential conviction that each one of us has parts of our personality which surface and affect our behaviour according to different circumstances. In 1951 Dr Wilder Penfield began a series of scientific experiments. Penfield proved, using conscious human subjects, by touching a part of the brain (the temporal cortex) with a weak electrical probe. Penfield's experiments went on over several years, and resulted in wide acceptance of the following conclusions: The human brain acts like a tape recorder, and whilst we may 'forget' experiences, the brain still has them recorded. Along with events the brain also records the associated feelings, and both feelings and events stay locked together. It is possible for a person to exist in two states simultaneously (because patients replaying hidden events and feelings could talk about them objectively at the same time). Hidden experiences when replayed are vivid, and affect how we feel at the time of replaying.

There is a certain connection between mind and body, i.e. the link between the biological and the psychological, e.g. a psychological fear of spiders and a biological feeling of nausea.

Early Transactional Analysis Theory and Model

In the 1950s Eric Berne began to develop his theories of Transactional Analysis. He said that verbal communication, particularly face to face, is at the centre of human social relationships and psychoanalysis. His starting-point was that when two people encounter each other, one of them will speak to the other. This he called the Transaction Stimulus. The reaction from the other person he called the Transaction Response. The person sending the Stimulus is called the Agent. The person

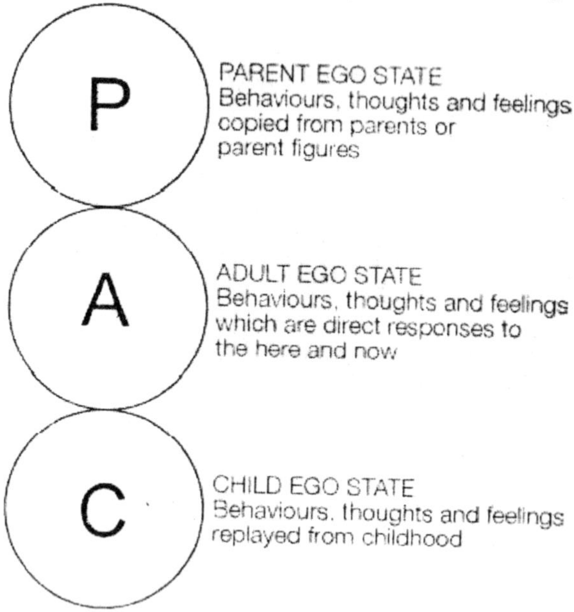

Fig. 15.1: Three Alter Ego States - Parent, Adult, Child.

who responds is called the Respondent. Transactional Analysis became the method of examining the transaction wherein: 'I do something to you, and you do something back'. Berne also said that each person is made up of three alter ego states - ***Parent, Adult, Child*** (Fig. 15.1).

Parent

This is our ingrained voice of authority, absorbed conditioning, learning and attitudes from when we were young. We were conditioned by our real parents, teachers, older people, next door neighbours, aunts and uncles, Father Christmas and Jack Frost. Our Parent is made up of a huge number of hidden and overt recorded playbacks. Typically embodied by phrases and attitudes starting with 'how to', 'under no circumstances', 'always' and 'never forget', 'don't lie, cheat, steal', etc, etc. Our parent is formed by external events and influences upon us as we grow through early childhood. We can change it, but this is easier said than done.

Child

Our internal reaction and feelings to external events form the 'Child'. This is the seeing, hearing, feeling, and emotional body of data within each of us. When anger or despair dominates reason, the Child is in control. Like our Parent we can change it, but it is no easier.

Adult

Our 'Adult' is our ability to think and determine action for ourselves, based on received data. The adult in us begins to form at around ten months old, and is the means by which we keep our Parent and Child under control. If we are to change our Parent or Child we must do so through our adult.

In other words: *Parent is our 'Taught' concept of life - Adult is our 'Thought' concept of life - Child is our 'Felt' concept of life.*

When we communicate we are doing so from one of our own alter ego states, our Parent, Adult or Child. Our feelings at the time determine which one we use, and at any time something can trigger a shift from one state to another. When we respond, we are also doing this from one of the three states, and it is in the analysis of these stimuli and responses that the essence of Transactional Analysis lies. A wonderful analogy - 'the person who had feelings' story - explains how experiences and conditioning in early life affect behaviour in later life. See also the poem by Philip Larkin about how parental conditioning affects children and their behaviour into adulthood.

At the core of Berne's theory is the rule that effective transactions (i.e. successful communications) must be complementary. They must go back from the receiving ego state to the sending ego state. For example, if the stimulus is Parent to Child, the response must be Child to Parent, or the transaction is 'crossed', and there will be a problem between sender and receiver. If a crossed transaction occurs, there is an ineffective communication. Worse still either or both parties will be upset. In order for the relationship to continue smoothly the agent or the respondent must rescue the situation with a complementary transaction. In serious break-downs, there is no chance of immediately resuming a discussion about the original subject matter. Attention is focused on the relationship. The discussion can only continue constructively when and if the relationship is mended.

Parent Ego State Transactions

The Parent ego state is a set of thoughts, feelings, and behaviors that are learned or "borrowed" from our parents or other caretakers. The Parent ego state can be divided into two functions. One part includes the nurturing side and can be soft, loving, and permission giving. This is called the Nurturing Parent ego state. It can also set limits in a healthy way. The other side of the Parent ego state is called the Critical Parent. (It is also sometimes called the Prejudiced Parent.) This part of our personality contains the prejudged thoughts, feelings, and beliefs that we learned from our parents.

Characteristics

We are all familiar with the parent. The parent is a status figure who has the power to direct other persons' lives by means

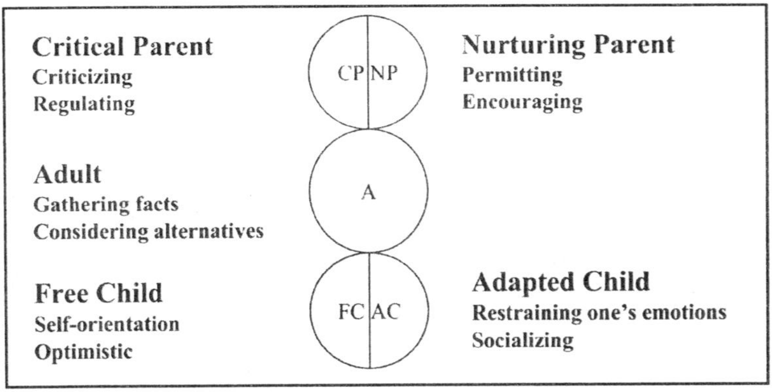

Fig. 15.2: Parent Ego State

of demanding conformity to certain behavioural norms, reinforced with sanctions or rewards (see the section on Learning). As we grow up, we learn our parents' behaviour patterns and communication styles and then apply them ourselves. For students of TA, this does not of course imply that we have to be parents to use these communication styles. A child may adopt the Parent ego state in a transaction with its toys or other people, a man may adopt it in a transaction with his girlfriend and, naturally, a parent may adopt it in a transaction with his or her own child.

The Nurturing Parent

As you can see from the graphic, Berne distinguishes between the Nurturing (or Natural) Parent and the Controlling Parent. Essentially, the Nurturing Parent's characteristics are quite positive, but can be overbearing and limiting. The Nurturing Parent is concerned with her child's welfare, so rewards, protects and cares for the child and try to pass on good moral standards: '"Always be on time", "Save your money", "Work hard" are some of the typical examples given by Berne. The Nurturing Parent can help the child feel OK about its relationships, but can also be overprotective, smothering the child in its development.

The Controlling Parent

The Controlling Parent is another kettle of fish entirely. This Parent is strict and judgmental, is quick to form opinions about the child's behaviour, may even have formed the judgements before the behaviour, and sees to it that the child should succeed on the parent's terms.

Communication Behaviour

The Nurturing Parent is likely to use comforting phrases, such as "Don't worry, it'll be OK" or "Let me see if I can help you with that", as well as offering frequent praise. The Controlling Parent will offer quite a number of orders, which, if necessary will be justified by appeal to some kind of moral criteria or principles of behaviour which appear to have some kind of absolute value. These verbal behaviours will of course be paralleled by appropriate non-verbal behaviours: encouraging gestures, indulgent smiles in the case of the Nurturing Parent, hostile glares and fixed stares in the case of the Controlling Parent.

Child Ego State of Transactions

The Child ego state is the part of our personality that is the seat of emotions, thoughts, and feelings and all of the feeling state "memories" that we have of ourselves from childhood. We carry around in our Child ego states all of the experiences we have had, and sometimes these childlike ways of being pop up in our grown-up lives. This can be fun when we are in a situation in which it is safe and right to play and enjoy ourselves. It can be a problem when our Child view of the world causes us to distort the facts in a current situation and prevents our Adult ego state from seeing things accurately. The Child ego state can also be divided into two parts: the Free Child ego state (also referred to as the Natural Child) and the Adapted Child ego state (which also contains the Rebellious Child ego state).

Characteristics

The Child is characterized by instinct, impulse and emotion, with these characteristics lying close to the surface. You will have noticed from the graphic, though, that Berne distinguishes three Child states:

The Natural Child

The Natural Child is pretty much as described above, generally uninhibited in its behaviour, loving and aggressive, afraid of the new as well as curious and inquisitive, sociable as well as egocentric.

The Adapted Child

The Adapted Child has learnt how to deal with adults. The self-expressive Natural Child is held in check. The Adapted Child may put things off (you don't get into trouble for your decisions if you don't take any); it may become withdrawn, dreaming is way through life; it may be compliant (doing as it's told) - however, it may be compliant, but look for ways around the 'law'. Berne describes the Child who adopts this last kind of behaviour as the Little Lawyer, seeking a way to transgress without breaking the letter of the 'law'. So a girl who is told by her parents not to lose her virginity may engage in mutual masturbation with boys, or perform fellatio; a boy who is told not to mess around with women may mess around with other boys, 'or in some cases with sheep or cows'.

Adult Ego State of Transactions

When in the Adult ego state the person functions as a human computer. It operates on data it collects and stores or uses to make decisions according to a logic-based program.

Characteristics

The Adult is detached, cool, calm, reasoning, unswayed by appeals to emotion. The Adult ego state is concerned with handling information and making decisions. It listens patiently in order to gather data and then bases a rational decision on the data collected, with reference to data and experiences previously gathered and decisions previously taken. It is most obviously predominant when we are engaged in solving problems. At the moment I have a bandage on my left thumb and keep hitting the CAPS LOCK key (if you're a competent typist, don't ask!). Any moment now, I'm going to thump the monitor out of sheer frustration - so I could do with a bit more of the Adult ego state at the moment!

Communication Behaviour

The above characteristics will be reflected in the Adult's behaviour. In a search for factual information, the Adult will ask questions: 'Why did you say that?', 'How did that happen?', 'How do you know that?', 'What makes you so sure?' The Adult will want to look at facts, saying 'Let's take a look at the facts', 'Let's just discuss it first to get the facts clear', 'OK, so what do we know now?' The Adult will resist false arguments and appeals to emotion and similarly will not appeal to emotion in either verbal or non-verbal behaviour. It is likely that the Adult will show the other person in the interaction calm acceptance and this acceptance will be apparent in active listening.

Transactions

A transaction is the basic unit of study of TA. The transaction (or interaction) when two people meet is the meeting place of six ego states (P-A-C plus P-A-C).

Complementary transactions

The simplest kind of transaction is the complementary transaction, where the arrows showing the communication of ego states with one another are parallel. You can see that in the diagram on the right, which shows a complementary transaction. In this example, Berne shows us a complementary transaction from the husband's Parent ego state to the wife's Child ego state. She responds from her Child ego state to his Parent ego state. This could be 'Look, you can't just go around spending my hard-earned money on new dresses whenever you feel like it', responded to by 'No, you're right. I'm sorry, I won't do it again.' (Sorry about the stereotyping!). Of course, the husband might not adopt the Controlling Parent ego state; he could equally speak from his Nurturing Parent state: 'You look really beautiful in that new dress', maybe at some later point suggesting that they really need to cut back for a while.

Crossed Transactions

Type I (AA-CP): In the graphic on the left, you see an example of a transaction where something has gone wrong - a crossed transaction. In this case, an initial Adult-to-Adult stimulus has been met with a Child-to-Parent response. Berne's example is a husband asking his wife, 'Have you seen my cuff-links?' to which he receives the response 'Why do you always blame me for everything?'. This is what Berne refers to as a crossed transaction Type I, the sort, he says, which causes most trouble in the world.

Type II (AA-PC): In a crossed transaction Type II (on the right), the Adult-to-Adult stimulus is met with a patronizing or pompous Parent-to-Child response, a response you as a student may be quite familiar with from certain teachers. As Berne points out, 72 different crossed transactions are mathematically possible. In fact, however, only four occur commonly. The other two are:

Type III (CP-AA): This is what Berne calls the 'exasperating response'. The stimulus is from Child to Parent, where someone is seeking sympathy, but gets facts instead (Adult-to-Adult).

Type IV PC-AA: Berne calls this 'impudence'. The stimulus is from Parent to Child, expecting compliance. Instead, however, the response is a 'smart aleck' response, in the form of a factual statement from Adult to Adult.

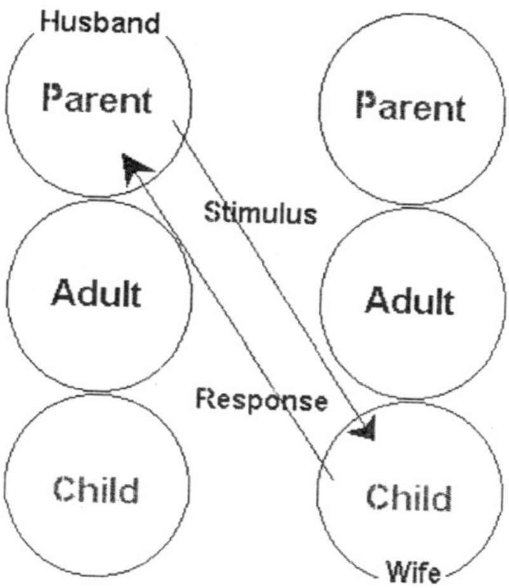

Fig. 15.3: Crossed Transactions

Angular Transactions

An angular transaction is what Berne also calls a two-level or ulterior transaction. In such a transaction, the speaker speaks as if to one ego state, but is in fact covertly addressing another. Berne takes the example (shown on the right) of a rational-sounding sales appeal, ostensibly Adult-to-Adult, which is in fact devised to 'hook' some other ego state, in this case the Child. If the response to the covert stimulus is from the ego state covertly addressed, then the angular transaction was successful, as shown in the graphic. Of course, it might well be unsuccessful, in which case the response in this example will be Adult-to-Adult.

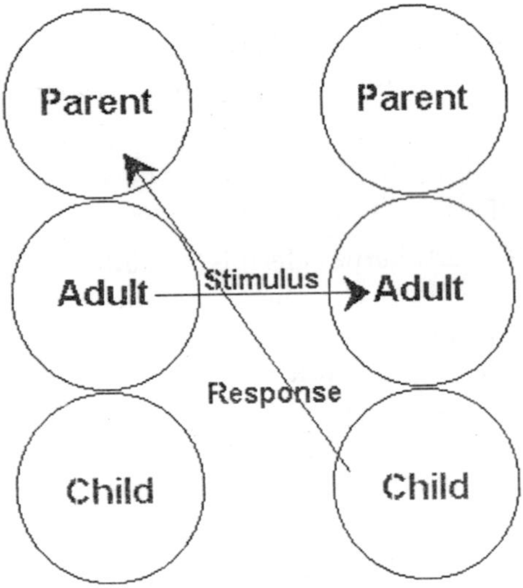

Fig. 15.4: Angular Transactions

One of my colleagues is particularly good at winding people up by dropping Adult-to-Adult factual remarks about the college, but which are in fact designed to throw his colleagues into a panic. You're probably quite familiar with this - 'I see Mark got off with Jo again last night.' Quite innocent at the social level, but if this is said to Lucy, who quite fancies Mark, then, at the psychological level, the transaction is Child-to-Child, the first of whom is a pretty spiteful Child at that.

Duplex Transactions

In a duplex transaction, there are two separate levels: an overt, social level and a covert psychological level. For example, in a group exercise I ran recently on the mass media, the two Sociology students in the group were confidently swapping comments about the Marxist view of ideology, hegemony theory and so on. Ostensibly, this was all very Adult-to-Adult. In fact, though, they were just as aware as I was that this was all something we hadn't yet dealt with in the Communication Studies class. At the psychological level, then, the transaction was Child-to-Child, saying to everyone else in the class, 'Look how clever we are!' It would be quite possible as well for a duplex transaction to take place in two separate channels. Typically the social level would be in the verbal channel and the psychological level in the non-verbal channel. For example, when a young man and woman fancy each other, the verbal channel may contain Adult-to-Adult talk about last night's TV movie, but the non-verbal channel a Child-to-Child transaction about their liking for each other.

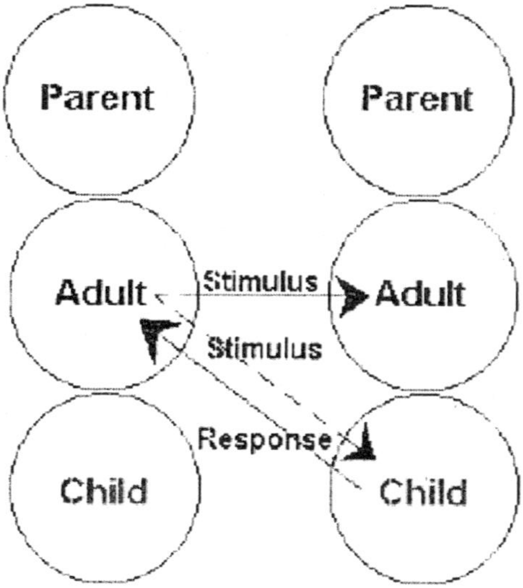

Fig. 15.5: Duplex Transactions

Understanding transactional analysis can help you understand yourself better. It can also help you see more clearly how you interact with others. One of the things that sets transactional analysis therapy apart from some other therapies is the belief that we are each responsible for our own future, regardless of what happened to us in the past. If you see things in yourself that you do not like or that do not serve you well, transactional analysis provides some tools to help you change. You can begin to change by deciding, for example, what kind of Parent ego state you would like to have and then practice using and developing that part of yourself. You can decide what ego state you would like to use more of and which one you might want to use less of.

REFERENCES

Berne, E. (1961). *Transactional analysis in psychotherapy: A systematic individual and social psychiatry.* New York: Grove Press.

Berne, E. (1972). *What do you say after you say hello?: The psychology of human destiny.* New York: Grove Press.

Berne, E. (1966). *Principles of group treatment.* New York: Oxford University Press.

Bowlby, J. (1969). *Attachment.* Vol. 1 of Attachment and loss. New York: Basic Books.

Crews, F., *et al.* (1995). *The memory wars: Freud's legacy in dispute.* New York: NYREV Collections.

Dellinger, S. (1989) *Psycho-geometrics. How to Use Geometric Psychology to Influence People.* Englewood Cliffs, NJ: Prentice-Hall.

Dusay, J. (1972). Egograms and the constancy hypothesis. *Transactional Analysis Journal,* 2(3): 37-41.

Goulding, M. M., and Goulding, R. L. (1997). *Changing lives through redecision therapy* (rev. ed.). New York: Grove/Atlantic Press.

Heinssen, R. K., Levendusky, P. G., and Hunter, R. H. (1995). Client as colleague: Therapeutic contracting with the seriously mentally ill. *American Psychologist,* 50(7): 522-532.

Karpman, S. (1968). Fairy tales and script drama analysis. Transactional Analysis Bulletin, 7(26): 39-43.

Levendusky, P. G., Berglas, S., Dooley, C. P., and Landau, R. J. (1983). Therapeutic contract program: A preliminary report on a behavioral alternative to the token economy. *Behavior Research and Therapy,* 21: 137-142.

Levendusky, P. G., Willis, B. S., and Ghinassi, F. A. (1994). The therapeutic contracting program: A comprehensive continuum of care model. *Psychiatric Quarterly,* 65: 189-208.

Loffredo, D. A., Harrington, R., Munoz, M. K., and Knowles, L. R. (2004). The ego state questionnaire-Revised. *Transactional Analysis Journal,* 34: 90-95.

Lynch, J., and Ford, J. (1977). *The broken heart: The medical consequences of loneliness.* New York: Basic Books.

Matlin, M., and Stang, D. (1978). *The pollyanna principle: Selectivity in language, memory, and thought.* Cambridge, MA: Schenkman.

Myers, I.B., McCaulley, M.H., Quenk, N.L., Hammer, A.L. (1998) *MBTI Manual: A guide to the development and use of the Myers Briggs type indicator.* 3rd ed. Mountain View, Calif: Consulting Psychologists Press.

Novey, T. (2002). Measuring the effectiveness of transactional analysis: An international study. *Transactional Analysis Journal,* 32: 8-24.

Ornish, D. (1998). *Love and survival: The scientific basis for the healing power of intimacy.* New York: HarperCollins.

Persons, J. B., Davidson, J., and Tompkins, M.A. (2001). *Essential components of cognitive-behavior therapy for depression.* Washington, DC: American Psychological Association.

Rowan, J., and Cooper, M. (1999). *The plural self: Multiplicity in everyday life.* London: Sage Publications.

Seligman, M., and Csikszentmihalyi, M. (2000). *Positive psychology.* American Psychologist, 55(1), 5-14.

Siegel, D. J. (1999). *The developing mind: How relationships and the brain interact to shape who we are.* New York: Guilford Press.

Spitz, R. (1945). Hospitalism: An inquiry into the genesis of psychiatric conditions in early childhood. In O. Fenichel et al. (Eds.), *The psychoanalytic study of the child* (Vol. 1, pp. 53-74). New York: International Universities Press.

Steiner, C. (1971). *Scripts people live: Transactional analysis of life scripts.* New York: Grove Press.

Stewart I, Joines V. *TA Today: A New Introduction to Transactional Analysis.* Chapel Hill, NC: Lifespace Publishing; 1987.

Suomi, S. J., Collins, M. L., Harlow, H. F., and Ruppenthal, G. (1976). Effects of maternal and peer separations on young monkeys. *Journal of Child Psychology and Psychiatry and Allied Disciplines,* 17(2), 101-112.

Tiger, L. (1979). *Optimism: The biology of hope.* New York. Simon and Schuster.

Tindall, W.N., Beardsley RS, Kimberlin CL. *Communication Skills in Pharmacy Practice.* 4th ed. Philadelphia, Pa: Lippincott Williams and Wilkins; 2003: 122.

Young, J.E. (1999). Cognitive therapy for personality disorders: A schema-focused approach. Sarasota, FL: *Professional Resource Exchange.*

16 Group Dynamics

> Speaking with kindness creates confidence, thinking with kindness creates profoundness, giving with kindness creates love.
>
> – *Lao Tseu*

Group Dynamics

The term "group dynamics" refers to the interactions between people who are talking together in a group setting. Group dynamics can be studied in business settings, in volunteer settings, in classroom settings, and in social settings. Any time there are three or more individuals interacting or talking together, there are group dynamics.

Meaning of Group

Group is defined as two or more individuals, interacting and interdependent, who have come together to achieve particular objectives. Group can be either formal or informal. By formal groups have organization's structure, with designated work assignments establishing tasks. In formal groups, the behaviours that one should engage in are stipulated by and directed toward organizational goals. The six members making up an airline flight crew are an example of a formal group. In formal groups are alliances that are neither formally structured nor organizationally determined. These groups are natural formations in the work environment that appear in response to the need for social contact. Three employees from different departments who regularly eat lunch together are an example of an informal group.

Tuckman and Jensen's Stages in Group Formation

Tuckman and Jensen draw on the movement known as group dynamics, which is concerned with why groups behave in particular ways. This offers various suggestions for how groups are formed and how they develop over time. The formation of some groups can be represented as a spiral; other groups form with sudden movements forward and then have periods with no change. Whatever variant of formation each group exhibits, they suggest that all groups pass through six sequential stages of development. These stages may be longer or shorter for each group, or for individual members of the group, but all groups will need to experience them. They are forming, storming, norming, performing, mourning and retiring.

The terms are pretty self-explanatory. When a group is forming, participants can feel anxious not knowing how the group will work or what exactly will be required of them. Storming, as the word suggests, is when things may get stormy. Conflict can emerge, individual differences are expressed and the leader's role may be challenged. The value and the feasibility of the task may also be challenged. After the storm comes the calm of norming, where the group starts to function harmoniously and where participants co-operate and mutual support develops. This enables the performing stage to occur where the work really takes off and the group accepts a structure and method for achieving the common task. When the group retires or adjourns, much learning happens through informal chat and feedback about the group performance. Tuckman and Jenson recognise that when groups dismantle themselves and the loose ends are all tied up, participants often go through a stage of mourning or grieving.

Stages of Group Development

Forming

What was the task? Did you all share the same expectations of the task? Did you all have the same attitude to working in a group? Did you feel any anxiety at the outset of the activity?

Storming

Was there any conflict in the group? Did you all agree on

the means of carrying out the task? Did you have a leader and was his/her authority challenged? Did any group members withdraw from the group?

Norming

Did you move on to agree methods of working? Did you have a common goal? Did you cooperate with each other? Did you work out how to proceed at all? (If not, you were probably still storming.)

Performing

Did everyone take on a functional role to achieve the task? Did you work constructively and efficiently? Did the group's activity focus on fulfilling the task? Did you experience a sense of achievement?

Retiring/Adjourning

Did you stop abruptly and all go your separate ways or did you finish the task and then go off together and socialize? Did you talk about the group and your experience of it? What sort of issues did you discuss or think about after the group activity? Was it more or less acceptable to give and receive feedback in a relaxed atmosphere when adjourning?

Mourning/Grieving

Have you experienced the mourning stage following the completion of a show or project? Have you ever felt empty or sad when a group activity has finished? Why might some people feel the mourning stage more acutely than others? How do you deal with your own feelings after the project or show? Do you recall any significant learning which took place outside of formal rehearsals and performances? Are you aware of any of your colleagues who experience the mourning stage acutely? If so, what might you do to support them?

The Need for Groups

There are several reasons why people want to come together:

- In a group, members have access to goods and services more easily than they would have on an individual basis;
- Group members pull together scarce resources, own and manage them themselves in order to fight against poverty, food shortage, powerlessness of an individual person against market forces, unemployment and low self esteem;
- Groups can be learning laboratories, promoting skills such as enterprise management and problem solving;
- Groups are useful receiving mechanisms for resources from Government and NGO development agencies;
- The group allows more small women entrepreneurs to be reached;
- It reduces on administrative transaction costs of lending;
- A group reduces default through collective risk taking; and
- Groups provide a channel for information.

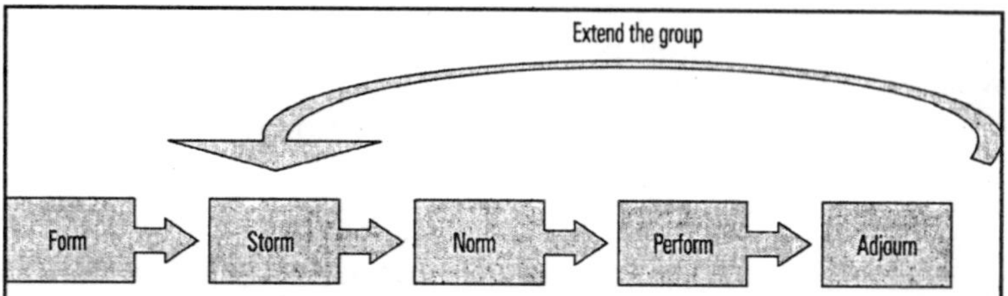

Fig. 16.1: Need for Groups

Characteristics of a Group

A gathering of people is a group when its members are collectively conscious of their existence as a group; when they believe it satisfies their needs; when they share aims, are interdependent, like to join in group activities, and want to remain with the group. Though groups occur in many forms and sizes, there seems to be a set of characteristics fairly common to them all. The following features are of consequence to any teacher involved in group teaching.

Cohesiveness

Cohesiveness is a measure of the attraction of the group to its members (and the resistance to leaving it), the sense of team spirit, and the willingness of its members to coordinate their efforts. Compared with members of a low-cohesive group, those in a high-cohesive group will, therefore, be keen to attend meetings, be satisfied with the group, use "we" rather than "I" in discussions, be cooperative and friendly with each other, and be more effective in achieving the aims they set for themselves. The low-cohesive group will be marked by absenteeism, the growth of cliques and factions, and a sense of frustration at the lack of attainment.

Participation

The degree of participation in a group is dependent to a large extent on its size and on the physical environment. The pattern of interaction may also vary. For instance, it may take the form of a one-way "mini" lecture by the leader or tutor, or be a two-way question-and-answer format, again directed by the tutor. In some cases, comments may be channelled through a member, not officially the leader, because of his or her dominant role outside the group, and in others a small clique may set up an interaction to the exclusion of the rest of the members. As a general rule communication is directed upwards in the status hierarchy and the upward communication tends to be more positive than that directed downwards. Consequently, the tutor may receive more rosy information than is appropriate: an important fact to remember in conducting an evaluation of the group or the tutor. Patterns of interaction in a group may be consistent over time or may vary. They can certainly be changed through the structuring of discussion with subgroups or by introducing helpful ground rules. The more widespread the participation in discussion, the better will be the interest and involvement.

Norms

Every group has a set of norms: a code of conduct about what is acceptable behaviour. They may apply to everyone in the group or to certain members only. Some norms will be strictly adhered to while others permit a wide range of behaviour. The group usually has sanctions (e.g., disapproval) which it may apply in the case of "deviation". Common norms in groups include: taboo subjects, open expression of feelings, interrupting or challenging the tutor, volunteering one's services, avoiding conflict, length and frequency of contributions. All of these are usually hidden or implicit and new members may find it difficult to adjust. Over the first few meetings of a group there may be confusion about the norms are with consequent frustration, discomfort, and lost momentum.

Physical Environment

Several critical factors in group dynamics - flow of communication, perception of status, emergence of leadership, for example - are affected by things like the physical position of group members, their distance apart, and their body orientations. These in turn are strongly influenced by the shape and size of the room in which a group meets, and the spatial arrangement of chairs and tables. A long, narrow room will probably limit eye contact along its length and impel members to talk to others across the room, but not along it. Anyone who sits at the end of a long table or behind the only desk in the room is likely to be accorded leadership status. Dominant members will tend to choose the more central seats in any group situation, and reticent ones may even try to sit outside the group. The further apart members are, the less talkative and more formal is the interaction likely to be. Tables create a physical barrier which may be reassuring in groups where formality is of the essence, or where there is a wish to maintain personal distance or space. They may also be invaluable as a writing surface. A lack of tables may be threatening to some but it usually encourages openness and informality.

Personal space, the area around a person which he or she regards as private, will of course vary from individual to individual, but it is clear that people of higher status often prefer, or are accorded, greater distance between them and others. (The seats on either side of a tutor in an otherwise undifferentiated circle of chairs are often the last to be filled by students.) The location of a group meeting has its effect too. The tutor's room is his or her territory and underlines the authority role. The student union bar on the other hand could be a more egalitarian venue but has the drawback of invasion by others, not to mention licensing limitations. Just as groups may assume territorial rights over physical space and objects, so members may act territorially about positions in a room.

Group Size

Two opposite tendencies exist with regard to the number of people in a group. The larger the group, the greater is the pool of talent and experience available for solving problems or sharing the effort. On the other hand as the size increases, fewer members have the chance to participate, and indeed the differences in relative participation increase to the point where one or two members begin to dominate. It thus becomes more likely that reticent members will fail to contribute, though they may well enjoy the relative anonymity a large group affords them. The smaller the group, the greater is the likelihood of close relationships, full participation, and consonance of aims. Whereas in a small group or team, leadership and other roles are likely to be shared or rotated, the formation of subgroups, and the increasing differentiation of roles in a large group will ensure the emergence of a leader. Where there is an agreed leader (e.g. the teacher) the need to counteract the above tendencies places special demands on his or her awareness of the problems and skills in coping with them. When does a group become "large" and does it still have any merits? Most theorists, researchers and practitioners agree that five to seven members is the optimum for leaderless groups. In the case of led groups, as for academic discussion, the maximum for member satisfaction according to students (NUS 1969) is 10 to 12. Larger groups are an advantage when it requires the combining of individual efforts as in brainstorming. They are of less value when everyone must accomplish the task, which is the general situation in most discussion groups.

Group Composition

As a general rule, a heterogeneous mix of students in each group provides the best chemistry for interaction and achievement of task. Such qualities as age, sex, nationality, and personality may be taken into account, though one can never be sure what mixture will lead to good participation. Individual students will contribute differently according to which other students they are grouped with: there occurs what is known as an "assembly effect" - a kind of convergence of needs and behaviours, which is often impossible to predict. Indeed the tutor may be part of it, for example when a group of dependent students are led by an authoritative tutor. From the point of view of cognitive learning, with problem solving for example, the mixing of quicker or more intelligent students with their slower counterparts can enable a teaching process between the students to take place. Yet often the most powerful influences are the personal likes and dislikes of fellow members. People tend to agree with individuals they like and disagree with those they dislike even though both may express the same opinion. By and large, groups composed of compatible people learn well when they want to learn. The opposite may often be the case with a disaffected group.

Communication

It is through communication that members of a group learn to understand one another and to influence, or be influenced by, each other. Yet communication is not just a matter of expressing ideas clearly. It is often suffused with unintended effects, fears and dislikes, and unconscious motives. Often the non-verbal part of communication is the most eloquent. A great deal is revealed about what a person is really thinking and feeling by their facial expression, posture, and gestures.

The content of communication is important too. In every subject area there is a specialised vocabulary which a newcomer may find off-putting. A clique within the group may sustain a private joke which intentionally excludes the rest. For any communication to take place, speaking must be complemented by listening. Students may often, through preoccupation with their own thoughts or scorn for another's opinions, fail to hear what is being said. Ground rules in which each speaker in turn has to summarise what the previous one said can encourage more purposeful listening.

Procedures

Procedures are really metarules or conventions for ensuring that what a group wants to happen does in fact happen. They are the means of handling problematic events like making decisions, conflict, distribution of tasks, assessment, and evaluation; and they may be invoked by, or applied to, any member or the whole group. Procedures may also be seen as devices for ensuring the smooth running of the group and the achievement of agreed aims. They may be formal and strictly codified, as in many committees, or informal and loose as for teams and working groups. The main virtue of a procedure is that it is usually set up before the event and this detaches discussions of how the group should handle problems in general from the problem-solving process itself. Typical rules and procedures for groups may be: All decisions should be made by consensus. Anyone may call time-out at any stage in order to review progress. The group starts and finishes on time. The first five minutes of every meeting are spent milling around the room and chatting. The group follows an agenda Members take on functional roles like timekeeper, summarizer, and so on each member has a maximum time-limit for contributions.

Structure

When a group comes together for the first time and begins to interact, various differences between the members begin to appear: differences in status, influence, role, ability, and so on. The pattern of relationships that is thus established is known as the group structure. The pattern will, of course, change according to the nature of the task or the stage of discussion and the most influential person for one purpose may not be so for another. A structure that emerges in these ways is known as the invisible structure. A visible structure exists when the group agrees a division of labour, roles, and responsibilities, in order to get essential tasks performed. You could for instance distribute a set of roles to the group: initiating, giving and asking for information, giving and asking for reactions, restating and giving examples, confronting and reality testing, clarifying, synthesising and summarising, gate-keeping and expediting, timekeeping, evaluating and diagnosing, standard setting, sponsoring and encouraging. Such a method, though it is valued by some students, may be too socially demanding. A structure that encourages participation is pyramiding, a sequence of stages involving individual work, followed by discussion in pairs, then in fours, and a final session with the whole group.

Aims

Aims are implicit in most, if not all, groups though they are not often thought about and even less often discussed. These aims may be intrinsic in nature: "to discuss environmental pollution", or they may be extrinsic: "to make decisions about the course" or "to prepare for an examination". Aims also have social and task dimensions. Social aims include "to develop group loyalty and a sense of belonging" while task aims refer to qualities like judging ideas and checking progress. They are complementary. If the social dimension is not given due regard, students may feel cool about the group and have no sense of commitment. If the task dimension is missing they may become dissatisfied and feel frustrated at not achieving anything worthwhile. The social dimension has an additional educational scope. It includes qualities like self-awareness, the ability to work independently yet cooperatively in a team-all important aspects of the students' personal development.

Members of any group are likely to have their own personal and, sometimes, hidden aims and these may have little to do with the aims of the group as a whole, where these are known. Sometimes these personal aims, for example, impressing the tutor, scoring off another student, wanting approval of the group, capitalising on other students' ideas, may undermine the intended aims of the tutor. It is the tutor's job to somehow accommodate or mobilise the personal aims within the overall aims; and there is usually no better way to do this than through as open discussion as possible of all the aims arising from the group.

Tasks

If an aim is to represent a bit more than good intentions, it must be related to a corresponding task. The task specifies the activity in which the students individually or collectively are engaged. It is what must be done in order to achieve an aim. Not enough attention or imagination is usually given to specifying tasks in group teaching. The tendency is to assume the task is simply one of discussing a topic. Yet a wealth of stimulating tasks, or their key verbs, may easily be found if one of the taxonomies of educational objectives is referred to, for example: identify, contrast, predict, select, differentiate, organise, judge, criticise, and so on.

Climate

Though it may be difficult to define, the social climate in which group discussion takes place is of enormous importance, and is usually fairly easy to sense. The tutor has an important role to play in creating a climate in which warmth, spontaneity, openness, and informality exist. A positive climate can not only release more energy and imagination in a group, but affect the way students feel about belonging to it.

Group Conformity

As a member of a group, you desire acceptance by the group. Because of your desire for acceptance, you are susceptible to conforming to the group's norms. Therefore, the conformity means adjusting one's behavior to align with the norms of the group. There is considerable evidence that groups can place strong pressures on individual members to change their attitudes and behaviors to conform to the group's standard.

The group influences the members to conform themselves by changing their behaviour and belief. It happens as a result of a real or imagined group pressure.

Influencing Sources

Group Factors

- Consensus
- Cohesion
- Characteristics of source
- Member in the group

- Interdependency
- Communication characteristics

Incentives

- Goals
- Rewards
- Punishments

Situation

- Presence of others
- New tasks
- Complex tasks
- Ambiguity

Group Deviance

Dentler and Erikson "The Functions of Deviance in Groups". In the early stages of a group's development, a group structures the range of behavior of its members (which behaviors are okay and which aren't), and in doing so defines some behaviors as deviant. D and E say that to a certain extent the group will accept and sustain this deviant behavior rather than eliminate it because it is functional and is a normal part of group formation.

Functions of Deviance

Deviant behavior functions to help maintain group equilibrium.

The presence of deviance in a group functions to maintain a group's normative boundaries.

- a group defines itself in relation to central norms which the group develops (e.g. the behaviors it will accept), and in reference to the range of possibilities it makes available.
- a norm becomes most evident in its occasional violation,
- so a group can maintain its stability by controlling the

balance of rewards for conformity and punishment for deviance.

- Thus, deviance is functional because by violating group norms the deviant person shows the rest of the group what behaviors are not appropriate, thus helping to define group norms and the range of acceptable group behavior - establishes group boundaries.
- Because deviance can serve a function, a group will maintain the deviant person until his or her behavior becomes so pronounced as to endanger group solidarity.
- This is because the deviant person increases group conformity, reaffirms its norms, and increases group solidarity.

Group Decision Making

Many managers like to believe that they are accomplished in such group decision-making processes as action planning, goal setting and problem-solving. However, their ability to implement such techniques effectively is often hindered by their lack of understanding of the dynamics of these group decision-making processes. As a result, these managers often end up perpetuating problems that they themselves create through their insensitivity to the needs of other group members. Hence, instead of achieving a consensus, such managers only serve their own interests by leading the group to situations such as decision-making by lack of response or by authority role. Sometimes, they lead the group toward decision-making by minority rule or by majority role, as the case might be. The better way to achieve consensus would be for them to track how decisions are made and ensure that they are achieved by true consultation.

Decision By Lack of Response

The most common—and perhaps least visible—group decision-making method is that in which someone suggests an idea and, before anyone else has said anything about it, someone else suggests another idea, until the group eventually finds one it will act on. This results in shooting down the original idea before it has really been considered. All the ideas that are bypassed have, in a sense, been rejected by the group. But because the "rejections" have been simply a common decision not to support the idea, the proposers feel that their suggestions have "plopped." The floors of most conference rooms are littered with "plops."

Decision by Authority Rule

Many groups start out with - or quickly set up - a power structure that makes it clear that the chairman (or someone else in authority) will make the ultimate decision. The group can generate ideas and hold free discussion, but at any time the chairman may say that, having heard the discussion, he or she has decided upon a given plan. Whether this method is effective depends a great deal upon whether the chairman is a sufficiently good listener to have culled the right information on which to make the decision. Furthermore, if the group must also implement the decision, then the authority-rule method produces a bare minimum of involvement by the group (basically, they will do it because they have to, not necessarily because they want to). Hence it undermines the potential quality of implementation.

Decision by Minority Rule

One of the most-often-heard complaints of group members is that they feel "railroaded" into some decision. Usually, this feeling results from one, two, or three people employing tactics that produce action—and therefore must be considered decisions—but which are taken without the consent of the majority.

A single person can "enforce" a decision, particularly if he or she is in some kind of chairmanship role, by not giving opposition an opportunity to build up. For example, the manager might consult a few members on even the most seemingly insignificant step and may get either a negative or positive reaction. The others have remained silent. If asked how they concluded there was agreement, chances are they will say, "Silence means consent, doesn't it? Everyone has a chance to voice opposition." If the group members are interviewed later, however, it sometimes is discovered that an actual majority was against a given idea, but that each one hesitated to speak up because she thought that all the other silent ones were for it. They too were trapped by "silence means consent."

Finally, a common form of minority rule is for two or more members to come to a quick and powerful agreement on a course of action, then challenge the group with a quick, "Does anyone object?," and, if no one raises their voice within two seconds, they proceed with "Let's go ahead then." Again the trap is the assumption that silence means consent.

Decision by Majority Rule *(Voting and Polling)*

More familiar decision-making procedures are often taken for granted as applying to any group situation because they reflect our political system. One simple version is to poll everyone's opinion following some period of discussion. If the majority of participants feel the same way, it is often assumed that is the decision. The other method is the more formal one of stating a clear alternative and asking for votes in favor of it, votes against it, and abstentions.

On the surface, this method seems completely sound, but surprisingly often it turns out that decisions made by this method are not well implemented, even by the group that made the decision. What is wrong? Typically, it turns out that two kinds of psychological barriers exist:

First, the minority members often feel there was an insufficient period of discussion for them to really get their point of view across; hence they feel misunderstood and sometimes resentful.

Second, the minority members often feel that the voting has created two camps within the group and that these camps are now in a win-lose competition: The minority feels that their camp lost the first round, but that it is just a matter of time until it can regroup, pick up some support and win the next time a vote comes up.

In other words, voting creates coalitions, and the preoccupation of the losing coalition is not how to implement what the majority wants, but how to win the next battle. If voting is to be used, the group must be sure that it has created a climate in which members feel they have had their day in court - and where all members feel obligated to go along with the majority decision.

The Better Way

Because there are time constraints in coming to a group decision and because there is no perfect system, a decision by consensus is one of the most effective methods. Unfortunately, it is one of the most time- consuming techniques for group decision-making. It is also quite important to understand that consensus is not the same thing as unanimity. Rather, it is a state of affairs where communications have been sufficiently open (and the group climate has been sufficiently supportive) to make everyone in the group feel that they have had their fair chance to influence the decision. Someone then tests for the "sense of the meeting," carefully avoiding formal procedures like voting. If there is a clear alternative to which most members subscribe and if those who oppose it feel they have had their chance to influence, then a consensus exists. Operationally, it would be defined by the fact that those members who would not take the majority alternative nevertheless understand it clearly and are prepared to support it in deference to any others that are probably about as good.

In order to achieve such a condition, time must be allowed by the group for all members to state their opposition—and to state it fully enough to get the feeling that others really do understand them. This condition is essential if they are later to free themselves of the preoccupation that they could have gotten their point of view across if others had understood what they really had in mind. Only by careful listening to the opposition can such feelings be forestalled, thereby allowing effective group decisions to be reached. Of course, recognizing the several types of group decision-making is only part of the process. Managers must be specific in their approach to the one that is best in their own situation.

Steps in Group Decision-making Process

Identify the Problem

Tell specifically what the problem is and how you experience it. Cite specific examples. "Own" the problem as yours – and solicit the help of others in solving it, rather than implying that it's someone else's problem that they ought to solve. Keep in mind that if it were someone else's problem, they would be bringing it up for discussion. In the identification phase of problem-solving, avoid references to solutions. This can trigger disagreement too early in the process and prevent the group from ever making meaningful progress. Once there seems to be a fairly clear understanding of what the problem is, this definition should be written in very precise language. If a group is involved, it should be displayed on a flip chart or chalkboard.

Clarify the Problem

This step is most important when working with a group of people. If the problem is not adequately clarified so that everyone views it the same, the result will be that people will offer solutions to different problems. To clarify the problem, ask someone in the group to paraphrase the problem as they understand it. Then ask the other group members if they see it essentially the same way. Any differences must be resolved before going any further. In clarifying the problem, ask the group the following questions: Who is involved with the problem? Who is likely to be affected? Can we get them involved in solving the problem? Who legitimately or logically should be included in the decision? Are there others who need to be consulted prior to a decision? These questions assume that commitment from those involved (and affected by the problem) is desirable in implementing any changes or solutions. The best way to get this commitment is to include those involved and affected by the problem in determining solutions.

Analyze the Cause

Any deviation from what should be is produced by a cause or interaction of causes. In order to change "what is" to "what is wanted," it is usually necessary to remove or neutralize the cause in some way. This calls for precise isolation of the most central or basic cause (or causes) of the problem and requires close analysis of the problem to clearly separate the influencing from the non-influencing factors. This is probably an easier process to follow when dealing with problems involving physical things rather than with interpersonal or social issues. Typically, interpersonal and social problems are more likely to spring from a dynamic constellation of causes that will be more difficult to solve if the causes are only tackled one at a time. Still, whether dealing with physical or social problems, it is important to seek those causes that are most fundamental in producing the problem. Don't waste energy on causes that have only a tangential effect.

Solicit Alternative Solutions to the Problem

This step calls for identifying as many solutions to the problem as possible before discussing the specific advantages and disadvantages of each. What happens frequently in problem-solving is that the first two or three suggested solutions are debated and discussed for the full time allowed for the entire problem-solving session. As a result, many worthwhile ideas are never identified or considered. By identifying many solutions, a superior idea often surfaces that reduces or even eliminates the need for discussing details of more debatable issues. These solutions may be logical attacks at the cause or they may be creative solutions that need not be rational. Therefore, it is important at this step to limit the time spent discussing any one solution and to concentrate instead on announcing as many as possible.

Selecting One or More Alternatives for Action

Before selecting specific alternatives for action, it is advisable to identify criteria the desired solution must meet. This can eliminate unnecessary discussion and help focus the group toward the solution (or solutions) that will most likely work. At this point, it becomes necessary to look for and discuss the advantages and disadvantages of options that appear viable. The task is for the group members to come to a mutual agreement on which solutions to actually put into action. It is desirable for positive comments to be encouraged (and negative comments to be ignored or even discouraged) about any of the solutions. One solution should be the best, of course, but none should be labeled as a "bad idea."

Plan for Implementation

This requires looking at the details that must be performed by someone for a solution to be effectively activated. Once the required steps are identified, it means assigning these to someone for action: it also means setting a time for completion. Not to be forgotten when developing the implementation plan: Who needs to be informed of this action?

Clarify the Contract

This is to insure that everyone clearly understands what the agreement is that people will do to implement a solution. It is a summation and restatements of what people have agreed to do and when it is expected they will have it done. It rules out possible misinterpretation of expectations.

The Action Plan

Plans are only intellectual exercises unless they are transformed into action. This calls for people assigned responsibility for any part of the plan to carry out their assignments according to the agreed upon contract. This is the phase of problem- solving that calls for people to do what they have said they would do.

Provide for Evaluation and Accountability

After the plan has been implemented and sufficient time has elapsed for it to have an effect, the group should reconvene and discuss evaluation and accountability. Have the agreed upon actions been carried out? Have people done what they said they would do? If they have not accomplished their assignments, it is possible that they ran into trouble that must be considered. Or it may be that they simply need to be reminded or held accountable for not having lived up to their end of the contract. Once the actions have been completed, it is necessary to assess their effectiveness. Did the solution work? If not, can a revision make it work? What actions are necessary to implement changes?

Techniques for Managing Group Dynamics

There are many techniques to assist the facilitator in managing the agenda and group dynamics. The following are just a few of the more common and frequently used techniques available to the facilitator. Be creative and adaptive. Different situations require different techniques. With experience will come an understanding of how they affect group dynamics and when is the best time to use them.

Equalizing Participation

The facilitator is responsible for the fair distribution of attention during meetings. Facilitators call the attention of the group to one speaker at a time. The grammar school method is the most common technique for choosing the next speaker. The facilitator recognizes each person in the order in which hands are raised. Often, inequities occur because the attention is dominated by an individual or class of individuals.

Listing

To help the discussion flow more smoothly, those who want to speak can silently signal the facilitator, who would add the person's name to a list of those wishing to speak, and call on them in that order.

Stacking

If many people want to speak at the same time, it is useful to ask all those who would like to speak to raise their hands. Have them count off, and then have them speak in that order. At the end of the stack, the facilitator might call for another stack or try another technique.

Pacing

The pace or flow of the meeting is the responsibility of the facilitator. If the atmosphere starts to become tense, choose techniques which encourage balance and cooperation. If the meeting is going slowly and people are becoming restless, suggest a stretch or rearrange the agenda.

Checking the Process

If the flow of the meeting is breaking down or if one person or small group seems to be dominating, anyone can call into question the technique being used and suggest an alternative.

Silence

If the pace is too fast, if energies and tensions are high, if people are speaking out of turn or interrupting one another, it is appropriate for anyone to suggest a moment of silence to calm and refocus energy.

Taking a Break

In the heat of discussion, people are usually resistant to interrupting the flow to take a break, but a wise facilitator knows, more often than not, that a five-minute break will save a frustrating half hour or more of circular discussion and fruitless debate.

Call for Consensus

The facilitator, or any member recognized to speak by the facilitator, can call for a test for consensus. To do this, the facilitator asks if there are any unresolved concerns, which remain unaddressed.

Summarizing

The facilitator might choose to focus what has been said by summarizing. The summary might be made by the facilitator, the note taker, or anyone else appropriate. This preempts a common problem, in which the discussion becomes circular, and one after another, speakers repeat each other.

Reformulating the Proposal

After a long discussion, it sometimes happens that the proposal becomes modified without any formal decision. The facilitator needs to recognize this and take time to reformulate the proposal with the new information, modifications, or deletions. Then the proposal is presented to the group so that everyone can be clear about what is being considered. Again, this might be done by the facilitator, the note taker, or anyone else.

Stepping Out of Role

If the facilitator wants to become involved in the discussion or has strong feelings about a particular agenda item, the facilitator can step out of the role and participate in the discussion, allowing another member to facilitate during that time.

Passing the Clipboard

Sometimes information needs to be collected during the meeting. To save time, circulate a clipboard to collect this information. Once collected, it can be entered into the written record and/or presented to the group by the facilitator.

Polling

The usefulness of polling within consensus is primarily clarification of the relative importance of several issues. It is an especially useful technique when the facilitator is confused or uncertain about the status of a proposal and wants some clarity to be able to suggest what might be the next process technique.

Censoring

If someone speaks out of turn consistently, the facilitator warns the individual at least twice that if the interruptions do not stop, the facilitator will declare that person censored. This means the person will not be permitted to speak for the rest of this agenda item. If the interrupting behaviour has exhibited over several agenda items, then the censoring could be for a longer period of time.

Expulsion

If an individual still acts very disruptively, the facilitator may confront the behaviour. Ask the person to explain the reasons for this behaviour, how it is in the best interest of the group, how it relates to the group's purpose, and how it is in keeping with the goals and principles. If the person is unable to answer

REFERENCES

Adolphs, R. (1999). "Social cognition and the human brain." *Trends in Cognitive Sciences, 3:* 469-479.

Browning, L. and Colman, A. (2004). Evolution of coordinated alternating reciprocity in repeated dyadic games. *Journal of Theoretical Biology, 229:* 549-557.

Buchanan, D. and Huczynski, A. (2004) *Organisational Behaviour: An Introductory Text,* 5th ed., Harlow: FT/Prentice-Hall

Buss, D. M. (2007). *Evolutionary psychology: The new science of the mind* (3rd ed.). Boston: Allyn and Bacon.

Fincham, R. and Rhodes, P. (2005) Principles of organizational behaviour. 4th ed. Oxford: Oxford University Press.

Gibson, J., Ivanchevich, J., Donnelly, J. and Konopaske, R. (2006) *Organizations: behavior, Structure, Processes.* 12th ed. McGraw-Hill

Hardy, C. L., and Van Vugt, M. (2006). Nice guys finish first: The competitive altruism hypothesis. *Personality and Social Psychology Bulletin, 32:* 1402-1413.

Huczynski, A. and Buchanan, D. (2007) *Organisational Behaviour: An Introductory Text,* 6th ed., Harlow: FT/Prentice-Hall.

Kerr X., and Levine, X. (2008). The detection of social exclusion: Evolution and beyond. *Group Dynamics: Theory, Research, and Practice, 12,* 39-52.

Kinicki, A. and Kreitner, R. (2006) *Organizational Behavior: Key Concepts. Skills, and Best Practices.* 2nd ed. McGraw-Hill.

Luthans, F. (2005) *Organisational Behaviour.* (10th ed.), McGraw-Hill Irwin.

Mullins, L. (2006) *Essentials of Organizational Behaviour.* Harlow: Prentice-Hall.

Mullins, L. (2007) *Management and Organizational Behaviour.* 8th ed. FT/Prentice-Hall.

Myers, D. (2005) *Social Psychology.* 8th ed. Boston: McGraw-Hill.

Nelson, D. and Quick, J. (2006) *Organizational Behavior: Foundations, Realities and Challenges*. 5th ed. Thomson South-Western.

Robbins, S. and Judge, T. (2008) Essentials of Organizational Behavior. 9th ed. New Jersey: Pearson/Prentice-Hall.

Robbins, S. (2005) *Organisational Behaviour: Concepts, Controversies and Applications*. 11th ed., New Jersey: Prentice-Hall.

Scott, P. (2005) Divisions of Labour. A Pearson Custom Publications

Stephen P. Robbins, (2003) *Organizational Behaviour*, 10th ed., Printice-Hall of India, New Delhi.

Thompson, P. and Warhurst, C. (ed), (2003) *Workplaces of the Future*. Palgrave: Macmillan,

Tuckman, B.W. and Jensen, M.A.C. (1977) Stages of small group development revisited. *Group andOrganizational Studies*, 2: 419-427.

Van Vugt, M., De Cremer, D., and Janssen, D. (2007). Gender differences in cooperation and competition: The male warrior hypothesis. *Psychological Science*, 18: 19–23.

17 Managing Conflict

> Common sense to most people is nothing more than their own opinions.
>
> – *William Hazlitt*

Meaning of Conflict

Conflict is a natural disagreement resulting from individuals or groups that differ in attitudes, beliefs, values or needs. It can also originate from past rivalries and personality differences. Other causes of conflict include trying to negotiate before the timing is right or before needed information is available.

Nature of Conflict

Conflict is when two or more values, perspectives and opinions are contradictory in nature and haven't been aligned or agreed about yet, including:

- Within yourself when you're not living according to your values;
- When your values and perspectives are threatened; or
- Discomfort from fear of the unknown or from lack of fulfilment.

Conflict is inevitable and often good, for example, good teams always go through a "form, storm, norm and perform" period. Getting the most out of diversity means often-contradictory values, perspectives and opinions.

Conflict is a natural outcome of human interaction. Conflict exists whenever there is disagreement and derives from differences in attitudes, beliefs, and expectations. Conflict can result from differences in perception as to what has happened or what needs to be done. Whenever two or more people disagree about a decision or action, conflict exists. Conflict is inevitable because not all persons think alike. Not all persons hold the same values or priorities. Not all persons react to situations in the same manner. Those facts make conflict resolution virtually impossible.

Conflict is often needed. It:

- helps raise and address problems.
- energizes work to be on the most appropriate issues.
- helps people "be real", for example, it motivates them to participate.
- helps people learn how to recognize and benefit from their differences.

Conflict is not the same as discomfort. The conflict isn't the problem - it is when conflict is poorly managed that is the problem.

It is important to remember that conflict is not inherently destructive. In fact, some conflict is desirable. In a constructive mode, conflict can improve problem solving, clarify issues or expectations, increase participant involvement and commitment, and result in a better decision or outcome. If all faculties held the same views on every issue, final decisions and recommendations would not account for the full range of ramifications. If all faculties thought alike, departments would experience little change. Change that results in improvement typically grows out of conflict.

Types of Managerial Actions that Cause Workplace Conflicts

- Poor communications

  a) Employees experience continuing surprises, they aren't informed of new decisions, programs, etc.

  b) Employees don't understand reasons for decisions, they aren't involved in decision-making.

c) As a result, employees trust the "rumor mill" more than management.

- The alignment or the amount of resources is insufficient. There is:

  a) Disagreement about "who does what".

  b) Stress from working with inadequate resources.

- "Personal chemistry", including conflicting values or actions among managers and employees, for example:

  a) Strong personal natures don't match.

  b) We often don't like in others what we don't like in ourselves.

Symptoms of Conflict

Before conflict develops people may simply feel unhappy about colleagues or issues that are troubling them. You might notice the following symptoms:

- ***Motivation*** drops: fewer people volunteer to take on new tasks and there is little employee input at team meetings or briefings
- ***Behaviour*** changes: people start to make derogatory remarks towards each other and there are fewer social events organised
- ***Productivity*** falls: there are likely to be more queries and complaints if people are not cooperating with each other
- ***Sickness absence*** increases: unhappiness may lead to depression or stress
- ***Responses to staff attitude surveys or questionnaires*** indicate underlying dissatisfaction.

Factors of Conflict

Some factors that can impact how we respond to conflict are listed below with explanations of how these factors might affect us.

- *Gender*: Some of us were socialized to use particular conflict modes because of our gender. For example, some males, because they are male, were taught "always stand up to someone, and, if you have to fight, then fight." If one was socialized this way he will be more likely to use assertive conflict modes versus using cooperative modes.
- *Self-concept:* How we think and feel about ourselves affect how we approach conflict. Do we think our thoughts, feelings, and opinions are worth being heard by the person with whom we are in conflict?
- *Expectations*: Do we believe the other person or our team wants to resolve the conflict?
- *Situation*: Where is the conflict occurring, do we know the person we are in conflict with, and is the conflict personal or professional?
- *Position (Power)*: What is our power status relationship, (that is, equal, more, or less) with the person with whom we are in conflict?
- *Practice:* Practice involves being able to use all five conflict modes effectively, being able to determine what conflict mode would be most effective to resolve the conflict, and the ability to change modes as necessary while engaged in conflict.
- *Determining the best mode:* Through knowledge about conflict and through practice we develop a "conflict management understanding" and can, with ease and limited energy, determine what conflict mode to use with the particular person with whom we are in conflict.
- *Communication skills:* The essence of conflict resolution and conflict management is the ability to communicate effectively. People who have and use effective communication will resolve their conflicts with greater ease and success.
- *Life experiences*: As mentioned earlier, we often practice the conflict modes we saw our primary caretaker(s) use

unless we have made a conscious choice as adults to change or adapt our conflict styles. Some of us had great role models teach us to manage our conflicts and others of us had less-than-great role models. Our life experiences, both personal and professional, have taught us to frame conflict as either something positive that can be worked through or something negative to be avoided and ignored at all costs.

Conflict Managing Skills

There are five steps to managing conflict. These steps are:

- Analyze the conflict
- Determine management strategy
- Pre-negotiation
- Negotiation
- Post-negotiation

Analyze the Conflict

The first step in managing conflict is to analyze the nature and type of conflict. To do this, you'll find it helpful to ask questions.

Answers may come from your own experience, your partners or local media coverage. You may want to actually interview some of the groups involved. Additional information regarding analyzing conflicts can be found in the Guide to Information and Resources.

Determine Management Strategy

Once you have a general understanding of the conflict, the groups involved will need to analyze and select the most appropriate strategy. In some cases it may be necessary to have a neutral facilitator to help move the groups toward consensus.

Conflict Management Strategies

- Collaboration

- Compromise
- Competition
- Accommodation
- Avoidance

These strategies divided into three categories: *win/lose, lose/lose* and *win/win*.

Win/Lose

There are three types of win/lose strategies: competing, accommodating and dominating. In all win/lose strategies the participants believe that in all conflicts someone is going to win and someone must therefore lose.

- *Competing* is depicted by a high desire to satisfy one's own concerns and a low desire to satisfy the concerns of the other party. It is also characterized as a personalized view of conflict where there must be a winner and a loser. The competing strategy focuses on the person and not on the issues of the conflict or problem. Often, one's authority is used to win one's own way, which leads to one party being satisfied at the expense of the other.
- ***Accommodating*** is characterized by a low desire to satisfy one's own desires and a high desire to satisfy the desires of the other party. A person who uses this strategy feels the need to preserve a harmonious relationship at all costs. He wishes to be accepted by others to the point that he will give in to others' desires when they are in conflict with his own. Confrontation is seen as destructive and painful. People who are high accommodators generally have low self-esteem. They don't believe they have a right to their beliefs, ideas, or values. They also feel responsible for how others feel.
- ***Dominating*** is characterized by a low level of cooperativeness and a high level of aggression. Personal attacks are on others, not on the issues. The person who uses this strategy is driven by a need to be in control or

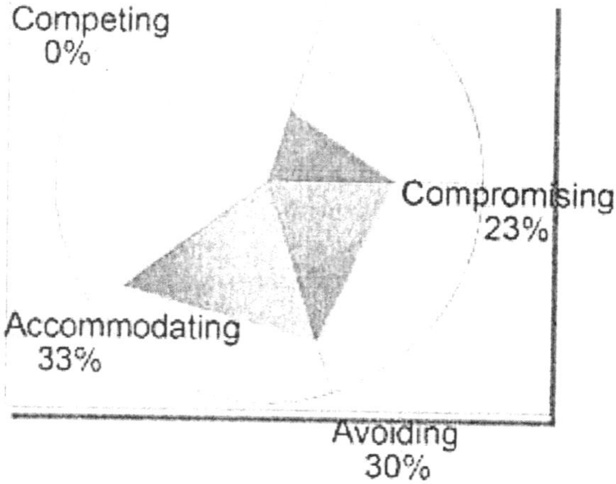

Fig. 17.1: Conflict Management Outcome

to control the behavior of others. He or she uses power and/or threats to win.

Lose/Lose

There are two types of lose/lose strategies: avoidance and compromising.

- ***Avoidance*** is characterized by a low level of cooperativeness and assertiveness. Conflict is seen as a useless and punishing experience. The avoidant person removes herself from the conflict both mentally (emotionally) and physically by literally sidestepping the disagreement and tension.

- ***Compromising*** is a widely used strategy characterized by a moderate desire to satisfy the concerns of oneself and a moderate desire to satisfy the concerns of the other party. Unfortunately, neither party is completely satisfied with the outcome. There is no direct confrontation of the issues and goals. The solution chosen is not the best, most effective choice. If compromise is a lose-lose strategy, why do people use it so often? And why do people feel such urgency about coming up with a solution right away?

To come up with a solution acceptable to all parties, questions have to be asked and feelings have to be explored. This requires effort, objectivity and risk-taking. The risks occur because when you ask someone about what he or she really wants and why, it may change you. And even though the change would be for the better, people often don't like to change.

Win/Win

There is only one type of win/win strategy: problem-solving. In problem-solving, both parties agree to an outcome that is acceptable.

There are five steps to the problem-solving process:

1. ***Identify the problem.*** It is important to identify the exact problem and its nature and who "owns" the problem. Keep in mind that we are not responsible for solving other people's problems. Pharmacists have an obligation to advise patients on medications and other health matters. But they cannot take responsibility when a patient consistently does not take their advice.

2. ***Identify all possible solutions.*** By brainstorming with others, multiple solutions to a problem are sought; parties understand that important decisions/solutions may take time; and all possible ideas must be expressed. Ideally in brainstorming, a relaxed atmosphere is desired, in which the problem is defined, all participants throw out as many ideas as they can, ideas are not criticized or ignored, and all ideas are recorded. Participants are striving for quantity at this point, not quality, and are free to seek combinations or improvements of ideas.

3. ***Decide which solution is best.*** After all the solutions have been identified, choose the one that is best for the problem at hand. Does this solution appeal to all?

4. ***Determine how to implement the solution.*** After choosing the best solution, decide on a plan of action for carrying it out.

5. ***Assess the outcome of the solution.*** Was it a win/win solution? Were both parties satisfied with the outcome? Could this problem have been prevented?

Pre-negotiation

To set the stage for effective negotiation, the groundwork must be laid. The following should occur prior to negotiation.

- *Initiation* - One partner raises the possibility of negotiation and begins the process. If no one is willing to approach the others to encourage them to reach an agreement, a trusted outsider could be brought in as a facilitator.
- *Assessment* - Conditions must be right for negotiation to be successful. Key players must be identified and invited. Each side must be willing to collaborate with the others. Reasonable deadlines and sufficient resources to support the effort must exist. Spokespersons for each group must be identified and involved. Parties need to determine which issues are negotiable and which are not.
- *Ground rules and agenda* - The groups must agree on ground rules for communication, negotiation and decision making. They should agree on the objectives of the negotiation process. An agenda of issues to be covered needs to be developed.
- *Organization* - Meeting logistics must be established, including agreed upon times and places. People must be contacted and encouraged to attend. Minutes must be taken so that information can be distributed before and after meetings.
- *Joint fact-finding* - The groups must agree on what information is relevant to the conflict. This should include what is known and not known about social and technical issues. Agreement is also needed on methods for generating answers to questions.

Negotiation

- *Interests* - When negotiating be sure to openly discuss interests, rather than stated positions. Interests include the reasons, needs, concerns and motivations underlying positions. Satisfaction of interests should be the common goal.

- *Options* - To resolve conflicts, concentrate on inventing options for satisfying interests. Do not judge ideas or favor any of the options suggested. Encourage creativity, not commitment.
- *Evaluation* - Only after the partners have finished listing options, should the options be discussed. Determine together which ideas are best for satisfying various interests.
- *Written agreement* - Document areas of agreement and disagreement to ensure common understanding. This helps ensure that agreements can be remembered and communicated clearly.
- *Commitment* - Every partner must be confident that the others will carry out their parts of the agreement. Discuss and agree upon methods to ensure partners understand and honor their commitments.
- ***When evaluating options*** - Use objective criteria for ranking ideas; Make trade-offs among different issues; and Combine different options to form acceptable agreements

Post-negotiation

Once negotiation is complete, the group will need to implement the decisions made. Some key steps include:

- *Ratification* - The partners must get support for the agreement from organizations that have a role to play in the agreement. These organizations should be partners and should have been involved in the previous steps. Each organization will need to follow its own procedures to review and adopt the agreement.
- *Implementation* - You and your partners' jobs are not done when you've reached agreement. Communication and collaboration should continue as the agreement is carried out. The partnership will need to have a plan to

monitor progress, document success, resolve problems, renegotiate terms and celebrate success.

- *Negotiation skills* -Negotiation is an important skill for coming to an agreement when conflicts develop at home, at work and when dealing with issues like those related to watershed management. When negotiating...

Separate People from the Problem

When negotiating, remember you're dealing with people who have their own unique needs, emotions and perceptions.

Some conflicts are based on differences in thinking and perceptions. These conflicts may exist mainly in peoples' minds. It helps for each party to put themselves into the other's shoes so they can understand each other's point of view. Identify and openly discuss differences in perceptions, being careful not to place blame. In addition, recognize and understand the other side's emotions as well as your own.

Interest vs. Position

People often confuse interests with positions. An interest may be reducing litter in roadside ditches. There are many possible ways of addressing this interest. One might be the position of mandatory recycling. Another position might be a deposit on bottles and cans. Still another could be organizing a clean-up day.

Focus on Interests, not Positions

Focusing on interests, rather than positions, makes it possible to come up with better agreements. Even when people stand on opposite positions, they usually have a few shared interests. It takes time and effort to identify interests. Groups may not even be clear about their own interests. It helps to write down each group's interests as they are discovered. It helps to ask why others take the positions or make the decisions they do. Partners will have multiple interests. Interests involving important human needs (such as security, economic well-being, a sense of belonging, recognition and control over one's life) are difficult to negotiate.

REFERENCES

Algert, N.E. (1996) "Conflict in the workplace" in *Proceedings: Women in Engineering Advocates Network*, Denver, Co., 123-127.

Algert, N.E. (2002). *The Center for Change and Conflict Resolution*, Bryan, TX: (979)775-5335 or e-mail cccr@bigfoot.com.

Algert, N.E., and Watson, K. (2002) *Conflict Management: Introductions for Individuals and Organizations*. Bryan, TX: (979)775-5335 or e-mail cccr@bigfoot.com.

Blake, R.R., and Mouton, J.S. (1964). *The Managerial Grid*. Houston: Gulf Publishing Co.

Bush, R. A., Baruch and Folger, J. P. (1994). *The Promise of Mediation*. San Francisco: Jossey-Bass Publishers.

Consulting Psychologists Press (CPP). *Thomas-Kilmann Conflict Mode Instrument*. Palo Alto, CA: (800)624-1765 or available on the World Wide Web at http://www.cpp-db.com.

Deetz, S. A., and Stevenson, S. L. (1986). *Managing Interpersonal Communication*. New York: Harper and Row Publishers.

Fisher, R., Ury, W., and Patton, B. (1991). *Getting to Yes: Negotiating Agreement Without Giving In* (2nd ed.). Penguin Books, and Deetz, S. A., and Stevenson, S. L. (1986). *Managing Interpersonal Communication*. New York: Harper and Row Publishers.

Jaworski, B. J. and Kohli, A. K. (1993) Market Orientation: Antecedents and Consequences *Journal of Marketing* 57(2): 53-70.

Johnson, D.W., and Johnson, F.P. (2000) *Joining together: Group Theory and Group Skills* (7th ed.), Boston, Allyn and Bacon.

Johnson, D.W., Johnson, R.T., and Holubec, E.J. (1986) *Circles of Learning: Cooperation in the Classroom* (rev. ed.), Edina, MN: Interaction Book Co.

Katzenbach, J.R., and Smith, D.K. (1992) *Wisdom of Teams*, Harvard Business School Press.

Lambert, J., and Myers, S. (1999) *50 Activities for Conflict Resolution*. Amherst, MA: HR Development Press.

Moore, C., "How Mediation Works" in *The Mediation Process: Practical Strategies for Resolving Conflict*.

Pondy, L. R. (1967) Organizational Conflict: Concepts and Models *Administrative Science Quarterly* 12(2): 296-320.

Putnam (1994). "Beyond third-party role: disputes and managerial intervention," *Employee Responsibilities and Rights J.* (7:1).

Raudsepp, E. (2002) "Hone Listening Skills To Boost Your Career," available on the World Wide Web at http://www.careerjournal.com/myc/ climbingladder/ 20021224-raudsepp.html, accessed on 28 January 2003.

Robert, M. (1982). *Managing Conflict From the Inside Out* (pp. 119-128). University Associates. Excellent suggestions are also provided on how to manage conflict among groups

Smith, K.A. (2000) *Project management and teamwork.* New York: McGraw-Hill BEST series.

alton, R. E. (1987). *Managing Conflict: Interpersonal Dialogue and Third-Party Roles* (2nd ed.) (p. 108). Addison-Wesley Publishing Company.

Winslade, J., and Monk, G. (2000). *Narrative Mediation: A New Approach to Conflict Resolution.* San Francisco: Jossey-Bass Publishers.

18 Authority, Power and Influence

A person without a purpose is like a ship without a rudder.

- *Thomas Carlyle*

Authority

The organizational structure provides the framework for the formal distribution of authority. Formalization is the degree to which tasks are standardized and rules and regulations govern employee behavior. It influences the amount of discretion an employee has over his or her job. In an organization with high degrees of formalization, job descriptions and policies provide clear direction. Where formalization is low, employees have a great deal of freedom in deciding how thy conduct their work. Within the same organization, different departments may have different degrees of formalization. For example, in a hospital, doctors have freedom in selecting treatments, drugs, and methods for treating patients. However, the hospital physical plant staff has a strict schedule for cleaning buildings, mowing lawns, and maintaining the facilities. Authority is the legitimate power of a manager to direct subordinates to take action within the scope of the manager's position. Formal authority in the organization can be traced all the way back to the U.S. constitutional right to own property. The owner of the organization has the authority to make decisions. For example, entrepreneurial firms have an informal arrangement of employees and centralization of decision-making authority, the owner.

Forms of Authority

Three forms of authority are line authority, staff authority, and team authority (Fig. 18.1).

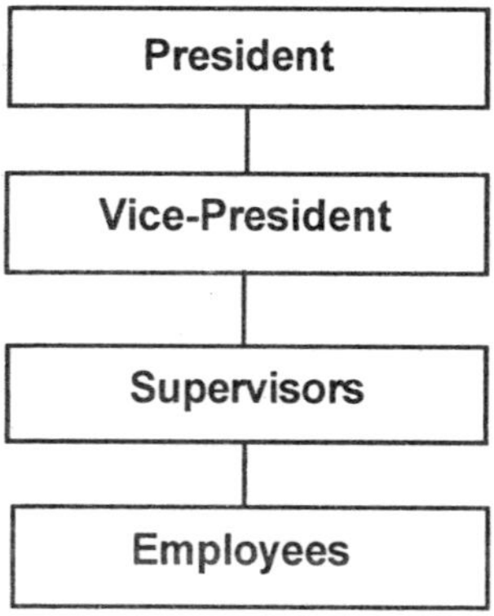

Fig. 4.4: Line Aothority: Chain of Command

Line Authority

Line authority is direct manager's authority from superior to subordinate. Authority flows in a direct chain of command from the top of the company to the bottom. Chain of command is an unbroken line of reporting relationships that extends through the entire organization that defines the formal decision-making structure. It helps employees know to whom they are accountable, and whom to go to with a problem. Line departments are directly linked to the production and sales of specific products. Managers - in line departments, such as marketing and production - give direct orders, evaluate performance, and reward or punish those employees who work for them. Unity of command within the chain states that each person in an organization should take orders from and reports to only one person. This helps prevent conflicting demands being placed on employees by more than one boss. However, the trend toward employee empowerment, fueled by advances in technology and changes in design from downsizing and reengineering have tempered the importance of being accountable to only one superior. Span of control refers to the number of employees that should be placed under the direction of one manager. Spans within effective organizations vary greatly. The actual number depends on the amount of complexity and the level of specialization. In general, a wide span of control is possible with better-trained, more experienced, and committed employees.

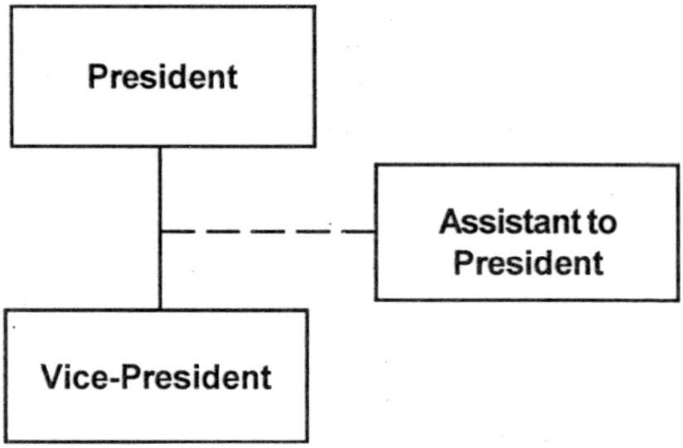

Fig. 4.5: Staff Authority

Staff Authority

Staff authority is more limited authority to advise. It is authority that is based on expertise and which usually involves advising line managers. Staff members are advisers and counselors who aid line departments in making decisions but do not have the authority to make final decisions. Staff managers help line departments decide what to do and how to do it. They coordinate and provide technical assistance or advice to all advisors, such as accounting, human resources, information technology, research, advertising, public relations, and legal services.

Team Authority

Team authority is granted to committees or work teams involved in an organization's daily operations. Work teams are groups of operating employees empowered to plan and organize their own work and to perform that work with a minimum of supervision. Team-Based structures organize separate functions into a group based on one overall objective. Empowered employees create their own schedules, design their own processes, and are held responsible for outcomes. This facilitates efficiencies in work process, and the ability to detect and react to changes in the environment. Employees with the skills and knowledge to manage more than one specialized task are able to promptly provide customers with quality products and services. Cross-functionally training team members allows any member to perform a variety of problem-solving tasks.

Power

In addition to authority, managers have more personal sources of power to draw upon for getting things done. Everyone has power in one form or another and it is by exercising this power that organizations get things accomplished. Managers who are capable of achieving their objectives independently of others are said to possess strength. When these "strong" managers involve and incorporate others into their plans and activities they are making use of power, and in fact increasing the total amount of power available to incorporate into a particular situation or problem. Involving employees in setting objectives and making decisions as it relates to their jobs empowers everyone, and results in greater job satisfaction and commitment, as well as increased productivity. Empowering employees provides them with greater autonomy.

Power is the ability to exert influence in the organization beyond authority, which is derived from position. The manager's personal power could include job knowledge, personal influence, interpersonal skills, and ability to get results, empathetic ability, persuasive ability, and physical strength. J.P. French and B. Raven ("The Bases of Social Power" in *Studies in Social Power*, edited by D. Cartwright, Institute for Social Research, 1959, pp. 150-167) identify six sources of power: legitimate, coercive, reward, expert, referent, and information. Legitimate power is a result of the position a person holds in the organization hierarchy. This position power is broader than the ability to reward and punish, as members need to accept the authority of the position. Coercive power is the threat of sanctions. It is dependent on fear and includes, but is not limited to the ability to dismiss, assign undesirable work, or restriction of movement. Reward power results in people doing what is asked because they desire positive benefits or rewards. Rewards can be anything a person values (praise, raises, and promotions). Expert power comes from expertise, skill, or knowledge. Referent power refers to a person who has desirable resources or personal traits. It results in admiration and the desire to emulate. Information power is based upon the persuasiveness or content of a communication and is independent of the influencing individual.

Power is the ability to get others to change their behavior even if they do not wish to do so. There are five bases of power defined by French and Raven (1960):

- Reward power: control over valued resources.
- Coercive power: ability to inflict punishment, possibly physical.
- Expert power: superior knowledge.
- Legitimate power: formal rank or position.
- Referent power: when people want to be like you.

Ten Types of Power

Several types of power can influence the outcome of a negotiation. We emphasize the word "can," because if you have power but don't use it, the power adds no value to the negotiation.

Position

Some measure of power is conferred on the basis of one's formal position in an organization. For example, a marketing manager can influence the decisions that affect the marketing department. However, the marketing manager has little power to influence the decisions that affect the finance department.

Knowledge or Expertise

People who have knowledge or expertise can wield tremendous power. Of course, knowledge in itself is not powerful.

It is the use of knowledge and expertise that confers power. Thus, you could be an incredibly bright person and still be powerless.

Character or Ethics

The more trustworthy individuals are, the more power they have in negotiations. The big issue here is whether they do what they say they are going to do—even when they no longer feel like doing it.

Rewards

People who are able to bestow rewards or perceived rewards hold power. Supervisors, with their ability to give raises, hold power over employees. Money can have power. But money, like anything else, holds very little power if it is not distributed.

Punishment

Those who have the ability to create a negative outcome for a counterpart have the power of punishment. Managers who have the authority to reprimand and fire employees hold this type of power. State troopers and highway patrol officers who have the ability to give out speeding tickets also have this power.

Gender

Dealing with someone of the opposite sex can confer power. We have videotaped many negotiation case studies in which the turning point came when a woman casually touched a man's hand or arm to make her point.

Powerlessness

In some instances, giving up all power can be very powerful. If a kidnapper threatens a hostage with death enough times, the hostage may just challenge the kidnapper to go ahead and kill him. At the point that the hostage gives up power, or control over his own death, the kidnapper actually loses power.

Charisma or Personal Power

When we ask participants in our seminars for examples of leaders who have had charisma or personal power, invariably the names of Mother Teresa, John F. Kennedy, and Ronald Reagan come up. When we ask, "What do all three of these leaders have in common?" participants usually respond, "Passion and confidence in what they believe in."

Lack of interest or desire

In negotiations, as in many other areas of life, the side with the least interest in what is being negotiated holds the most power. If you are buying a house and you really do not care if you purchase the house you are currently negotiating for or the one down the street, you will most likely hold more power in the negotiation—unless, of course, the sellers could care less if they sell the house today or live in it for another ten years!

Craziness

This may sound funny, but bizarre or irrational behavior can confer a tremendous amount of power. Every organization has someone who blows up or behaves irrationally when confronted with problems. Those who have been exposed to this type of behavior tend to avoid such individuals. As a result, these individuals are not given many tasks to accomplish because others are afraid to ask them.

Influence

Influence is simply the capacity to effect a choice made. In other words anything that will value or devalue a certain choice is an influence. As an example if I'm hungry and thinking of stopping someplace to get something to eat I will be influenced by the type of restaurants I come across. If there is nothing but taco stands I may be less likely to indulge my whim. An important factor here is that influence is a purely internal equation. The influences have no inherent value but instead are determined in so much as they play on the variable psychologies of the observer. One person may find taco stands an incentive to stop while the next wouldn't touch them.

Power on the other hand is a totally different matter. Power over an individual is the capacity to make their decisions for them. An individual's only inherent power is the ability to make their own decisions. Giving that up is how power is ceded to others. As an example as a condition of employment I have given tacit agreement that I will do what my boss says while on the job. I have surrendered aspects of my ability to decide things for myself. My boss has power over me. Power then is not purely internal as with influence. Power is not filtered by the individual psychology. If my boss tells me one day to work on job x then I do that. Its not a matter of influencing my choices but rather making them for me. Naturally I can withdraw that power by forfeiting my job.

Self Concept Influences on Behavior

The structure of the self concept may be thought of as a relatively stable set of cognitions that provide the basis for the expectancies, instrumentalities, and valences in instrumental or calculative motivation. However, there is also an expressive component of the self concept, which refers to how an individual processes information (feedback, observations, etc.) and uses the structure of the self concept to filter incoming information and translate this information into action. Much of the work in motivation relies heavily on cognitive models of behavior, and while many behaviors are the result of thought processes that are open to the individual's conscious inspection, other behaviors are the result of a process that is not entirely understood or conscious to the individual. We will refer to these acognitive processes, as the expressive component of the self concept. Both the expressive or acognitive processes, as well as the cognitive processes, are important in understanding the link between the self concept and behavior.

The Anxiety of Influence

On the surface of things, the concept of influence seems straightforward. An artist trying to define a space for himself or herself under the weight of tradition is inspired by precursors. She or he selects elements that are useful or admired, interpolates them with implicit commentary of his or her own, and arrives at an "original" production that nevertheless grasps what has gone before. Influence is pervasive and inescapable, even if the artist is a revolutionary and acknowledges the past only to condemn it. In this way history in the arts makes progress.

REFERENCES

Adam-Smith, D. and Peacock, A. (1994) *Cases in Orgasational Behaviour*. London: Pitman.

Bennett, R. (1997) *Organizational Behavior*. 3rd ed. London: Pitman.

Cohen, A. *et al.* (1995) *Effective Behaviour in Organisations: Cases, Concepts, and student Experiences*. 6th ed. Irwin/McGraw-Hill.

Cowling, A., Stanworth, M., Bennett, R., Curran, J. and Lyons, P. (1993) *Behavioural sciences for managers*. 2nd ed. London: Edward Arnold.

Falbraith, J. (1977) *Organization design*, Reading, MA: Addision-Wesley.

Fincham, R. and Rhodes, P. (1996) *The individual, work and organization: behavioral studies for business and management*. 2nd ed. Oxford: Oxford University Press.

Gordon, J. (1993) *A diagnostic approach to organizational behaviour*. 4th ed. Boston: Allyn and Bacon.

Greenberg, J. and Baron, R. (1993) *Behavior in Organizations: Understanding and Managing the Human side of Work*. 4th ed. Boston: Allyn and Bacon

Henry L. Tosi, John R. Rizzo, Stephen J. Carroll, (1998) *Organizational Behaviour – A Comprehensive Mannual*, Becon Books, New Delhi.

Luthans, F. (1992) *Organisational behaviour*. 6th ed. McGraw-Hill.

Macionis, J. and Plummer, K. (1997) *Sociology: A Global Introduction*. New York: Prentice-Hall.

Mullins, L. (1996) *Management and Organizational Behaviour*. 4th ed. FT/Prentice-Hall.

Pfeffer, J. (1981) *Power in organizations*, Boston, Pitman Publishing.

Plender, J. (1997) *A Stake in the future: the Stakeholding Solution*, Nicholas Breadley Publishing

Pugh, D. (1997) *Organization theory: selected readings*. 4th ed. London: Penguin books.

Robbins, S. (1998) *Organisational Behaviour: Concepts, Controversies and Applications.* 8th ed. New Jersey: Prentice-Hall.

Rollinson, , D. and Edwards, D. and Broadfield, A. (1998) *Organisational behaviour analysis: an integrated approach.* Harlow: Addison Wesley

Stephen P.Robbins, *Organizational Behaviour,* 10th ed., Printice-Hall of India Private Limited, New Delhi, 2003.

Tyson, S. and Jackson, T. (1992) *The Essence of Organizational Behavior.* New York: Prentice-Hall.

Vecchio, R. (1995) *Organisational Behaviour.* 3rd ed. The Dryden Press.

Weiss, J. (1996) *Organisational Behavior and Change: Managing Diversity, Cross-cultural Dynamics and Ethics.* New York: West Publishing.

19 Work Stress and Yoga

"Nothing gives one person so much advantage over another as to remain always cool and unruffled under all circumstances." – *Thomas Jefferson*

Stress is the "wear and tear" our bodies experience as we adjust to our continually changing environment; it has physical and emotional effects on us and can create positive or negative feelings. As a positive influence, stress can help compel us to action; it can result in a new awareness and an exciting new perspective. As a negative influence, it can result in feelings of distrust, rejection, anger, and depression, which in turn can lead to health problems such as headaches, upset stomach, rashes, insomnia, ulcers, high blood pressure, heart disease, and stroke. With the death of a loved one, the birth of a child, a job promotion, or a new relationship, we experience stress as we readjust our lives. In so adjusting to different circumstances, stress will help or hinder us depending on how we react to it.

Definition of Stress

Stress is your body's way of responding to any kind of demand. It can be caused by both good and bad experiences. When people feel stressed by something going on around them, their bodies react by releasing chemicals into the blood. These chemicals give people more energy and strength, which can be a good thing if their stress is caused by physical danger. But this can also be a bad thing, if their stress is in response to something emotional and there is no outlet for this extra energy and strength.

This class will discuss different causes of stress, how stress affects you, the difference between 'good' or 'positive' stress and 'bad' or 'negative' stress, and some common facts about how stress affects people today.

Selye and Levi have defined stress as a non-specific, conventional phytogenetic basic response pattern, the primary function of which is to prepare the body for physical activity such as fight or flight (this is eustress). If, however, the subject lacks the means of resorting either to fight or flight, i.e. of relieving the stress reaction, eustress develops into distress, which manifests in the form of psychosomatic symptoms or disorders. There are two types of stress as distinguished by Selye and Levi: eustress (healthy, essential stress) and distress (morbid stress), e.g. mental or physical strain, anger, frustration, tension, all seemingly without hope.

Stress can be defined as a form of tension or strain in the body or the mind for which there is no release or outlet. When under stress, one is like a car in the neutral gear with the accelerator on, trying to exert initially, but unable to do so . Stress is also defined as mental, physical, emotional tension, strain or distress. Stress is a fact of life. However too much stress can result in the breakdown of a person's physical, mental and emotional health. It has physical and emotional effects on us and can create positive or negative energy.

But not all stress is bad. Stress can have positive effects too. In fact, stress is a very natural and important part of life. Human body is designed to react to two types of stress. Good stress helps keep us alert, motivates us to face challenges, and drives us to solve problems. These low levels of stress are manageable and can be thought of as necessary and normal stimulation. However, Distress, on the other hand, results when our bodies overreact to events. Most people think of stress as a mental state but it is in fact, very largely, a physical condition. When a person is subjected to a stress- producing effect known as stressor (a challenge, pressure, stimulus, external influence, etc.) it is registered in the brain. The brain gives various parts of the body instructions for a chain of reactions known as stress reaction or stress response. Different People can tolerate different levels of stress. Each person needs to work on their own stress control techniques according to their tolerance levels.

Types of Stress

There are five main types of stress that people experience. They are: Eustress, Distress, Hyperstress, Hypostress, and Neustress.

Eustress

When a stressor puts demand on our resources and we experience stress that need not always lead to distress. If the stressor is within limits and we have enough resources we will be able to cope up with the stress. When a stress makes us cope up with it, there is a feeling of satisfaction and joy. Stresses that make us cope up with them culminate in better integration of our personality. Such stresses are called 'Eustress' or useful stress. The child who prepared well for the examination, wrote it effectively and came out successfully experiences better self worth and increased self-esteem. The examination though a stress had indeed beneficial effects on him. Such beneficial stresses are required for our motivation and growth. No wonder it is then called a useful stress.

Distress

When a stressor becomes too demanding or when we do not have adequate resources to meet the demands, we get 'stressed up'. The stressed up experience is called a 'Distress'. Distress is bad and unhealthy. Prolonged distress initiates a number of reactions at the level of the body and mind. As it depletes our resources we become impoverished and susceptible to diseases and disorders. The child who has poor resources to write an examination falls ill. The executive who went on worrying depleted his resources and developed hypertension. The housewife spent a sizable portion of her resources to suppress her constant anger and ended up with bronchial asthma. Thus any stress that becomes distressing is unhealthy.

Hyperstress

Hyperstress is an excessive amount of stress. It occurs when an individual is pushed beyond what he or she can handle.

Hyperstress results from being overloaded or overworked. When someone is hyperstressed, even little things can trigger a strong emotional response. A Wall Street trader is likely to experience hyperstress. he most common sufferers of hyperstress are those who are overloaded trying to juggle children, careers, marriages, so much so, that one more little incidence could very easily push them over the edge. Mothers are often victims of hyperstress, as they may work and care for the home, husband, and children, or they may stay at home, plus juggle marriage and the demands of motherhood.

Hypostress

Hypostress is the opposite of hyperstress. Hypostress occurs when an individual is bored or unchallenged. People who experience hypostress are often restless and uninspired. A factory worker who performs repetitive tasks might experience hypostress. Hypostress happens when you suffer from extreme boredom, or when you have nothing in your life that stimulates you anymore. If you go to work everyday at the same time, same place, and perform the same repetitive work, then you are likely to suffer from hypostress. When you lack stimulation or have an unchallenging job or if you are over satisfied with your job, you might be suffering from hypostress.

Neustress

Neustress is neutral stress, neither good nor bad. Neustress describes sensory stimuli that have no consequential effect, neither good nor bad. This kind of stress arises when a tornado hits an unoccupied island. It is a kind of stress which has no significant consequence. Also, from the scientific point of view, it has no real meaning.

Causes of Stress

Many different things can cause stress from physical (such as fear of something dangerous) to emotional (such as worry over your family or job). Identifying what may be causing you stress is often the first step in learning how to better deal with your stress. Some of the most common sources of stress are:

Survival Stress

You may have heard the phrase "fight or flight" before. This is a common response to danger in all people and animals. When you are afraid that someone or something may physically hurt you, your body naturally responds with a burst of energy so that you will be better able to survive the dangerous situation (fight) or escape it all together (flight). This is survival stress.

Internal Stress

Have you ever caught yourself worrying about things you can do nothing about or worrying for no reason at all? This is internal stress and it is one of the most important kinds of stress to understand and manage. Internal stress is when people make themselves stressed. This often happens when we worry about things we can't control or put ourselves in situations we know will cause us stress. Some people become addicted to the kind of hurried, tense, lifestyle that results from being under stress. They even look for stressful situations and feel stress about things that aren't stressful.

Environmental Stress

This is a response to things around you that cause stress, such as noise, crowding, and pressure from work or family. Identifying these environmental stresses and learning to avoid them or deal with them will help lower your stress level.

Fatigue and Overwork

This kind of stress builds up over a long time and can take a hard toll on your body. It can be caused by working too much or too hard at your job(s), school, or home. It can also be caused by not knowing how to manage your time well or how to take time out for rest and relaxation. This can be one of the hardest kinds of stress to avoid because many people feel this is out of their control. Later in this course we will show you that you DO have options and offer some useful tips for dealing with fatigue.

Managing Stress

The following are stress managing practice, which can reduce stress in life and help to live with more balanced life:

Exercise regularly

Exercise has so many stress management and health benefits, and for many of us, nighttime is when it best fits our schedules. Light exercise like yoga or walking at night can also help sleep as it releases tension without over-stimulating the body. Exercise in water can reduce stress even more.

Breathing

The amazing stress-reducer that you have with you right now is your breathing. That's right. The method in which you take air into your body is an essential part of you releasing stress and becoming more relaxed.

Laughter therapy

Laughter therapy is gaining grounds firmly in India. Medical research has shown that laughter decreases blood pressure and heart rate, increases oxygen in the blood, creates an enzyme that protects your stomach from stress, and strengthens the immune system.

Eat a good breakfast

Studies show that eating breakfast is one of the healthiest habits we can adopt. Yet, most people do not pay attention to their breakfast and some don't even bother having it. Having a good breakfast is very healthy! Remember unless you put fuel to your car, it does not run. Same is the case with human body...

Cultivate a hobby

Start something you always wanted, it can be working in the garden (amazing) or learning how to make pots (even more amazing), working out is good, running or swimming, in fact almost any kind of regular physical activity is good.

Listen to music

Music can soothe your mind and body to the point that it's now being used as a therapeutic tool by many practitioners. You can use music to your benefit by playing.

Yoga and meditation

Some powerful practices like *yoga*, meditation or tai chi are the best herb for being stress free. *Yoga* is a wonderful practice for reducing stress. It gives complete relaxation to body as well as mind. It helps you to concentrate and focus on some particular things. It's the best relief for stress.

Yoga and Stress

Stress, long considered alien to the Indian lifestyle, is now a major risk factor for various cardiac and non-cardiac ailments. The victims are not just high-pressured executives but also slum dwellers, working women, businessmen, professionals and even children. With the fast pace of modern life, stress-related disorders such as heart attacks, peptic ulcers, arthritis, allergies, sexual problems, bowel disorders and so on are greatly on the increase. People across the country are in search of measures to cope with this menace. That is why more and more stress management workshops are being organized for executives, *yoga* and meditation centres are mushrooming and the demand for anxiolytic and antidepressant drugs has been escalating.

Benefits of Yoga

There are two major benefits of *yoga:*

Preventive Value

Yoga helps to bring natural order and balance to the neuro-hormones and metabolism in the body. At the same time, these exercises improve endocrine metabolism, thus providing you with a preventive shield.

Curative Value

Yogic postures activate the energies that have accumulated

and stagnated in the energy pockets of the body - since left inert, these energies create various ailments. Yogic exercises cleanse your body, mind and consciousness by venting toxins from the body.

Principles of Yoga

Patanjali's Eight Principles of *Yoga* are:

1. Abstinence (*yama*)
2. Observance (*niyama*)
3. Posture (*asana*)
4. Regulation of breath (*pranayama*)
5. Withdrawal of Senses (*pratyahara*)
6. Concentration (*dharana*)
7. Meditation (*dhyana*)
8. Super Consciousness (*samadhi*)

Swami Sivananda's Modified Five Principles of Yoga

Proper relaxation

Releases tension in the muscles, Helps letting go of all worries, and Ensures conservation of energy.

Proper exercise

Yoga postures - to be performed as per body constitution. Yogic consultation is a must. Correct postures work systematically on all parts of the body. Stretching and toning the muscles & ligaments. Keeping the spine and joints flexible. Improving the blood circulation.

Proper breathing (pranayama)

Brings an extraordinary balance in the consciousness. Teaches you to control your mental state by regulating the flow of the life force.

Proper diet

Chart out a well-nourished balanced diet. Keeps the body light and supple and the mind calm. Resists ailments.

Positive Thinking and Meditation

Removes negative thoughts. Stills the mind. You attain superconsciousness. A state beyond time, space and causation.

Yogic Solutions to Stress

Stress hazards decrease the quality of life and can lead to many ailments. Four distinct stress attack stages or phases are recognized: psychic, psychosomatic, somatic and organic. Anxiolytic/antidepressant drugs are available to treat the somatic and organic phases of stress, while *yoga* is most useful in controlling and treating the psychic and psychosomatic phases, thereby nipping the cause in the bud in the early stages.

In 1988 a study was carried out at Charing Cross Medical School, London, by Dr A.K. Ghosh (Swami Mangaltirtham Saraswati), which showed that meditation (especially *yoga* nidra) can modify stress-induced EEG patterns and bring about progressive and systematic relaxation by inducing a high degree of alpha brain wave rhythms. *Yoga nidra* has the capacity to induce deep sleep in only twenty minutes.

The basic aim of the yogic approach towards stress is not to deal with the manifest symptoms (like fear, anger, palpitation, sleeplessness, etc.) but rather to eliminate the root cause. According to *yoga,* stress is an imbalance at the mental, physical or emotional level. Stress is not the cause of our ills; the cause is our inability to cope with a changing condition.

Maintenance of physical body with asana

Yoga balances, harmonizes, and brings integration between physical and mental health. The definition of asana, in traditional texts, is '*Sthiram sukham asanam*'. The word sthiram means homeostasis, balance; *sukham* means pleasure; and *asanam* means physical posture. It is the posture that produces homeostasis in the system - restores endocrinal balance, balances the inhibitors and stimulator circuits, regulates secretions and optimizes the functions of the entire system of the body.

'*Sukham*' also relates to the state of mind, which is relaxed. Muscles contain stretch receptors; the stretching movements of asanas send relaxing impulses to the brain, which induce a relaxed state of mind.

Simple asanas to relieve tension

When we stand or sit for prolonged periods in chairs, our muscles accumulate stress and consequently lactic acid, which causes a feeling of stiffness when we wake up in the morning. To remove this stiffness the practice of simple asanas like *tadasana, tiryaka tadasana, kati chakrasana,* and *pawanmuktasana* part I are very useful. These postures stretch the muscles and massage the joints. As a result circulation improves and toxins are drained away. Thus *asanas* activate, tone and revitalize the organs, massage the joints, stretch and relax the muscles, optimize endocrine gland secretions, develop stamina and promote internal awareness. Concentration, awareness and relaxation are integral parts of performing *asanas*. Asanas are not just mechanical performances.

Power of pranayama

Pranayama is generally defined as breath control. Although this interpretation may seem correct in view of the practices involved, it does not convey the full meaning of the term. The word *pranayama* is comprised of two roots: '*prana*' plus '*ayama*'. Prana means 'vital force' or 'life force' and ayama is defined as 'extension' or 'expansion'. Thus, the word pranayama means 'extension or expansion of the dimension of prana'. The techniques of *pranayama* provide the method whereby flow of *prana* in the nadis is regulated, activated and purified, inducing physical and mental stability.

Pranayama and lifestyle

Physical activities such as exercise, work, sleep, intake of food and sexual relations all affect the distribution and flow of prana in the body. Faculties of mind such as emotion, thought and imagination affect the pranic body even more. Irregularities in lifestyle, dietary indiscretions and stress deplete and obstruct the pranic flow. This results in what people experience as being drained of energy. Depletion of energy in a particular *prana* leads to the devitalization of the organs and limbs which prana governs and ultimately to disease or metabolic dysfunction. The techniques of pranayama reverse this process, energizing and balancing the different pranas within the *pranamaya kosha. Pranayama* practices should be performed after *asana.*

Relaxation and concentration through yoga nidra

One of the prime needs of today is to learn how to relax. Sleep is not relaxation. According to *yoga,* sleep is wilfully and consciously becoming aware of how the mind and consciousness are interacting with the body, senses and objects and experiences. *Yoga* aims to achieve and maintain clarity of mind and awareness (*sajagata*). When we attain this awareness then naturally existing turbulences and distractions will settle down. In *yoga,* the experience of relaxation means moving from outside to inside, becoming aware of this introversion and maintaining balance and stability. Psychology indicates that activity and stimulation is the nature of the mind. Relaxing the disturbed, agitated mind can be achieved through the relaxation practice of *yoga* nidra. It is therefore evident from the above discussion that asanas relax the body and mind, and through meditation (*yoga nidra*) one attains relaxation, concentration and awareness.

Change in attitude and lifestyle

Change in attitude and modification of lifestyle are the two pillars on which the management of stress through *yoga* is based. Attitude change can be achieved by developing positive attitudes. This is explained in yogic literature on the basis of *asakti* (attachment), *anasakti* (non-attachment) and vairagya (detachment). *Asakti* literally means attraction with expectation and ego involvement towards certain individuals or objects.

This leads to *raga* (attraction), *dwesha* (repulsion) and *ahamkara* (ego involvement), which often manifests as insecurity, aggression, a high need for recognition, possessiveness and anxiety. As a result, a person high in asakti often suffers from frustration, tension, psychological stress and other neurotic tendencies. On the other hand, vairagya is the height of the nivritti way of life. It means detachment or non-dependence on worldly material things and personalized relationships. This is very difficult for the average householder to achieve. Devoted saints and seers may be able to achieve *vairagya*. However, for most people, who live normal social and family lives, *anasakti* (non-attachment) is the middle path which may be followed in order to improve the quality of life and social well-being. This provides lasting happiness and peace without being disturbed by *asakti* (attachment).

Yogic lifestyle

Living according to the laws of the body and the laws of nature is the concept of yogic lifestyle. This includes diet, sleep, relaxation, exercise and a daily work schedule. The best way to learn the yogic lifestyle is to spend a few days in a yogashram. Yogic lifestyle does not mean just adding the practice of a few asanas and/or pranayama to one's daily schedule of activities. It actually means living a self-disciplined life of anasakti.

Practice of Yoga

Short sessions of twenty minutes each, after one's bath in the morning, in the afternoon and at bedtime can be devoted to *yoga* practice. The effect of *yoga* is never evident immediately, rather it is experienced slowly. Slowly one will start to experience that one's power of concentration and relaxation has increased. The mental and emotional tensions that are generated in day to day life slowly start settling down. It is here that *yoga* begins. *Yoga* does not begin by standing upside down or by wearing geru clothes. *Yoga* begins by becoming self-aware (*sajagata*).

According to *yoga* one becomes a victim of stress not on account of a stressful situation but on account of one's inability to cope with it. Do not fight stress and in the effort fall prey to alcohol, cigarettes or anxiolytic drugs, rather develop and enhance your potential and capacity to cope with stress. Learn to alter your attitude and lifestyle. Practise asana, pranayama and *yoga* nidra regularly to bring about a change in attitude and to correct imbalances at the mental, physical and emotional levels. Anxiolytic/antidepressant drugs do not bring lasting relief, they only help manage some of the somatic and organic phase symptoms of stress, while *yoga* is most useful in controlling and treating stress in the early psychic and psychosomatic phases.

REFERENCES

Arnold, H. & Feldman, D. (1986) *Organizational Behavior.* New York: McGraw Hill.

Arpita, (1996) "Physiological and Psychological Effects of Hatha *Yoga*: A Review of the Literature", *The Journal of the International Association of Yoga Therapists,* Vol..1, Nos.I & II.

Bhala, Balmakund, (1996) "*Yoga* in Modern Medicine", *International Journal of Alternative and Complementary Medicine,* April, 1996 (Reprinted in *Yoga* & Health, August.

Gerloff, E. (1985) *Organizational theory and design: a strategic approach for management.* New York: McGraw Hill.

Griffin, R. & Moorhead, G. (1986) *Organizational behavior.* Boston Houghton Mifflin.

Huczynski, A. & Buchanan, D. (1991) *Organisational Behaviour: An Introductory Text.* New Jersey: FT/Prentice Hall.

Lasater, Judith, (1992) "10 Ways to relax deeply", *Yoga Journal,* Jan/ Feb, pp.74-81.

Manjunath, NK *et al,* (1999) "Factors influencing changes in tweezer dexterity scores following *yoga* training.", *Indian J Physiol Pharmacol,* April;43(2): 225-9

Rajkumar S. Adukia, (2010) *Handbook on Stress Management with Self Care Techniques,* a part of the book accessed through www. carajkumarradukia.com/ *development /hb**stressmanagement**. doc,visisted this website on February 10.*

Robbins, S. (1998) *Organisational Behaviour: Concepts, Controversies and Applications.* 8th ed. New Jersey: Prentice Hall

Rollinson, , D. & Edwards, D. & Broadfield, A. (1998) *Organisational behaviour analysis: an integrated approach.* Harlow: Addison Wesley

Singh, Shettiwar, Udupa, "Physiological and Therapeutic Studies on *Yoga*", *The Yoga Review*, Vol. II, No.4, 1982

Udupa, K.N., Stress and Its Management by *Yoga*, Motilal Banarsidass, Delhi 1985 Selvamurthy *et. al.*, "A New Physiological Approach to Control Essential Hypertension", Indian J Physiol Pharmacol, 1998 April; 42 (2): 205-13; Cole, Roger, "Relaxation, Physiology and Practice, self-published by Synchrony Applied Health Sciences, 1994 Ways Stress Affects Individuals", http://www.drkoop.com/conditions/stress

White, D. and Bednar, D. (1986) Organizational behavior: understanding and managing people at work. Boston: Allyn & Bacon www.MyDailyYoga.com

20 Organizational Creativity and Innovations

Be creative. Be innovative. Think differently.
There is Always A Better Way.

Innovation and Creativity

In Webster's Dictionary, *Innovation* discovers that its root is innovâre—to renew. Today's definition reads: to introduce something new, make changes. innovation is adding something new to an existing product or process. The key words here are adding and existing. The product or process has already been created from scratch and has worked reasonably well. When we change it so that it works better or full-fills a different need, we are innovating on what already exists.

Whereas, *Creativity,* on the other hand, is defined as to cause something to come into being, as something unique. It is the process that created the product in the first place. The product or process didn't exist before it was created. It is original, unique and usually novel. So, we believe that creativity is a process that produces an original outcome or product, while innovation is the change, modification or improvement of an existing product.

Although creativity and innovation are closely intertwined in the public eye, they have often been studied in isolation by researchers using different methodologies and models. Creativity has been the province of psychology, with its emphasis on individuals and small groups, while innovation has been the focus of sociologists, economists, and others who take a larger, systems perspective. Creativity is generally defined as useful novelty - not novelty for its own sake, but novelty that can be applied and add value to an organization's products and services. Creativity includes the generation of ideas, alternatives, and possibilities.

Four Types of Innovation

There are four distinct types of innovation, these are: invention, extension, duplication and synthesis. *Invention* has been described as the creation of a new product, service or process. *Extension* is said to be the expansion of a product, service or process. *Duplication* has been defined as replication of an already existing product, service or process. Finally, the combination of existing concepts and factors into a new formulation has been identified as *synthesis*.

Issues of Innovation

We now know that innovation is the total process of generating new knowledge and converting that knowledge into a commercial product or service. Sources of innovation in terms of the main areas are where new ideas come from. The main areas are: unexpected occurrences, process needs, and gaps between expectations and reality. The market is one of the main sources of innovation. In a constantly changing market new ideas are always presenting themselves. Other sources include demographic changes and changes in perception.

Five Myths of Innovation

There are several *myths* associated with innovation that are covered in the literature. Five myths are presented:

1. Innovation is planned and predictable;
2. Technical specifications should be thoroughly prepared in advance;
3. Creativity relies on dreams and blue-sky ideas;
4. Big projects will develop better innovations than smaller ones, and
5. Technology is the driving force of innovation and success.

Principles of Innovation

While innovation encompasses a large area, it is pertinent to point out that there are a number of *principles* of innovation. An important message here is that entrepreneurs must realize that these principles exist and that they can be learned. One of the principles is to be action-oriented. Making the product, process or service simple and understandable is another example of a principle of innovation. A few more include: make the product, process or service customer-based, start small, aim high, follow a milestone schedule, and the like.

The Three Components of Creativity

Within every individual, creativity is a function of three components: expertise, creative-thinking skills, and motivation. Can managers influence these components? The answer is an emphatic yes - for better and for worse - through workplace practices and conditions. *Expertise* is, in a word, knowledge - technical, procedural and intellectual. *Creative thinking skills* determine how flexibly and imaginatively people approach problems. Do their solutions up-end the status quo? Do they persevere through dry spells? Not all *motivation* is created equal.

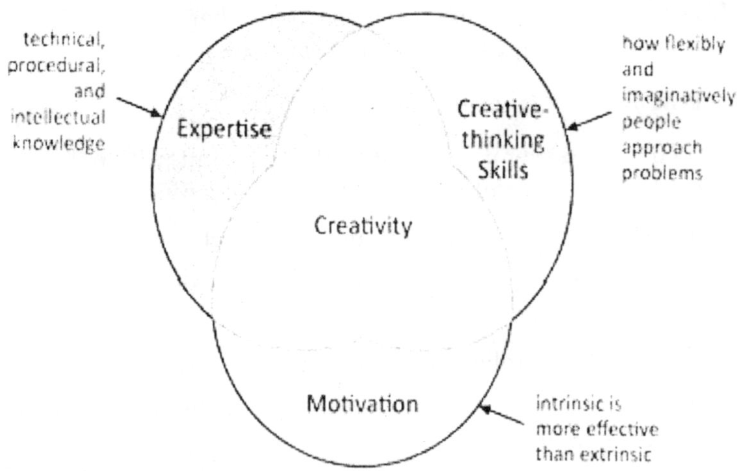

Fig. 20.1: Three Components of Creativity

An inner passion to solve the problem at hand leads to solutions far more creative than external rewards, such as money. This component - called intrinsic motivation - is the one that can most immediately be influenced by the work environment.

Managing Creativity

Challenge

Of all the things managers can do to stimulate creativity, perhaps the most efficacious is the deceptively simple task of matching people with the right assignments. Managers can match people with jobs that play to their expertise and their skills in creative thinking, and ignite intrinsic motivation. Perfect matches stretch employees' abilities. The amount of stretch, however, is crucial: not so little that they feel bored but not so much that they feel overwhelmed and threatened by a loss of control.

Freedom

When it comes to granting freedom, the key to creativity is giving people autonomy concerning the means - that is, concerning the process - but not necessarily the ends. People will be more creative, in other words, if you give them freedom to decide how to climb a particular mountain. You needn't let them choose which mountain to climb. In fact, clearly specified strategic goals often enhance people's creativity.

Resources

The two main resources that affect creativity are time and money. Managers need to allot these resources carefully. Like matching people with the right assignments, deciding how much time and money to give to a team or project is a sophisticated judgment call that can either support or kill creativity.

Work-group features

If you want to build teams that come up with creative ideas, you must pay careful attention to the design of such teams. That is, you must create mutually supportive groups with a diversity of perspectives and backgrounds. Why? Because when teams comprise people with various intellectual foundations and approaches to work - that is, different expertise and creative thinking styles - ideas often combine and combust in exciting and useful ways.

Supervisory encouragement

Most managers are extremely busy. They are under pressure for results. It is therefore easy for them to let praise for creative efforts - not just creative successes but unsuccessful efforts, too - fall by the wayside. One very simple step managers can take to foster creativity is to not let that happen.

Organizational support

Encouragement from supervisors certainly fosters creativity, but creativity is truly enhanced when the entire organization supports it. Such support is the job of an organization's leaders, who must put in place appropriate systems or procedures and emphasize values that make it clear that creative efforts are a top priority. For example, creativity-supporting organizations consistently reward creativity, but they avoid using money to 'bribe' people to come up with innovative ideas.

Organizational Factors that Inhibit or Facilitate Creativity

The organizational context - including the management practices, job design, and human resource policies - plays an important role in creativity. Amabile's model of organizational creativity is one of the most widely cited in psychological studies of organizations. Although not explicitly stated, the assumption behind the model is that creativity and innovation are important for all organizations and jobs.

Key organizational factors related to creativity include "proximate factors" that are close to daily experience "distal factors" that are more remote, such as organizational structure and climate.

Proximal Factors

According to Amabile (1988), complex and challenging jobs that enable workers to decide how to carry out tasks are more likely to encourage intrinsic motivation that, in turn, increases creativity. Motivation is also aided by a sense of urgency that increases the perception that the project or task is valuable and worth pursuing. In contrast to complex, challenging jobs, routine work can readily be accomplished by adhering to well-known processes and information. In such circumstances creativity may actually incur a cost if it reduces efficiency by introducing unnecessary change.

Distal Factors

Distal factors, which set the overall context in which creative behaviors occur, include resources, organizational adaptability, organizational culture, and levels of internal strife. Resources are important not only for functional support, but also because having an adequate level of resources for the task/project influences workers' perceptions that the project is valuable and worthy of organizational support. Resources include financial support as well as time, physical space, and information.

The Role of the Physical Environment

The physical environment or setting can influence the degree to which divergent thought processes are used. Divergent thinking has a broad, relaxed focus of attention that requires a sense of psychological safety and peacefulness. Distractions and time pressures can inhibit this process. In addition, creative problem solving takes time. A person or group may stop short of achieving a creative solution if there are strong external time pressures; under these circumstances, the first solution that appears to be good enough is likely to be selected. Also, problem solving tools, equipment, and technology available to workers can aid the ability to switch perspectives by providing display space, visual aids, analogies, and metaphors.

REFERENCES

Allen, Thomas J. (1973). "Communication Networks in R& D Laboratories." *R&D Management* 1:14-21.

Allen, Thomas J. (1977). *Managing The Flow of Technology*. Cambridge, MA: MIT Press.

Amabile, T. (1998) *Harvard Business Review*, September, 77–87.

Amabile, Teresa and Regina Conti. 1999. Changes in the Work Environment for Creativity during Downsizing. *Academy of Management Journal* 42(6):630-640.

Amabile, Teresa. 1988. A Model of Creativity and Innovation in Organizations. In *Research in Organizational Behavior*. B. M. Staw and L.L. Cummings (eds.). Vol 10: pp. 123-167. Greenwich, CT: JAI Press.

Amabile, Teresa. (1998) How to Kill Creativity. *Harvard Business Review* Sept-Oct:77-87.

Antonovsky, A. (1987) The Salutogenic Perspective: Toward a New View of Health and Illness. *Institute for the Advancement of Science* 4(1):47-55.

Basadur, Min. (1997) Managing Creativity: A Japanese Model. In R. Katz (Ed). *The Human Side of Managing Technological Innovation: A Collection of Readings*. New York: Oxford University Press.

Buchanan, Bruce. 2001. Creativity at the Metalevel. AAAI -2000 Presidential Address. *AI Magazine*, Fall. www.findarticles.com

Carland, J.W., Hoy, F., Boulton, W.R. & Carland, J.A. (1984). Differentiating entrepreneurs from small business owners: A conceptualization. *The Academy of Management Review*, 9(2), 354-359.

Chi, M. 1997. Creativity: Shifting Across Ontological Categories Flexibly. In *CreativeThought: An Investigation of Conceptual Structures and Processes*. T. Ward, S. Smith and J

Dacey, John S. and Kathleen H. Lennon. 1998. *Understanding Creativity: The Interplay of Biological, Social and Psychological Factors*. San Francisco: Jossey-Bass.

Dahl, Cheryl. (2000). Have You Seen the Five Faces of Genius? Fast Company October:54-62. de Bono, Edward. 1970. *Lateral Thinking: Creativity Step by Step*. New York: Harper-Collins.

Drazin, Robert, Mary Ann Glynn, and Robert Kazanjian, (1999). Multilevel Theorizing about Creativity in Organizations: A Sensemaking Perspective. *Academy of Management Review*, April. Available URL: www.findarticles.com.

Drucker, P.F. 1984, „Our entrepreneurial economy , *Harvard Business Review*. Drucker, P.F. (1985). *Innovation and entrepreneurship: practice and principles*. New York: Harper and Row. von Oech,

Dunbar, Kevin. 1997. How Scientists Think: On Line Creativity and Conceptual Change in Science. In Creative Thought: An Investigation of Conceptual Processes and Structures.T.S. Ward, S.M. Smith and J. Vaid (eds). Washington D.C: American Psychological Association.

Ford, Cameron. 1996. A Theory of Individual Creative Action in Multiple Social Domains. *Academy of Management Review.* 21(4):1112-1142.

Gryskiewicz, Stanley S. 2000. Cashing in on Creativity at Work. Psychology Today September/October:63-65.

Hargadon, Andrew B. (1999). *Group Cognition and Creativity in Organizations. Research on Managing Groups and Teams.* Vol 2. Pp. 137-155. Greenwich, CT: JAI Press Inc.

Hargadon, Andrew, and Robert Sutton. 2000. Building an Innovation Factory. *Harvard Business Review* May-June:157-166.

Hillier, Bill, and A. Penn. 1991. Visible Colleges: Structure and Randomness in the Place of Discovery. Science in Context 4(1):23-49.

Isaksen, Scott. 1983. Toward a Model for the Facilitation of Creative Problem Solving. Journal of Creative Behavior 17(1):18-31.

Isen, Alice M. 1990. The Influence of Positive and Negative Affect on Cognitive Organization: Some Implications for Development. In Psychological and Biological Approaches to Emotion. N.L .Stein, B. Leventhal, T. Trabasso (eds.). Hillsdale, NJ: Erlbaum.

Kelly, Robert and Janet Caplan. 1997. How Bell Labs Creates Star Performers. In The Human Side of Managing Technological Innovation: A Collection of Readings. R. Katz (ed.). New York: Oxford University Press

Penn, A., J. Desyllas, and J. Vaughan. (1999). The Space of Innovation: Interaction and Communication in the Work Environment. Environmental and Planning B: *Planning and Design* 26:193-218.

Roberts, Edward. (1997). Managing Invention and Innovation: What We've Learned. In R. Katz (ed.). *The Human Side of Managing Technological Innovation: A Collection of Readings.* New York: Oxford University Press.

Roger. (1991). *A Kick in the Seat of the Pants.* New York: Harper & Row Publisher Schumpeter, J. 1934, *The Theory of Economic Development,* Harvard University Press, Cambridge, MA.

Shalley, Christina E., Lucy Gilson, and Terry C. Blum. 2000. Matching Creativity Requirements and the Work Environment: Effects on Satisfaction and Intentions to Leave. Academy of Management Journal 43(2):215-243.

Simonton, Dean K. 1977. "Creative Productivity, Age, and Stress: A Biographical Time-series Analysis of Ten Classical Composers." *Journal of Personality and Social Psychology* 35: 791-804.

Simonton, Dean K. 2000. "Creativity: Cognitive, Personal, Developmental, and Social Aspects." *American Psychologist* 55(1):151-158.

Smith, Gerald F. (1998). Idea-Generation Techniques: A Formulary of Active Ingredients. *Journal of Creative Behavior* 32(2): 107-133.

Stacey, Ralph D. (1996). *Complexity and Creativity in Organizations.* San Francisco: Berrett- Koehler.

Sternberg. Robert. (1988). The Nature of Creativity: Contemporary Psychological Perspectives. Cambridge, UK: Cambridge University Press.

Tesluk, Paul E., James L. Farr, and Stephanie A. Klein. (1997). Influences of Organizational Culture and Climate on Individual Creativity. *Journal of Creative Behavior.* 31(1): 27-41.

Woodman, Richard W., John E. Sawyer, and R.W.Griffin. (1993). "Toward a Theory of Organizational Creativity." *Academy of Management Review* 18(2):293-321.

21 Contemporary Trends in Organizational Behaviour

What less behind us and what before us are tiny matters compared to what lies within us.

International Dimensions

As it is becoming increasingly clear that the work is shrinking and requires new business strategies, it is also becoming increasingly evident that organizational behaviour plays an important role in this globalization process. For instance, a recent analysis noted: many companies that rushed into cross-border mergers and acquisitions in the last two decades realize that such projects are more complicated than they appeared. The missing element is the human factor.

Although there is a trend towards similar clothes, entertainment, and material possessions, and even a growing acceptance of English as the international business language, there are still important differences in the ways in which people think and behave around the world. There are even differences in the way in which knowledge about organizational behaviour is accumulated. For example, it has been pointed out that the European behavioral scientists tend to be more cognitive and/or psychologically based, while their American counterparts are more behavioristic and/or humanistically oriented. In understanding and applying organizational behaviour concepts in other countries around the world, one must be aware of the similarities and differences.

Cultural Differences

In cross-cultural interactions, people should consider and understand the cultural background of each other in order to have successful interactions. Much research has shown that in cross-cultural communication and negotiation the cultural differences between communicators affect the outcome of the negotiation. In the negotiation among different countries, small misunderstandings caused from cultural differences lead the whole negotiation to bad results. Herring showed cross-cultural counselors should understand cultural differences and apply those differences to their non-verbal communication styles to avoid misunderstandings. Condon emphasized the importance of understanding cultural differences relative to that of understanding language differences in that the misunderstandings from language differences could easily be recognized but misunderstandings from cultural differences could not easily be deciphered and corrected. Thus, the consideration of cultural contexts in cross-cultural communication is essential to successful interactions. However, a systematical method to automate analysis of cultural differences has not been completed yet.

The Impact of Culture on International Organizational Behaviour

Cultural differences are a two way street. Cultural differences must be understood and mangers must be sensitive to them in order to be successful in the global economy. There are several basis dimensions that differentiate cultures. They are:

- *How people see themselves:* In some countries of the world, people are viewed as basically honest and trustworthy. In others, people are regarded with suspicion and distrust. For example, a reason some Third World people regard the United States with suspicion and distrust may result form the way these people view themselves.
- *People relationship to their world:* In some societies people attempt to dominate heir environment. In other societies they try to live in harmony with it or are

subjugated by it. People from the United States and Candida, for example, attempt to dominate their environment.

- *Individualism versus Collectivism:* Some counties of the world encourage individualism. The United States, Great Britain, and Canada re examples. In other counties collectivism, or group orientation, is important. Japan, China, and the Israeli kibbutzim emphasize group harmony, unity, commitment, and loyalty. The differences felt themselves in many ways, such as in hiring practices.
- *Time Dimension:* In some societies people are oriented towards the past. In others they tend to be more focused on the present. People from the United States and Canada are most interested in the present and the near future. Business people in these countries are particularly interested in where their companies are today and where they will be in five to ten years.
- *Public and Private Space:* Some cultures promote the use of pubic space; others favour private space. For example, in Japan bosses often sit together with their employees in the some large room. The ***heads*** of some of the biggest Japanese firms may leave their chauffeur-driven limousines at home and ride the crowded public subways to work in the morning so that they can be with their workers.

Dimensions of Culture

Hofstede's dimensions of culture have become the most widely used model for explaining various effects across cultures. Hofstede's five dimensions include the following.

Power Distance

The power distance dimension has to do with inequality in a society. In a high power distance environment there would be greater tolerance for, and expectation of, inequality in prestige, wealth and power.

Uncertainty Avoidance

Hofstede focuses on uncertainty at the organizational level looking at the use of rules and strategies to reduce exposure to an unsure future.

Individualism and Collectivism

This dimension has to do with the relationship the individual has with the group and more generally with society. Hofstede points out that the nature of this relationship determines not only how people think about themselves and their immediate group but the "structure and functioning of many institutions aside from the family".

Masculinity and Femininity

There seem to be two elements to this dimension. One deals with the values held and the other with role expectations. Hofstede notes that in a work setting, males value "advancement, earnings, training, up-to-dateness" while females' value "friendly atmosphere, position security, physical conditions and manager cooperation". The second aspect of this dimension has to do with what people in a culture expect of sex roles. In a very masculine culture, sex roles would be differentiated while in a feminine culture sex roles would be more similar.

Long-term Orientation (LTO)

This is a recent addition to the Hofstede model, added as a new dimension to the model in the second edition (2001). It is based on the philosophy of Confucius and has to do with "persistence, thrift, personal stability and respect for tradition" (p. 351). It describes a longer term, higher level view of life.

Cultural Crossings

In order to approach the cross-cultural organisations of the companies studied, the present study introduces a new concept of cultural crossing. Cultural crossing is that layer in a cross-cultural organisation in and through which the cultural codes of communication and patterns of management are transformed from one cultural "language" to another. Cultural crossing appears to have two main elements, its locus and mode.

The locus of the cultural crossing is the organizational location where the two cultures meet. In foreign subsidiary management it can, by definition, be in four paradigmatic locations:

1. Between a foreign subsidiary and its foreign customers,
2. Within the foreign subsidiary,
3. Between the foreign subsidiary and the company headquarters and
4. Within the company headquarters. In real life, the locus of the cultural crossing is often multi-local, for instance when the locally hired managers of a foreign subsidiary do pursue management activity at the same time with the expatriate managers within the subsidiary and the parent country national managers at the company headquarters.

The modus of the cultural crossing is the way how this process of transformation is done. According to the present study the modus or mode has three alternative patterns:

1. If the mode is segregated, the both parties of a cross-cultural setting operate among themselves using their own cultural styles and patterns of management and no integration has been done in order to bridge the cross-cultural gap.
2. In companies that use integrated or gradual mode of cultural crossing, the two cultures are gradually bridged to each other so that a "buffer-zone" exists in which "mixed management" is used in order to achieve good integration.
3. Finally, it is also possible to hire a truly bi-cultural individual, a cultural mediator, to act as the bridge in a cross-cultural organisation. In such case, the mode is mediated.

Behaviour Across Cultures

In human interactions, it is important to know what is

expected of each other. People are expected to behave in certain ways in certain situations, and the failure of behaving in the expected manner is often regarded rude and impolite. For example, when a person goes to an American shop, he expects someone to help his shopping, helping him find a product in the shop and suggesting which products would be the best for his purpose. If the attendant gives a map of the warehouse to the customer and asks him to search for it by himself, the customer will be infuriated. The expected behaviors differ by culture; people in different cultures will expect different things even in the same situation. Thus, it is important to understand the different expectations of the different cultures to avoid misunderstandings and misled communication.

Dimensions of Cultural Difference

One way of examining organizational behaviour across cultures and explaining the differences that this is to look at important dimensions such as those identified by Geert Hofstede, a well-known Dutch researcher. There are numerous subcultures and individual differences.

- Individualism/Collectivism and Power Distance
- Uncertainty Avoidance
- Masculinity/Femininity

Communication in an International Environment

Communication breakdown across cultures: There are a number of contributing factors leading to communication breakdown across cultures. Perhaps the best way to get at the root causes of this breakdown is through the concepts of perception, stereotyping, and ethnocentrism.

- Perceptual Problems
- Stereotyping Problems
- Ethnocentric Problems.

Motivational Differences across Cultures

What contributes to the motivational differences cross culture?

The roles of *religion, uncertainty avoidance, and power distance* provide some insights into this question.

Managerial Leadership across Cultures

The contributing factors to the differences in effective managerial leadership across cultures are:

- Personal Values
- Managers' Background
- Interpersonal skills
- Decision Making
- Transnational competent managers.

Tactics for Removing Cross-Cultural Communication Barriers

Once we have established the prerequisites for understanding communication issues, we should then seek to remove cross cultural communication barriers from the school environment. The major tactics that might be employed for this purpose fall under two categories:

- Removing language which appears to stereotype students; and
- Reducing violations of cultural rules during discussions and conversations.

With respect to removing stereotypical language, the following strategies might be useful:

- **Be aware of words, images and situations that suggest that all or most members of a racial group are the same.** Example: "Why can't Joe ever be on time?" "He's African American, isn't he?"
- **Avoid using qualifiers that reinforce racial and ethnic stereotypes.** Example: "The articulate African American student" implies that African American students typically have low verbal skills.
- **Avoid racial identification except when it is essential to communication.** Example: "Judy, an outgoing student" is preferable to "Judy, an outgoing African American

female student."

- **Be aware of possible negative implications of color symbolism and usage that could offend people or reinforce bias.** Example: Terms such as "black magic" or "black market" can be offensive.
- **Avoid language that has questionable racial or ethnic connotations.** Example: Phrases such as "culturally deprived," "culturally disadvantaged" and "you people" have racist overtones. With respect to changing communicative behaviors which violate the cultural rules of others, the following strategies may be useful:

1. **Be aware of rules for attentiveness during conversation.** Example: The constant maintenance of eye contact while listening during a conversation often violates a conversational rule in working class African American and Hispanic cultures.
2. **Be aware of rules regarding the distance between speakers during conversation.** Example: In some cultures, speakers stand close enough to touch often. In other cultures, distance is maintained to denote respect.
3. **Be aware that objects, characters and symbols may reflect different beliefs or values for different groups.** Example: The confederate flag and Uncle Remus stories may offend African Americans because they reflect the culture of slavery and the Old South.
4. **Be aware that cultures may vary in what they consider humorous or taboo.** Example: Ethnic humor is often perceived by many groups as evidence of racial prejudice. Discussion of in group cultural rules and behaviors with outsiders is considered taboo within many cultures.
5. **Be aware of different rules for taking turns during conversations.** Example: African American children frequently perceive "breaking in" to reinforce or

disagree with another's point to be perfectly permissible, indeed desirable. **Cultures may use different standards for loudness, speed of delivery, silence, attentiveness and time to respond to another's point.** Example: Many Native American societies place high value on contemplation and tend, therefore, to feel little responsibility to make immediate responses during conversation.

6. **Be aware of different cultural rules for entering into conversations in progress.** Example: African American students tend to consider conversations as private between recognized participants. Therefore, anyone, including the teacher, who "butts in" is viewed as an eavesdropper and rebuked.

One way to improve relationships across cultural lines, particularly in the upper grades, is to develop a unit on "Communicating with One Another." The purpose of such a unit would be to teach students how to communicate more effectively across cultural lines and how to address and negotiate differences.

It is also useful for teachers to brainstorm with one another on how to remove communication barriers. In addition, a well designed staff development program can lead to better relations among staff and generate effective cross cultural communication activities for the classroom.

It can also be useful for teachers to ask parents to identify sources of miscommunication and socially offensive behavior or language. Parents may be asked to suggest ways that school personnel can improve communication with students, adults and the communities.

While schools have a responsibility to teach students the behavioral codes of the society at large and to expect students to adhere to them, they have a similar responsibility to reduce culturally induced discipline problems and to avoid misinterpreting cultural differences as behavioral problems.

Managing Behaviour in 21st Century

Managing people in the 21st century is also about embracing something change. In many ways, the manager's job is still the same—to motivate, inspire, and influence, among other things. What's different today is the increasing complexity of the work environment and the breakneck pace of change. The complex variety of social, demographic, and technological change makes managing people more challenging than ever. There's nothing more important to corporate success than valuing people highly and managing them well. Ironically, the increasing pace of change in information technology (IT) underscores the value of people like never before. Because it evolves so rapidly and yet is so cheap and available, technology is rarely a source of sustainable competitive advantage for companies. Granted, firms must stay abreast of technological advances and hope to pull ahead of competitors in doing so.

Organizational Behaviour : Key to Effective Management

At this point, it is clear that the effective management of people is the key to corporate success. But now we need to explain how an understanding of organizational Behaviour is the key to meeting that challenge. Organizational Behaviour examines how and why people act, think, and feel in corporate and other organized settings. The field is concerned with timeless questions such as the nature of leadership, how to motivate people, how to resolve interpersonal conflicts, and how to develop effective teams. At the same time, we know organizational Behaviour has an empirical bias that makes everything seem complex. Most scholars in the field rely on the same approaches and data collection methods used in other sciences to conduct research. As a result, knowledge in organizational Behaviour accumulates incrementally through scientific study, just like it does in physics or biology.

At a broader level, many people have a difficult time viewing Behaviour as something that can be "studied" in the first place. And that makes empirical approaches all the more attractive for those of us "in the business." But there's really no substitute for using the basic principles and methods found in all sciences to study Behaviour in the workplace. While experience, opinions, and common sense are valuable starting points for understanding organizational behavior, they provide notoriously inconsistent information about how to manage people.

Framework for Effective Behavioural Management

We believe that a contingency approach to organizational Behaviour can provide a great deal of practical help to managers. In this section we present a framework that will guide your exploration of organizational Behaviour from a managerial perspective. There are four sets of skills provide the building blocks for effective Behaviour management in organizations.

Outstanding self-insight and perceptual skills

Excellent managers understand their own behavioral styles and tendencies as well as their unique strengths and weaknesses. They know, for instance, what their preferred style or approach is when leading, resolving conflicts, communicating, and so on. But they also grasp the fact that what's comfortable for them may not be the best fit in all situations. Likewise, excellent managers are aware of the assumptions that they make about the people around them and how this impacts their decision making.

The ability to analyze situations correctly

Effective Behaviour management also requires the ability to analyze the context accurately. People don't work in a vacuum. They operate in a multilayered organizational situation that includes groups, task requirements, the company culture, and the competitive environment, just to name a few. This is where a contingency perspective clearly comes into play.

The ability to inspire, motivate, and lead people

But there's more to Behaviour management than knowing "what makes other people tick" and being able to diagnose situations. You may have excellent perception and diagnostic skills but still fail to effectively manage behavior. For instance, knowing what motivates subordinates in a particular context is useless unless the manager also has the ability to lead.

Personal flexibility and adaptability

That brings us to what is often the biggest Behaviour management challenge. Let's say that you've thought about how to motivate a subordinate and now feel that the best solution requires a behavioral approach that you are uncomfortable with, perhaps because it intersects with one of your weaknesses.

Issues of Effective Behaviour Management

In any event, effective Behaviour management involves addressing four sets of issues in sequence:

Identify the behavioral challenge: Maintain, improve, or redirect behavior

This first step requires that managers understand what types of behaviors are critical for outstanding performance in their organizational context. Once that's done, managers should assess whether the behaviors they're currently seeing are consistent with those criteria. And "consistency" can be defined in a variety of ways. For example, if appropriate customer service behaviors are missing, management should redirect employees and encourage a different set of behaviors.

Identify the causes of current behaviour

After determining the behavioral challenge in step 1, managers must identify what drives employees' current behavior. In part, this means understanding what is important to employees and what motivates them. It also means looking at yourself in the mirror and asking how your goals, skills, and characteristics might be impacting employee behavior. So good perception skills and self-insight continue to be extremely important.

Choose a solution or strategy for achieving behavioral goals

The third step involves generating options and selecting a strategy for maintaining, improving, or redirecting behavior. Of course, managers' analytical and diagnostic skills remain critical here, especially as they pertain to devising possible alternatives for responding to behavioral challenges. It's at this point that a thorough grasp of what theories and practices "work" in organizational Behaviour proves helpful. Managers are able to generate better solutions if they know what organizational Behaviour has to offer and can accurately weigh the pros and cons of alternatives within the demands of the context.

Implement the strategy, then monitor and adjust as needed

In many ways, this last step is the toughest of all. Implementation means that managers must develop a clear time frame for taking specific action steps. Managers also must be prepared to inspire, persuade, and motivate subordinates to embrace the steps necessary to actually modify existing behavior. Plus, it may be that the steps required fall outside managers' personal styles or comfort zones. Managers need to be prepared for that possibility and able respond in an adaptive fashion.

Summary

Organizational Behaviour is the study of how people act, think, and feel in organized settings. The roots of the field go back thousands of years. Since the 1900s, major perspectives on organizational Behaviour have included scientific management, the human relations approach, and the contingency approach. Adopting a contingency orientation means recognizing that organizational Behaviour is complex and driven by a variety of factors. Consequently, pat answers are elusive. Managers must develop their own answers, at least to an extent. Outstanding managers possess four sets of skills that allow them to effectively navigate the process of managing behaviour.

That process involves:

- Identifying the behavioral challenge;
- Identifying the causes of current behavior;
- Choosing a strategy for attaining behavioral goals; and

- Implementing and adjusting the chosen strategy as needed.

The behavioral challenges managers face today are exacerbated by the increasing complexity of the work environment and the fast pace of demographic and technological changes. The workforce is becoming increasingly diverse. Most of the growth in the work force is being driven by women and various racial or ethnic minorities. Increasing internationalization is also bringing people from a variety of cultural backgrounds together in the workplace.

Being able to manage diversity well is more important than ever because decisions are increasingly made in cross-functional teams and task forces. But most corporations still have a long way to go to create a work environment in which diversity is embraced. Likewise, managers need to understand that people who traditionally have been discriminated against (e.g., gays, people with disabilities) represent valuable pools of employee talent. Business practices, cultural values, and market structures usually vary—sometimes dramatically—from country to country. These factors impact all aspects of Behaviour management and raise the bar when it comes to managers' skills. As workplace demands continue to increase, they may spill over into family life. Exacerbating the issue is the fact that family structures have shifted over the years toward more dual-career couples and single parents. Managers who can recognize these work-family issues and craft flexible solutions will be rewarded with greater employee loyalty and performance.

REFERENCES

Adler, N.J. and John L. Graham, (1989) "Cross-Cultural Interaction: the International Comparison Fallacy?," *Journal of International Business Studies,* 20(3), 515-537.

Edmondson, G. (2000). See the world, erase its borders. *Business Week,* August 28, 113–114.

Fang, Tony (2003), "A Critique of Hofstede's Fifth National Culture Dimension", *International Journal of Cross Cultural Management,* 3, 347 - 368.

Gentile, M. C. (1996). *Managerial excellence through diversity*. Chicago, IL: Irwin; and Joplin, J.R.W., and C.S.

Harris, P. R, and Moran, R. T. (2000). *Managing cultural differences: Leadership strategies for a new world of business*. Houston, Texas: Gulf , 5th Edition.

Herring, R.D., (1990) "Nonverbal Communication: A Necessary Component of Cross-Cultural Counseling," *Journal of Multicultural Counseling and Development*, 18(4), 172-179.

Hofstede, Geert H. (1980), *Culture's Consequences: International Differences in Work-Related Values*, Beverly Hills: Sage Publications.

Hofstede, Geert H. (2001), *Culture's Consequences: Comparing Values, Behaviors, Institutions, and Organizations across Nations*, Thousand Oaks: Sage Publication Inc.

Inglehart, Ronald and Wayne E. Baker (2000), "Modernization, Cultural Change and the Persistence of Traditional Values", *American Sociological Review*, 65, Feb, 19-51.

Lewis, R. D. (2000). *When cultures collide: Managing successfully across cultures*. London: Nicholas Brealy.

Peterson, B. (2004) Cultural intelligence: A guide to work and life with people from other cultures. London: Intercultural Press.

Pfeffer, J., and J. F. Veiga (1999). Putting people first for organizational success. *Academy of Management Executive*, 13, 37-48.

Shellenbarger, S. (1997). Work gets wilder as employees insist on stable family life. *The Wall Street Journal*, July 16, B1.

Tung, R. L. (1996). Managing in Asia: Cross-cultural dimensions. In Joynt, P. and Warner, M. (eds.), *Managing across cultures: Issues and perspectives*. London: International Thomson Business.

Valbrun, M. (2000). Immigrants find economic boom brings more than higher pay. *The Wall Street Journal*, August 16, B1, B4.

Bibliography

Adam-Smith, D. and Peacock, A. (1994), *Cases in Orgasational Behaviour*. London: Pitman

Adler, N.J. and John L. Graham (1937), *Administration*, pp. 161–9. See Volume 8: 236–47.

Adler, N.J. and John L. Graham (1989), "Cross-Cultural Interaction: the International Comparison Fallacy?," *Journal of International Business Studies*, 20(3): 515-537.

Adolphs, R. (1999), Social cognition and the human brain. *Trends in Cognitive Sciences*, 3: 469–479.

Adukia, Rajkumar S. (2010), *Handbook on Stress Management with Self Care Techniques*, a part of the book accessed through www.carajkumarradukia.com/development/hbstress-management.doc,visisted this website on February 10.

Ajzen, I., and Fishbein, M. (1980), *Understanding attitudes and predicting social behavior*. Englewood Cliffs, NJ: Prentice-Hall.

Akhouri, N (2002), "Aligning HRM Strategies with Competitiveness". In: Singh, S. (ed.), *High Performance Organizations*, New Delhi: New Age, pp. 333-343.

Alexander, J. and Ciaschi, E. (2002), *Leadership Development in the Digital Age*. Presented at the Human Resource Planning Society Annual Conference.

Algert, N.E. (1996) "Conflict in the workplace" in *Proceedings: Women in Engineering Advocates Network*, Denver, CO., 123–127.

Algert, N.E. (2002), *The Center for Change and Conflict Resolution*, Bryan, TX: (979)775-5335 or e-mail cccr@bigfoot.com.

Algert, N.E., and Watson, K. (2002) *Conflict management: introductions for individuals and organizations*. Bryan, TX: (979)775-5335 or e-mail cccr@bigfoot.com.

Allen, LA. (2002), *Management and Organization*, McGraw-Hill Publishing Co., Ltd.,

Allen, Thomas J. (1973), *Communication Networks in R& D Laboratories*. R&D

Allen, Thomas J. (1977), *Managing the Flow of Technology*. Cambridge, MA: MIT Press.

Allpot, G.W. (1961), *Pattern and Growth in Personality*, New York, Holt.

Alton, R.E. (1987), *Managing Conflict: Interpersonal Dialogue and Third-Party Roles*.

Amabile, T. (1998) *Harvard Business Review*, September, 77–87.

Amabile, Teresa (1988), A model of creativity and innovation in organizations. In: B.M. Staw and L.L. Cummings III (Eds.), *Research in organizational behavior*: vol. 10, pp. 123-167, JAI Press.

Amabile, Teresa (1998), How to Kill Creativity. *Harvard Business Review*; Sept-Oct:77-87.

Amabile, Teresa and Regina Conti (1999), Changes in the Work Environment for Creativity during Downsizing. *Academy of Management Journal* 42(6): 630-640.

Antonovsky, A. 1987. The Salutogenic Perspective: Toward a New View of Health and Illness. *Institute for the Advancement of Science* 4(1):47-55.

Arnold, H. and Feldman, D. (1986), *Organizational Behavior*. New York: McGraw-Hill.

Arpita (1990), "Physiological and Psychological Effects of *Hatha Yoga*: A Review of the Literature", *The Journal of the International Association of Yoga Therapists*, Vol..1, Nos.I and II.

Arvey, R.D., Bouchard, T.J., Jr., Segal, N.L. and Abraham, L.M. (1989), "Job satisfaction: Environmental and genetic components." *Journal of Applied Psychology*, 74: 187-192.

Associates, V (1999), "Cultural Influences on Leadership and

Organizations: Project Globe." In: W.H. Mobley, M. J. Gessner, and V. Associates. *Excellent suggestions are also provided on how to manage conflict among groups.*

Atkinson, J.W. and Birch, D. (1970), *The Dynamics of Action*. New York: Wiley.

Bailey, E.P., (1996), *Plain English at Work: A guide to business writing and speaking*, Oxford University Press, UK.

Barnard, C. (1938), *The Functions of the Executive*. Cambridge, MA: Harvard University Press.

Barrett, A. and Beeson, J. (2002), *Developing Business Leaders for 2010*. The Conference Board, New York.

Barton, Cunningham J. and Ted Eberle (1990) "A Guide to Job Enrichment and Redesign," *Personnel* (February): 56–61.

Bartunek, Jean M., (1981) "Why Did You Do That? Attribution Theory in Organizations", *Business Horizons*, September-October.

Basadur, Min. (1997), Managing Creativity: A Japanese Model. In: R. Katz (Ed), *The Human Side of Managing Technological Innovation: A Collection of Readings*. New York: Oxford University Press.

Bass, Bernard (1989), *Stogdill's Handbook of Leadership: A Survey of Theory and Research*. New York: Free Press.

Bateman, Snell (2002), *Management: Competing in the New Era*, McGraw-Hill, Irwin, 2002.

Baugh, L.S., Fryar, M., Thomas, D.A., (1999), *How to Write First-Class Business Correspondence*, NTC Publishing Group, USA

Beatty, R.H. (1986), *The Five-Minute Interview*, John Wiley and Sons, USA.

Becker, T.E. (1992), Foci and bases of commitment: Are they distinctions worth making? *Academy of Management Journal*, 35, 232-244.

Bennett, R. (1997) *Organizational Behavior*. 3rd ed. London: M&E Pitman.

Bennis, W. (1989): *On Becoming a Leader*, Reading, MA: Addison-Wesley Publishers

Berne, E. (1961), *Transactional Analysis in Psychotherapy: A Systematic Individual and Social Psychiatry*. New York: Grove Press.

Berne, E. (1966), *Principles of Group treatment*. New York: Oxford University Press.

Berne, E. (1972), *What do you say after you say hello?: The Psychology of Human Destiny*. New York: Grove Press.

Bhala, Balmakund (1996) "*Yoga* in Modern Medicine", *International Journal of Alternative and Complementary Medicine*, April, (Reprinted in *Yoga and Health*, August.

Black, Stewart and Lyman W. Porter, (2000), *Management – Meeting New Challenges*, Prentice-Hall.

Blake and Mouton (n.d.), *The Versatile Manager: A Grid Profile*, pp.239-161

Blake, R.R., and Mouton, J.S. (1964), *The Managerial Grid*. Houston: Gulf Publishing Co.

Blake, Robert R. and Mouton, Janse S. (1985), *The Managerial Grid III: The Key to Leadership Excellence*. Houston: Gulf Publishing Co.

Blanchard, B.S. and W.J. Fabrycky (1990) *System Engineering and Analysis*, 2nd ed., Prentice-Hall, Englewood Cliffs, N.J.

Bolman, L. and Deal, T. (1991), *Reframing Organizations*. San Francisco: Jossey-Bass.

Borsenik, Frank D. and Alan T. Stutts, (1997), *The Management of Maintenance and Engineering Systems in the Hospitality Industry*, 4th ed. New York: John Wiley and Sons, Inc.

Bovee, Courtland L. (2008), *Business Communication Today*, 9th edition.

Bowditch, James L. and Anthony F. Buono, (1997) *A Primer on Organizational Behavior*, 4th, John Wiley and Sons.

Bowers, K. S. (1973), Situationism in psychology: An analysis and a critique. *Psychological Review*, 80: 307-336.

Bowlby, J. (1969), *Attachment*. Vol. 1 of Attachment and loss. New York: Basic Books.

Brief, A.P. and Aldag, R.J. (1981), The self in organizations: A conceptual review. *Academy of Management Review*, 6, 75-88.

Browning, L., and Colman, A. (2004), Evolution of coordinated alternating reciprocity in repeated dyadic games. *Journal of Theoretical Biology,* 229: 549–557.

Buchanan, Bruce (2001), Creativity at the Metalevel. AAAI -2000 Presidential Address. *AI Magazine,* Fall. www.findarticles.com

Buchanan, D. and Huczynski, A. (2004), *Organisational Behaviour: An Introductory Text,* 5th ed., Harlow: FT/Prentice-Hall.

Budhwar, P. (2001), Doing business in India, Thunderbird *International Businesss Review,* 43(4): 549–568.

Burns, Tom and Stalker, G.M. (1961) *Management of Innovation,* London: Tavistock Publications, p. 19.

Bush, R. A., Baruch and Folger, J. P. (1994), *The Promise of Mediation.* San Francisco: Jossey-Bass Publishers.

Buss, D.M. (2007), *Evolutionary Psychology: The New Science of the Mind* (3rd ed.), Boston: Allyn and Bacon.

Cacioppe, R. (1998), "An Integrated Model and Approach for the Design of Effective Leadership Development Programs." *Leadership and Organization Development Journal,* 19(1): 44-53.

Cantor, N. and Kihlstrom, J.F. (1985), Social intelligence: The cognitive basis of personality. *Review of Personality and Social Psychology,* 6: 15-33.

Carland, J.W., Hoy, F., Boulton, W.R. and Carland, J.A. (1984), Differentiating entrepreneurs from small business owners: A conceptualization. *The Academy of Management Review,* 9(2), 354-359.

Certo (2002), *Modern Management,* 9th Edition, Prentice-Hall of India.

Chambers, R. (2002), *Participatory Workshops: A Sourcebook of 21 Sets of Ideas and Activities,* Earthscan, UK.

Chandra Bose, D. (2002), *Principles of Management and Administration,* Prentice-Hall of India.

Chi, M. 1997. Creativity: Shifting Across Ontological Categories Flexibly. In: *Creative Thought: An Investigation of Conceptual Structures and Processes. et al.* T. Ward, S. Smith.

Cleland, D.I. and W.R. King (1972), *Management: A Systems Approach*, McGraw-Hill, New York, N.Y.

Cohen, A. *et al.* (1995) *Effective Behaviour in Organisations: Cases, Concepts, and Student Experiences.* 6th ed. Irwin/McGraw-Hill.

Cole, Roger (1994), *Relaxation, Physiology and Practice*, Synchrony Applied Health Sciences, Ways Stress Affects Individuals", http://www.drkoop.com/conditions/stress.

Collier, J. and Esteban, R. (2000), "Systemic Leadership: Ethical and Effective." *Leadership and Organization Development Journal*, 21(4): 207-215.

Combs, Arthur W. and Donald Snygg (1949), *Individual Behavior: A Perceptual Approach To Behavior*, Harper and Row: NY.

Consulting Psychologists Press (CPP), *Thomas-Kilmann Conflict Mode Instrument.* Palo Alto, CA: (800) 624-1765 or available on the World Wide Web at http://www.cpp-db.com.

Cowling, A., Stanworth, M., Bennett, R., Curran, J. and Lyons, P. (1993), *Behavioural Sciences for Managers.* 2nd ed. London: Edward Arnold.

Crews, F., *et al.* (1995), The memory wars: Freud's legacy in dispute. New York: NYREV Collections.

Dacey, John S. and Kathleen H. Lennon (1998), *Understanding Creativity: The Interplay of Biological, Social and Psychological Factors.* San Francisco: Jossey-Bass.

Dahl, Cheryl (2000), Have You Seen the Five Faces of Genius? *Fast Company* October: 54-62.

Dance, Frank E. X., and Larson, Carl (1976), *The Functions of Human Communication: A Theoretical Approach.* New York: Holt, Rinehart and Winston.

Dance, Frank E. X., and Zak-Dance, Carol (1986), *Public Speaking.* New York: Harper and Row.

Dann and Timothy Hornsey, D. (1986), "Towards a Theory of Interdepartmental Conflict in Hotels," *International Journal of Hospitality Management*, 23.

Davis, Keith (1957), *Human Relations at Work: The Dynamics of Organizational Behavior*, New York: McGraw-Hill.

Davis, Keith (1969), Management Communication and the Grapevine, *Harvard Business Review*, Vol. 31.

Day, D.V. (2001), "Leadership Development: A Review in Context." *Leadership Quarterly*, 11(4): 581-613.

de Bono, Edward (1970), *Lateral Thinking: Creativity Step by Step*. New York: Harper-Collins.

DeCharms, R. (1968), *Personal Causation: The Internal Affective Determinants of Behavior*. New York: Academic Press.

Deci, E.L., and Ryan, R.M. (2000), The "what" and the "why" of goal pursuits: Human needs and the self-determination of behavior. *Psychological Inquiry*, 11: 227-268.

Deetz, S. A. and Stevenson, S. L. (1986), *Managing Interpersonal Communication*. New York: Harper and Row Publishers.

Dellinger, S. (1989), *Psycho-geometrics. How to Use Geometric Psychology to Influence People*. Englewood Cliffs, NJ: Prentice-Hall.

Drazin, Robert, Mary Ann Glynn, and Robert Kazanjian, (1999), *Multilevel Theorizing about Creativity in Organizations: A Sensemaking Perspective*. Academy of Management Review, April. Available URL: www.findarticles.com.

Drucker, P. (1992), *Innovation and Entrepreneurial Practices and Principles*, New York: Harper Business: 19.

Drucker, Peter F. (1988), "The Coming of the New Organizations," *Harvard Business Review*, 88(1): 45 - 53.

Dumaine , Brian (1984), "A Checklist of Qualities That Make a Good Boss," *Nation's Business* (November).

Dumaine, Brian (1984), "The New Non-Managers," *Fortune*, February 22, 1993, pp. 80–84.

Dunbar, Kevin. (1997), How Scientists Think: On Line Creativity and Conceptual Change in Science. In: T.S. Ward, S.M. Smith and J. Vaid (eds), *Creative Thought: An Investigation of Conceptual Processes and Structures*. Washington D.C: American Psychological Association.

Dusay, J. (1972), Egograms and the constancy hypothesis. *Transactional Analysis Journal*, 2(3), 37-41.

Eagly, A. and Chaiken, S. (1993), *The Psychology of Attitudes.* Fort Worth, TX: Harcourt, Brace.

Edelman, Gerald (1992), *Bright Air, Brilliant Fire: On the Matter of the Mind.* Basic Books.

Edmondson, G. (2000), See the world, erase its borders. *Business Week,* August 28, 113–114.

Edwards, J.R. (1996), An examination of competing versions of the person-environment fit approach to stress. *Academy of Management Journal*, 39: 292-339.

Eisenberger, R., Rhoades, L., and Carmeron, J. (1999), Does pay for performance increase or decrease perceived self-determination and intrinsic motivation? *Journal of Personality and Social Psychology*, 77: 1026-1040.

Ernest R. Hilgard, Richard C. Atkinson and Rital L. Atkinson (1975), *Introduction to Psychology*, Oxford and IBH Publication Co. Pvt. Ltd.

Etzioni, A. (1975), *Comparative Analysis of Complex Organizations.* New York: Macmillan Publishing Co.

Etzioni, A. (1988), *The Moral Dimension: Toward a New Economics.* New York: Free Press.

Eysenck, H.J., (1971) *The Structure of Human Personality* (3rd ed.), New York , Methuen.

Falbraith,J. (1977), *Organization Design, Reading*, MA: Addision - Wesley.

Fang, Tony (2003), "A Critique of Hofstede's Fifth National Culture Dimension", *International Journal of Cross Cultural Management*, 3: 347-368.

Fayol, H., *General and Industrial Administration,* Sir Isaac Pitman and Sons, London, UK, 1949.

Festinger, L. (1957), *A Theory of Cognitive Dissonance.* Stanford, CA: Stanford University Press.

Fincham, R. and Rhodes, P. (1996), *The Individual, Work and Organization: Behavioral Studies for Business and Management.* 2nd ed. Oxford: Oxford University Press.

Fincham, R. and Rhodes, P. (2005), *Principles of Organizational Behaviour*. 4th ed. Oxford: Oxford University Press.

Fisher, R., Ury, W., and Patton, B. (1991), *Getting to Yes: Negotiating Agreement Without Giving In*, (2nd ed.), Penguin Books.

Floyd, F. J., and Widaman, K. F. (1995), Factor analysis in the development and refinement of clinical assessment instruments. *Psychological Assessment*, 7: 286-299.

Foote, N.N. (1951), Identification as the basis for a theory of motivation. *American Sociological Review*, 16: 14-21.

Ford, Cameron. (1996), A Theory of Individual Creative Action in Multiple Social Domains. *Academy of Management Review*. 21(4): 1112-1142.

Foster, T., 2001. *101 Ways to Better Business Writing*, Kogan Page, India.

Freiberg, Kevin and Jackie Freiberg, (1996), *NUTS! Southwest Airlines' Crazy Recipe for Business and Personal Success*, Bard Press, p. 298).

French, W. and Bell, C. (1984) *Organization development: behavioral science interventions for organization improvement*. 3rd ed. New Jersey: Prentice-Hall.

Friesen and J.A. Johnson, M. (1995): *The Success Paradigm*, Westport, CT: Quorum Books.

Fulmer, R.M. (1997), "The Evolving Paradigm of Leadership Development." *Organizational Dynamics*, 25(4).

Gallagher, K. *et al.* (1999) People in Organisations: An Active learning Approach: Blackwell.

Galvin, Kathleen M. and Charles A. Wilkinson (2006), *The Communication Process: Impersonal and Interpersonal*, Roxbury Publishing Company.

Gecas, V. (1982), The self-concept. *Annual Review of Sociology*, 8: 1-33.

Gentile, M.C. (1996), *Managerial Excellence through Diversity*. Chicago, IL: Irwin; and Joplin, J. R. W., and C. S.

Gerhardt, B. (1987), How important are dispositional factors as determinants of job satisfaction – Implications for job design and other personnel programs. *Journal of Applied Psychology*, 72: 366-373.

Gerloff, E. (1985), *Organizational theory and design: a strategic approach for management*. New York: McGraw-Hill

Gibson, J., Ivanchevich, J., Donnelly, J. and Konopaske, R. (2006), *Organizations: Behavior, Structure, Processes*. 12th ed. McGraw-Hill.

Gilsdorf, J.W. (1989), *Business Correspondence for Today*, John Wiley and Sons, USA.

Goleman, D., Boyatzis, R., and McKee, A. (2002), *Primal Leadership*. Boston: Harvard Business School Press.

Gordon, J. (1993), *A Diagnostic Approach to Organizational Behaviour*. 4th ed. Boston: Allyn and Bacon.

Gottfredson, L.S. (1981), Circumscription and compromise: A Developmental Theory of Occupational Aspirations. *Journal of Counseling Psychology*, 28: 545-579.

Goulding, M. M., and Goulding, R. L. (1997), *Changing Lives through Redecision Therapy* (rev. ed.), New York: Grove/ Atlantic Press.

Graesser, A.C., Woll, S.B., Kowalski, D.J. and Smith, D.A. (1980), Memory for typical and atypical actions in scripted activities. *Journal of Experimental Psychology*, 6: 503-515.

Greenberg, J. and Baron, R. (1993), *Behavior in Organizations: Understanding and Managing the Human Side of Work*. 4th ed. Boston: Allyn and Bacon.

Greenwald, A.G. and Pratkanis, A.R. (1984) The self. In: R.S. Wyer and T.S. Srull (Eds), *Handbook of Social Cognition*. Hillsdale, NH: Earlbaum.

Griffin, R. and Moorhead, G. (1986), *Organizational Behavior*. Boston Houghton Mifflin

Gryskiewicz, Stanley S. (2000), Cashing in on Creativity at Work. *Psychology Today*, September/October: 63-65.

Hager, P. and Scheiber, H. (1997), *Designing and Delivering Scientific, Technical, and Managerial Presentations*, John Wiley and Sons, USA.

Hammer, Michael, (1996) *Beyond Reengineering*, New York: HarperBusiness.

Hammer, Michael, (2002) "Process Management and the Future of Six Sigma", *MIT Sloan Management Review*, 42:2, Winter.

Hardy, C. L., and Van Vugt, M. (2006), Nice guys finish first: The competitive altruism hypothesis. *Personality and Social Psychology Bulletin*, 32: 1402–1413.

Hargadon, Andrew and Robert Sutton (2000), Building an Innovation Factory. *Harvard Business Review*, May-June: 157-166.

Hargadon, Andrew B. (1999), *Group Cognition and Creativity in Organizations. Research on Managing Groups and Teams.* Vol 2. pp. 137-155. Greenwich, CT: JAI Press Inc.

Harold, Koontz (1961), "The Management Theory Jungle", *Journal of the Academy of Management*, December.

Harold, Koontz (1962), "Making Sense of Management Theory", *Harvard Business Review*, July-August.

Harold, Koontz (1980), "The Management Theory Revisited", in *Academy of Management Review*, April.

Harold, Koontz , (2001), *Essentials of Management*, Tata McGraw-Hill, 5th Edition.

Harold, Koontz and C. O'Donnell, (1972), *Principles of Management: An Analysis of Managerial Functions*, 5th ed., McGraw-Hill, New York, N.Y.

Harold, Koontz and Weihrich Heinz (1990), *Essentials of Management*, Fifth Edition, McGraw-Hill.

Harold, Koontz, C. O'Donnell, and H. Weihrich, (1980), *Management*, 7th ed., McGraw-Hill, New York, N.Y.

Harris, P. R. and Moran, R. T. (2000), *Managing Cultural Differences: Leadership Strategies for a New World of Business.* Houston, Texas: Gulf , 5th Edition.

Heinssen, R. K., Levendusky, P. G., and Hunter, R. H. (1995), Client as colleague: Therapeutic contracting with the seriously mentally ill. *American Psychologist*, 50(7): 522-532.

Hellriegel, Jackson and Slocum, (2002), *Management: A Competency-Based Approach*, South Western, 9th edition.

Hennagan (1997), *Management Concepts and Practices*, Macmillan India, Ltd.

Henry, I. Tosi, John R. Rizzo, Stephen J. Carroll, (1998) *Organizational Behaviour - A Comprehensive Mannual*, Becon Books, New Delhi.

Herbert, Samir, Chatterjee and Mark. (2006), *Management in India: Trends and Transition*, Response Books, New Delhi.

Herring, R.D. (1990), "Non-verbal Communication: A Necessary Component of Cross-Cultural Counseling," *Journal of Multicultural Counseling and Development*, 18(4): 172-179.

Hersey and Blanchard (2002), *Management of Organisational Behaviour*, 8th Edition, Prentice-Hall.

Hersey, P. and K.H. Blanchard (1982) *Management of Organisational Behaviour: Utilizing Human Resources*. 4th Edition. Prentice-Hall of India Pvt. Ltd., New Delhi, p. 343.

Hersey, Paul, Kenneth H. Blanchard, Dewy E. Johson, (2004), *Management of Organizaitonal Behaviour - Leading Human Resources*, Prentice-Hall of India Private Limited, New Delhi,

Hertzberg, F. (1966), *Work and the Nature of Nan*. Cleveland: World Publishing.

Hillier, Bill and A. Penn (1991), Visible Colleges: Structure and Randomness in the Place of Discovery. *Science in Context* 4(1): 23-49.

Hodge, B. and Anthony, W. (1984), *Organization Theory*. 2nd ed. Boston: Allyn and Bacon.

Hofstede, Geert H. (1980), *Culture's Consequences: International Differences in Work-related Values*, Beverly Hills: Sage Publications.

Hofstede, Geert H. (2001), *Culture's Consequences: Comparing Values, Behaviors, Institutions, and Organizations Across Nations*, Thousand Oaks: Sage Publication Inc.

Holt, David H. (1993), *Management - Principles and Practices*, Prentice-Hall, Englewood Cliffs, New Jersey.

Holt, David H. (n.d.), *Personal Communication And Consulting Withy Falcooner Glass Industries*, Inc,. Jamestown, New York.

Homans G. C. (1958) *The Human Group* New York: Harcout, Brace and World.

Huczynski, A. and Buchanan, D. (2007) *Organisational Behaviour: An Introductory Text*, 6th ed., Harlow: FT/Prentice-Hall.

Hull, C.L. (1943), *Principles of Behavior. Appleton-Century*, New York.

Hurlock, E.B. (2006), *Personality Development*, 28th Reprint. New Delhi: Tata McGraw-Hill.

Inglehart, Ronald and Wayne E. Baker (2000), "Modernization, Cultural Change and the Persistence of Traditional Values", *American Sociological Review*, 65, Feb, 19 - 51.

Intagliata, J., Ulrich, D. and Smallwood, N. (2000), "Leveraging Leadership Competencies to Produce Leadership Brand: Creating Distinctiveness by Focusing on Strategy and Results." *Human Resource Planning*, 23(3),

Isaksen, Scott. 1983. Toward a Model for the Facilitation of Creative Problem Solving. Journal of Creative Behavior 17(1):18-31.

Isen, Alice M. 1990. The Influence of Positive and Negative Affect on Cognitive Organization: Some Implications for Development. In N.L .Stein, B. Leventhal, T. Trabasso (eds.) *Psychological and Biological Approaches to Emotion*. Hillsdale, NJ: Erlbaum.

Jaworski, B. J. and Kohli, A. K. (1993) Market orientation: antecedents and consequences *Journal of Marketing* 57(2) pp.53-70.

John M. Ivancevich, Peter Lorenzi, and Steven J. Skinner, with Philip B. Crosby, *Management: Quality and Competitiveness* (Boston: Richard D. Irwin, 1996), 254.

John P. Kotter , *A Force for Change: How Leadership Differs From Management* (The Free Press, 1990),

John W. Newstrom and Keith Davis, (1999) *Organizational Behaviour- Human Behaviour at Work*, Tata McGraw-Hill Edition, (11th Edition), New Delhi.

Johnson, J. A. (1998), "Interview with Warren Bennis," *Journal of Healthcare Management* (July/ August): 293.

Kakabadse, A. (1991) The Wealth Creations: *Top Peoples, Top Teams and Executive Best Practice*. Kogan Page.

Kameda, T., and Tindale, R. S. (2006), Groups as adaptive devices: Human docility and group aggregation mechanisms in evolutionary context.

Kandel, E. R., Schwartz, J. H., and Jessell, T. M. (Eds.), (1991), *Principles of Neural Science* (Third edition), Elsevier, New York.

Kanungo, R.N. and Mendonca, M. (1994), Culture and performance improvement, *Productivity*, 35(3): 447-453

Karpman, S. (1968), Fairy tales and script drama analysis. *Transactional Analysis Bulletin*, 7(26): 39-43.

Katz, D. (1960), The functional approach to the study of attitudes. *Public Opinion Quarterly*, 24: 163-204.

Katzenbach, J.R., and Smith, D.K. (1992) *Wisdom of Teams*, Harvard Business School.

Kaul, Asha (2009), *Business Communication*, Prentice-Hall of India New Delhi. 2nd edition.

Kelley, Harold H., (1973), "The Processes of Casual Attribution", *American Psychologist*, February.

Kelly, Robert and Janet Caplan (1997), How Bell Labs Creates Star Performers. In: R. Katz (ed.), *The Human Side of Managing Technological Innovation: A Collection of Readings*, New York: Oxford University Press.

Kerr, X., and Levine, X. (2008), The Detection of Social Exclusion: Evolution and beyond. *Group Dynamics: Theory, Research, and Practice*, 12: 39–52.

Kerzner, H., (1989), *Project Management: A Systems Approach to Planning, Scheduling, and Controlling*, 3rd ed., Van Nostrand Reinhold, New York, N.Y.

Kincaid, S.B. and Gordick, D. (2003), "The Return on Investment of Leadership Development: Differentiating Our Discipline." *Consulting Psychology Journal: Practice and Research*, 55(1): 47-

57.

Kinicki, A. and Kreitner, R. (2006) *Organizational Behavior: Key Concepts, Skills, and Best Practices.* 2nd ed. McGraw-Hill

Klein, S. B. (1991), *Learning: Principles and Applications* (second edition), McGraw-Hill, New York.

Kolb, D.A., I.M.. Rubin and J.M. Mc Intyre (1979), *Organizational Psychology – an experiential approach.* Third edition Prentice-Hall, INC., Englewood cliffs, New Jersey 07632. p. 496.

Komaki, J. (1982), Managerial effectiveness: Potential contributions of the behavioral approach. *Journal of Organizational Behavior Management*, 3: 71-83.

Koontz, Harold, Cyril O and Donnell, (1968), *Principles of Management*, McGraw-Hill Publishing Co. Ltd.

Kouzes, James M. and Posner, Barry Z. (1987), *The Leadership Challenge.* San Francisco: Jossey-Bass.

Lasater, Judith, (1992), "10 Ways to relax deeply", *Yoga Journal*, Jan/Feb, pp.74-81

Leavitt, Harold J., *Managerial Psychology*, University of Chicago Press: Chicago IL 1964 (2nd Ed.),

Leighton, Alexander H. (1949), *Human Relations in a Changing World*, New York: E. P. Dutton and Co. Inc., pp 156-161.

Levendusky, P. G., Berglas, S., Dooley, C. P., and Landau, R. J. (1983), Therapeutic contract program: A preliminary report on a behavioral alternative to the token economy. *Behavior Research and Therapy*, 21: 137-142.

Levendusky, P. G., Willis, B. S., and Ghinassi, F. A. (1994), The therapeutic contracting program: A comprehensive continuum of care model. *Psychiatric Quarterly*, 65: 189-208.

Levine, Michael W., and Jeremy M. (1991), *Shefner, Fundamentals of Sensation and Perception*, (2nd Ed), Brooks/Cole, Pacific Grove,CA.

Lewis, R. D. (2000), *When Cultures Collide: Managing Successfully Across Cultures.* London: Nicholas Brealy.

Livingston, J. Sterling, (1969), "Pygmalion in Management", *Harvard Business Review*, July/August.

Locke, E.A. (1976), The nature and causes of job satisfaction. In M.D. Dunette (Ed.), *Handbook of Industrial and Organizational Psychology*: 1297-1350. Chicago: Rand McNally.

Loffredo, D. A., Harrington, R., Munoz, M. K., and Knowles, L. R. (2004), The ego state questionnaire - Revised. *Transactional Analysis Journal*, 34, 90-95.

London, Manuel (Ed.) (2001), *How People Evaluate Others in Orgnizations*, Mahwah NJ: Erlbaum.

Luthans, F. (2005), *Organisational behaviour*. (10th ed.) McGraw-Hill Irwin.

Luthans, Fred (1988), Successful Vs. Effective Real Mangers, *The Academy of Management Executive*, 2(2): 1988.

Luthans, Fred (1995), *Organizational Behaviour*, McGraw-Hill, New York.

Lynch, J., and Ford, J. (1977), The broken heart: The Medical Consequences of loneliness. New York: Basic Books.

Macionis, J. and Plummer, K. (1997), *Sociology: A Global Introduction*. New York: Prentice-Hall.

MacKenzie, R.A., (1969), "The Management Process in 3-D," *Harvard Business Review*, Nov.-Dec.: 80-87.

Madhukar (2008), *Business Communication*, Vikas Publishing House, New Delhi.

Majchrzak, Ann and Qianwei Wang (1996), "Breaking the Functional Mindset in Process Organizations", *Harvard Business Review*, Sept - Oct.

Manjunath, NK *et al*, (1999), "Factors influencing changes in tweezer dexterity scores following yoga training.", *Indian Physiol Pharmacol*, April; 43(2): 225-9

Markham, R., (1998), *Excellence in Public Speaking*, Simon and Schuster, USA.

Maslow, A.H. (1943), "A Theory of Human Motivation", *Psychological Review*, 50: 370-396.

Matlin, M., and Stang, D. (1978), *The pollyanna principle: Selectivity in language, memory, and thought*. Cambridge, MA: Schenkman.

Matteson, M. and Ivancevich, J. (1999) *Management and Organisational Behavior Classics*. 7th ed. Irwin/McGraw-Hill.

Meenakshi Raman& Prakash Singh, (2006), *Business Communication*, Oxford Higher Education.

Miller, L. (1989), *Barbarians to Bureaucrats: Corporate Lifestyle Strategies*, New York: Fawcett.

Mintzberg, H. (1973), *The Nature of Managerial Work*, New York: Harper and Row.

Mintzberg, H. (1996), "The Manager's Job: Folklore and Fact". In: F.H. Maidment (ed), *Management 96/97*, 4th ed., Sluice Dock, Guilford, CT: Brown and Benchmark Publishers.

Mintzberg, Henry (1973), *The Nature of Managerial Work*, Harper and Row.

Morgen Witzel, (2000), *Human Resource Management*, ed., 8 vols. Bristol: Thoemmes Press.

Morris, C.G., and Maisto, A.A. (1999), *Understanding Psychology*. 4th ed. New Jersey: Prentice-Hall, Inc.

Mort, S., 1997. *Professional Report Writing*, Gower Publishing, USA.

Mowrer, O. H. (1960), *Learning Theory and Behavior*. Wiley, New York.

Moxley, R.S. and O'Connnor Wison, P. (1998), "A Systems Approach to Leadership Development." In: C.D. McCauley, R.S. Moxley, and E. Van Velsor (eds.), *The Center for Creative Leadership Handbook of Leadership Development*. San Francisco: Jossey-Bass, pp. 217-241.

Mullins, L. (2006), *Essentials of Organizational Behaviour*. Harlow: Prentice-Hall.

Mullins, L. (2007), *Management and Organizational Behaviour*. 8th ed. FT/Prentice-Hall

Munn, N.L, (1967), *Introduction to Psychology* , Oxford and IBH (Indian Ed.), New Delhi, 1967.

Murphy, H.A. and Hilderbrandt, H.W., (1997), *Effective Business Communication*, McGraw-Hill, Singapore.

Myers, D. (2005), *Social Psychology*. 8th ed. Boston: McGraw-Hill.

Myers, I.B., McCaulley, MH (1998), *Quenk NL, Hammer AL. MBTI Manual: A guide to the development and use of the Myers Briggs type indicator*. 3rd ed. Mountain View, Calif: Consulting Psychologists Press.

Naomi Stuart, (2008), *5DM, Salisbury House*, 15-17 The Broadway, Old Hatfield, Herts AL9 5HZ.

Nelson, D. and Quick, J. (2006) *Organizational Behavior: Foundations, Realities and Challenges*. 5th ed. Thomson South-Western

Nevins, M., and Stumpf, S. (1999), "21st-Century Leadership: Redefining Management Education." *Strategy, Management, Competition*, 3rd Quarter: 41-51.

Nicholson, Nigel (2003), "How to Motivate Your Problem People", *Harvard Business Review*, January: 62.

Novey, T. (2002), Measuring the effectiveness of transactional analysis: An international study. *Transactional Analysis Journal*, 32: 8-24.

Ornish, D. (1998), *Love and survival: The scientific basis for the healing power of intimacy*. New York: HarperCollins.

Ostroff, Frank, (1999), *The Horizontal Organization* (New York, Oxford University Press.

Penn, A., J. Desyllas, and J. Vaughan. 1999. The Space of Innovation: Interaction and Communication in the Work Environment. Environmental and Planning B: *Planning and Design* 26: 193-218.

Persons, J. B., Davidson, J., and Tompkins, M. A. (2001), Essential components of cognitive-behavior therapy for depression. Washington, DC: American Psychological Association.

Peterson, B. (2004), *Cultural intelligence: A guide to work and life with people from other cultures*. London: Intercultural Press.

Pfeffer, J. (1981), *Power in organizations*, Boston, Pitman Publishing.

Pfeffer, J. and J. F. Veiga (1999), Putting people first for organizational success. *Academy of Management Executive*, 13: 37–48.

Plender, J. (1997) *A Stake in the future: the Stakeholding Solution*, Nicholas Breadley Publishing.

Poe, R.W. (1994), *The McGraw-Hill Handbook of Business Letters*, 3rd edition, McGraw-Hill, USA.

Pondy, L. R. (1967), Organizational Conflict: Concepts and Models *Administrative Science Quarterly* 12(2) pp.296-320.

Prahalad, C K and Ramaswamy, Venkatram (2004), *The Future of Competition: Co-creating Value with Customers*, Harvard Business School Press.

Prahalad, C.K. (2004), *The Fortune at the Bottom of the Pyramid: Eradicating Poverty through Profit*, Wharton Business Publishing.

Pretty, J., *et al.* (1995), *Participatory Learning and Action: a trainers guide*, IIED, UK.

Prince, Morton (1992), *The Unconscious* (2nd ed.), New York, Macmillan.

Pugh, D. (1997), *Organization Theory: Selected Readings.* 4th ed. London: Penguin Books.

Rai, Urmila and S.M. Rai (2008), *Business Communication*, Himalaya Publishing House, Mumbai.

Rangnekar, S. (2006), The Temple ethos in Indian Management, *Science Tech Entreprenurship*, January: 4-7 31.

Raymond J. Aldag and Timothy M. Stearns (1987), *Management*, Cincinnati: Southwestern.

Reiser, Paul (1994), *Couplehood.* New York: Bantam Books.

Robbins, S (1998), *Organizational Behaviour*, 8th ed, New Delhi: Prentice-Hall of India, 16th Indian reprint.

Robbins, S. (2005) *Organisational Behaviour: Concepts, Controversies and Applications.* 11th ed. New Jersey: Prentice-Hall

Robbins, S. and Judge, T. (2008) *Essentials of Organizational Behavior.* 9th ed. New Jersey: Pearson/Prentice-Hall.

Robbins, S.B. (2005), *Organizational Behaviour.* New Delhi: Prentice-Hall of India.

Robert D. Dewar and Donald P. Simet, "A Level-Specific Prediction of Spans of Control Examining the Effects of Size, Technology, and Specialization," *Academy of Management Journal* (March 1981): 5.

Robert Katz, (1974), "Skills of an effective administrator," *Harvard Business Review*, September-October: 90-101

Roberts, Edward (1997), Managing Invention and Innovation: What We've Learned. In: R. Katz (ed.), *The Human Side of Managing Technological Innovation: A Collection of Readings.* New York: Oxford University Press.

Roger (1991), *A Kick in the Seat of the Pants.* New York: Harper and Row Publisher.

Rollinson, D. and Edwards, D. and Broadfield, A. (1998) *Organisational behaviour analysis: an integrated approach.* Harlow: Addison Wesley.

Rosenfeld, R. and Wilson, D. (1999) *Managing Organisations: Text, Readings and Cases.* 2nd ed. London: McGraw-Hill

Rowan, J., and Cooper, M. (1999), *The plural self: Multiplicity in everyday life.* London: Sage Publications.

Sahay, S. and Walsham, G. (1997), Social structure and managerial agency in India, *Organiziaton Studies*, 18: 415-444.

Sansone, C., and Harackiewicz, J.M. (2000), *Intrinsic and extrinsic motivation: The search for optimal motivation and performance.* San Diego: Academic Press.

Sathyaraju (2002), *Management : Text and Cases*, Prentice-Hall of India Publishers

Schein, Hdgar H. (1997), *Organizational Culture and Leadership*, 2nd ed. San Francisco, CA: Jossey Bass Publishers.

Schermerhorn, (2001), Hunt and Osborn, Organisational Behavior, John Wiley, 7th edition.

Schwartz, M.D. (1973), *Physiological Psychology*, Englewood Cliffs, N.J.: Prentice-Hall.

Scott, P. (2005), *Divisions of Labour.* A Pearson Custom Publications

Seashore, S. E., Lawler, E. E., Mirvis, P., and Cammann, C. (eds.) (1982), *Observing and Measuring Organizational Change: A Guide to Field Practice.* Wiley, New York.

Seligman, M., and Csikszentmihalyi, M. (2000), Positive psychology. *American Psychologist*, 55(1): 5-14.

Shalley, Christina E., Lucy Gilson, and Terry C. Blum. 2000. Matching Creativity Requirements and the Work Environment: Effects on Satisfaction and Intentions to Leave. *Academy of Management Journal* 43(2): 215-243.

Shellenbarger, S. (1997), Work gets wilder as employees insist on stable family life. *The Wall Street Journal,* July 16, B1.

Shippes, Frank and Charles C. Manz (1988), "Employee Self-Management Without Formally Designated Teams: An Alternative Road to Empowerment," *Organizational Dynamics* (Winter 1992): 48–61.

Siegel, D. J. (1999), The developing mind: How relationships and the brain interact to shape who we are. New York: Guilford Press.

Simonton, Dean K. (1977), Creative Productivity, Age, and Stress: A Biographical Time-series Analysis of Ten Classical Composers. *Journal of Personality and Social Psychology* 35: 791-804.

Simonton, Dean K. (2000), Creativity: Cognitive, Personal, Developmental, and Social Aspects. *American Psychologist,* 55(1): 151-158.

Sims, H. P., Szilagyi, A. D., and McKemey, D. R. (1976), Antecedents of work-related expectancies. *Academy of Management Journal,* 19: 547-559.

Singh, Shettiwar, Udupa (1982), "Physiological and Therapeutic Studies on Yoga", *The Yoga Review,* 2(4).

Smith, B. (2004), *Body Language.* Delhi: Rohan Book Company.

Smith, Gerald F. (1998), Idea-Generation Techniques: A Formulary of Active Ingredients. *Journal of Creative Behavior* 32(2): 107-133.

Smith, K.A. (2000), *Project Management and Teamwork.* New York: McGraw-Hill BEST

Smith, M. *et al.* (1982) *Introducing organizational behavior.* London: Macmillan.

Smith, M.J. (1982), *Persuasion and human action.* Belmont, CA: Wadsworth.

Spiro, L.N. (2003), "In Search of Leaders." *CEO Magazine*, October: 25-30.

Spitz, R. (1945), Hospitalism: An inquiry into the genesis of psychiatric conditions in early childhood. In: O. Fenichel *et al.* (eds.), *The Psychoanalytic Study of the Child*, 1: 53-74, New York: International Universities Press.

Stacey, Ralph D. (1996), Complexity and Creativity in Organizations. San Francisco: Berrett- Koehler. Sternberg. Robert. 1988. *The Nature of Creativity: Contemporary Psychological Perspectives*. Cambridge, UK: Cambridge University Press.

Staw, B.M. (1995), *Psychological Dimensions of Organizational Behaviour*, 2nd Edition, Engle Wood Cliffs, Prentice-Hall.

Staw, B.M., and Ross, J. (1978), Commitment to a policy decision: A multi-theoretical perspective. *Administrative Science Quarterly*, 23: 40-64.

Steiner, C. (1971), *Scripts people live: Transactional analysis of life scripts*. New York: Grove Press.

Stephen P. Robbins (1980), *The Administrative Process*, 2nd ed. Englewood Cliffs, NJ, Prentice-Hall, pp. 194-195.

Stephen P. Robbins, (2003), *Organizational Behaviour*, 10th ed., Prentice-Hall of India Private Limited, New Delhi.

Stephen P.Robbins, (1998), *Organizational Behaviour, Concepts, Controversies and Applications*, Prentice-Hall of India Private Limited, New Delhi, (Eight Edition),

Stewart I, Joines V. (1987), *TA Today: A New Introduction to Transactional Analysis*. Chapel Hill, NC: Lifespace Publishing.

Stoner (2002), *Management*, 6th Edition, Prentice-Hall of India Publishers

Stoner James A. F., Freeman R. Edward, and Gilbert, Jr. Daniel R. (2003), *Management*, New Delhi: Prentice-Hall of India, Sixth Edition.

Suomi, S. J., Collins, M. L., Harlow, H. F., and Ruppenthal, G. (1976), Effects of maternal and peer separations on young monkeys. *Journal of Child Psychology and Psychiatry and Allied Disciplines,* 17(2): 101-112.

Sushil Bahl, (2009), *Business Communication Today,* Response Books, Reprint.

Sutton, R. S., and Barto, A. G. (1990), Time-derivative models of Pavlovian reinforcement. In: Moore, J. W., and Gabriel, M. (Eds.), *Learning and Computational Neuroscience.* MIT Press.

Swaminathan. V.D and Kaliappan. K.V. (2001), *Psychology for Effective Living.* Chennai. The Madras Psychology Society.

Sylwester, Robert (1393), "What the Biology of the Brain Tells Us About Learning," *Education Leadership,* December.

Taber, Mark (1992), 'Systems Management Beyond the Glass House', *Datamation,* March 15: 63-67.

Tesluk, Paul E., James L. Farr, and Stephanie A. Klein. (1997), Influences of Organizational Culture and Climate on Individual Creativity. *Journal of Creative Behavior.* 31(1): 27-41.

Thayer, R.H. and A.B. Pyster, (1984), "Guest Editorial: Software Engineering Project Management," *IEEE Transactions on Software Engineering,* Vol. SE-10, No. 1, Jan.

Thompson, P. and McHugh, D. (2002), *Work Organisations: a Critical Introduction.* 3rd ed. Palgrave

Thompson, P. and Warhurst, C. (ed) (2003), *Workplaces of the Future.* Palgrave: Macmillan

Thompson, R.F. (1967), *Foundations of Physiological Psychology,* N.Y. Harper and Row.

Tichy, N.M., DeRose, C. (1996), "The Pepsi Challenge: Building a Leader-Driven Organization." *Training and Development,* 50(5): 58-66.

Tierney, E.P., (1996), *How to make Effective Presentations,* SAGE Publications, UK.

Tiger, L. (1979), *Optimism: The Biology of Hope.* New York. Simon and Schuster.

Tim Hannagan, (1997), Management Concepts and Practices, Macmillan India Ltd.

Tindall, WN, Beardsley, RS, Kimberlin, CL. (2003), *Communication Skills in Pharmacy Practice.* 4th ed. Philadelphia, Pa: Lippincott Williams and Wilkins; 122.

Tronpenaars, F. and Hampden-Turner, C. (2001), *21 leaders for the 21st Century: how innovative leaders manage in the digital age.* Capstone

Tuckman, B.W. and Jensen, M.A.C. (1977), Stages of small group development revisited. *Group andOrganizational Studies,* 2: 419-427.

Tung, R. L. (1996), Managing in Asia: Cross-cultural dimensions. In: Joynt, P. and Warner, M. (eds.), *Managing across cultures: Issues and perspectives.* London: International Thomson Business.

Tyson, S. and Jackson, T. (1992), *The Essence of Organizational Behavior.* New York: Prentice-Hall

Udupa, K.N., Stress and Its Management by Yoga, Motilal Banarsidass, Delhi 1985 Selvamurthy et. al., "A New Physiological Approach to Control Essential Hypertension", *Indian J Physiol Pharmacol,* 1998 April; 42 (2): 205-13.

Valbrun, M. (2000), Immigrants find economic boom brings more than higher pay. *The Wall Street Journal,* August 16, B1, B4.

Van Vianen, A.E.M. (2000), Person-organization fit: The match between newcomers' and recruiters' preferences for organizational cultures. *Personnel Psychology,* 53: 113-149.

Van Vugt, M., De Cremer, D., and Janssen, D. (2007), Gender differences in cooperation and competition: The male warrior hypothesis. *Psychological Science,* 18: 19–23.

Van, Fleet David D. and Peterson Tim O. (1994) *Contemporary Management,* Houghton Mifflin Company, Third Edition.

Vecchio, R. (1995), *Organisational Behaviour.* 3rd ed. The Dryden Press

Vicere, A.A. (2002), "Leadership and the Networked Economy." *Human Resource Planning,* 25(2): 26-33.

Vilanilam, J.V., (2000), *More Effective Communication: a manual for professionals,* Response Books, India

Watson, J.B., (1930), *Behaviorism,* London, Kegan Paul, 1930

Weick, K. E. (2001), *Making Sense of the Organization,* Blackwell Publishing.

Weihrich, H. and H. Koontz, (1993), *Management: A Global Perspective,* 10th ed., McGraw-Hill, New York.

Weiss, J. (1996) *Organisational behavior and change: Managing Diversity, Cross-cultural Dynamics, and Ethics.* New York: West Publishing.

White, D. and Bednar, D. (1986), *Organizational behavior: understanding and managing people at work.* Boston: Allyn and Bacon.

Wilder, L. (1986), *Professionally Speaking,* Simon and Schuster, USA.

Winslade, J. and Monk, G. (2000), *Narrative Mediation: A New Approach to Conflict*

Witzel, Morgen (ed.), (2001), *'Introduction', Organization Behaviour, 1890-1940* (Bristol: Thoemmes Press, pp. v-xvii.

Wood, Julia (2000), *Relational Communication.* 2nd ed. Belmont, CA: Wadsworth.

Woodman, Richard W., John E. Sawyer, and R.W.Griffin (1993), Toward a Theory of Organizational Creativity. *Academy of Management Review,* 18(2): 293-321.

Woodworth, R.S. (1984), *Contemporary Schools of Psychology,* Londaon, Methuen.

World Wide Web at http://www.careerjournal.com/myc/climbingladder/ 20021224-raudsepp.html, accessed on 28 January 2003.

Wright, C. (ed.), (1995), *Communication Skills: a practical handbook,* The Industrial Society, UK.

Yasin Olum, (2004), *Modern Management Theories And Practices,* a paper presented at the 15th East African Central Banking Course, held on 12th July 2004, at Kenya School of Monetary Studies.

Young, J. E. (1999), *Cognitive Therapy for Personality Disorders: A Schema-focused Approach*. Sarasota, FL: Professional Resource Exchange.

Zaleznik, Abraham, and Manfred F. R. Kets de Vries (1985), *Power and the Corporate Mind*, Bonus Books, Chicago IL (2nd Ed.).

Zimbardo, P. and Leippe, M. (1991), *The Psychology of Attitude Change and Social Influence*. Philadelphia, PA: Temple University Press.

Index

D

E